SIBLING RELATIONSHIPS

Also by Robert Sanders

An Introduction to Working with Children: A Guide for Social Workers (with M. Colton and M. Williams)

The Management of Child Protection: Context and Change

Area Child Protection Committees (with N. Thomas)

Sibling Relationships

Theory and Issues for Practice

ROBERT SANDERS

Consultant Editor
JO CAMPLING

First published 2004 by
PALGRAVE MACMILLAN
Houndmills, Basingstoke, Hampshire RG21 6XS and
175 Fifth Avenue, New York, N.Y. 10010
Companies and representatives throughout the world

PALGRAVE MACMILLAN is the global academic imprint of the Palgrave
Macmillan division of St. Martin's Press LLC and of Palgrave Macmillan Ltd.
Macmillan* is a registered trademark in the United States, United Kingdom
and other countries. Palgrave is a registered trademark in the European
Union and other countries.

ISBN 0–333–96410–1 hardback
ISBN 0–333–96411–X paperback

This book is printed on paper suitable for recycling and made from fully
managed and sustained forest sources.

A catalogue record for this book is available from the British Library.

Library of Congress Cataloging-in-Publication Data
Sanders, Robert, 1946–
     Sibling relationships: theory and issues for practice / Robert Sanders;
  consultant editor, Jo Campling.
       p. cm.
     Includes bibiliographical references and index.
     ISBN 0–333–96410–1 (cloth) – ISBN 0–333–96411–X (pbk.)
     1. Brothers and sisters. 2. Developmental psychology. I. Campling, Jo. II.
     Title.
     BF723.S43S159 2004
     306.875–dc22   2003062092

10   9   8   7   6   5   4   3   2   1
13 12 11 10 09 08 07 06 05 04

Transferred to digital printing 2005

This book is dedicated to the memories of my sister, Sandy,
and my brother, Tony

Contents

List of Figures

List of Tables

List of Practice Notes

Foreword

Relationships between brothers and sisters have been much less researched and observed than most other kinds of family relationships. Yet our relationships with our siblings are likely to be, as this book points out, the longest-lasting in our lives. No wonder the theme recurs so often in legend and literature, not to mention the Bible. Brothers and sisters may be best friends, a source of support and advice in times of trouble or alternatively a cause of irritation and conflict. In childhood they may be competitors for adult attention and role models for better or worse. In old age they often become the most important informal resource when ill-health or disability strike.

Most practitioners are well aware of this, but until now they have been operating largely in the dark, with no evidence base to guide their decision making. The vast literature on child development and the mother–child relationship mostly seems to assume that the child in question is the only one, although 80 per cent of children grow up in families with at least one brother or sister and the parents of a newborn baby are, as often as not, coping with a demanding toddler at the same time. Birth order too can have lifelong consequences, but the impact may be quite different depending on the number and gender of the other siblings and how they are distributed in the family.

What this book does is to disentangle the innumerable facets of the relationships between brothers and sisters, tracking down and analysing an elusive body of research and making it accessible to the reader. It then becomes possible to move beyond bland assessments of the quality of these relationships towards understanding them in all their complexity, both as they exist at a particular point in time and as they evolve through the life cycle.

Social workers have to make many difficult decisions which depend on their view of sibling relationships, in particular when there is a question of splitting a family so that one or more of the children may have a chance of adoption or a promising long-term foster placement. The assumption that brothers and sisters should always be kept together needs to be re-examined; the mere fact of relationship is not enough to settle the question. Similar issues arise when parents divorce. Skilled and careful assessment is essential, but until now there has not been a readily available text to help achieve it.

Another myth dispelled by Robert Sanders' own research is that in abusive or dysfunctional families siblings provide support for each other. This may sometimes be true, but often children model their behaviour on that of their parents and become aggressive and violent towards each other, or one of the siblings may be scapegoated.

Conflict between siblings can be a severe source of stress for parents even in ordinary families. They may be faced many times a day with the dilemma of when to step in to stop a fight or defend a smaller child, when to sort out the rights and wrongs of the dispute, and when to look the other way and let the warring pair work it out for themselves. There are no easy answers to these questions but the increasing number of professionals providing different forms of support to families, from a social work, health, educational or legal perspective, all need a deeper understanding of sibling relationships and what they can do to improve them when necessary. I am sure that they will find this book a most valuable resource.

Professor Sonia Jackson, OBE, AcSS

PART I

An Introduction to Sibling Relationships

Why is it important to study sibling relationships? There are a number of reasons. First, sibling relationships are an important aspect of child development, although they have received relatively little attention in the study of family relationships (Dunn, Slomkowski, Beardsall and Rende, 1994; Eno, 1985). Dunn (1988a, p. 119) describes the sibling relationship as 'distinctive in its emotional power and intimacy, its qualities of competitiveness, ambivalence and of emotional understanding'. The sibling relationship affects how children develop, particularly socially and emotionally. Historically, we have placed so much emphasis on the parents as the architects of the child's character that we have neglected sibling influences. Judith Rich Harris (1999) has controversially suggested that parents are in fact not very significant in children's development. Both genetics and peer groups, she argues, are more significant influences on how we develop. She may perhaps overstate the case, but it is probably true that we have neglected other influences on children's development because of pre-eminence given to parents. It is time to redress the balance.

Secondly, siblings spend more time with each other than with anyone else. They may spend more time with each other during the day than either spends with their mother, and they will almost certainly spend more time together than they do with their father (Kosonen, 1999).

Thirdly, sibling relationships are likely to be the longest standing that any of us has (Freeman, 1992; McGoldrick and Gerson, 1985). For most people, their siblings will outlive their parents, and indeed many sibling relationships begin to take on a different dimension when the parents die. Ross and Milgram (1982) question whether it is ever possible to dissociate oneself psychologically from one's siblings in a way that former friends and even marriage partners can be forgotten.

Fourthly, sibling relationships are pervasive relationships. Most of us have brothers and sisters. Wedge and Mantle (1991), in their review of the sibling literature, inform us that 80 per cent of children in the population belong to sibling groups. Smith and Adler (1991) reported that 83 per cent of children in Australia are either first- or second-born suggesting that the overall rate for siblings might even be somewhat higher there than the 80 per cent described by Wedge and Mantle (1991).

Fifthly, sibling relationships are an ingrained part of the collective psyche. As such they represent an archetypal image passed down to us through myths, legends, the Bible, fairy tales and other received sources of folk wisdom. The diverse nature of sibling relationships is also exemplified in the archetypal images.

Sixthly, the problems of dealing with sibling squabbling, bickering, rivalry, hostility and conflict are among the major headaches that parents have to cope with on a daily basis (Newson and Newson, 1978). Therefore this is likely to be an important consideration for professionals working with families.

Finally, there are times when decisions need to be made in relation to children and their siblings, and the lack of knowledge may disadvantage many children. As early as 1985, Jones and Niblett suggested that continuing to make decisions about whether to place siblings together or separately, in the light of such little knowledge about sibling relationships was unacceptable. If it was unacceptable in the 1980s, how much more so is it today?

But what exactly are siblings? As Perlman (1967) tells us, the Anglo-Saxon origins of the word ('sibb', 'gesib', 'sib') suggested a kind of duality of meaning, both of kin being born of the same parents and a relationship within which there is a degree of intimacy (she notes the connection with the word 'gossip'). But there is a vast array of relationships that could be described as 'sibling'. As noted by Kosonen (1999, p. 33):

> Considering the biological, emotional and social connections between siblings, and the child's and siblings' residential arrangements, there is potentially a range of different types of sibling arrangements. Treffers et al. (1990) identified . . . 26 types of sibling a child can have.

She notes the Oxford dictionary definition of siblings as indicating people having one or more parents in common, but this rules out quite a few relationships that might justifiably be regarded as siblings. She notes for example that in addition to the biologically related siblings there are those who become siblings through socio-legal arrangements, for example fostering and adoption. She makes a distinction between 'core siblings' (those regarded as siblings with whom one has lived in the past, or is living with in the present) and 'kin' siblings (those with whom one has not lived, but where there may be strong ties). An example of 'kin' siblings that she provides is a child whose father has started a new family that has produced four children, who are regarded as brothers and sisters by the child. Akhtar and Kramer (1999) refer to 'social siblings', describing children who are being raised together but who are not biologically related. In addition to children being adopted, they cite children being reared together in a kibbutz as an example.

One classification of sibling relationships is according to how many parents the children share. Full siblings have two parents in common, half-siblings have one parent in common, and stepsiblings have no parents in common. But the last category can be quite difficult to define, as noted in my research into sibling relationships in families involved with social services departments:

> If stepsiblings were to be included would the parents have to be married in order for them to be properly considered as a stepfamily? If not, is a long-term stable, but non-marital relationship sufficient? If so, how long does it need to be for it to be considered 'long-term'? What factors would indicate that it was a stable relationship? (Sanders, 2002, p. 161)

As we see, simply defining who is one's brother or sister is not easy, and may be something upon which people's views may differ.

Let us begin with a quite simple assertion. It needs to be simple, because as we get into the consideration of sibling relationships, we very quickly find that issues become exceedingly complex. Our simple assertion is: the vast majority of material that has been written about siblings has not focused on the quality of the relationships between siblings. That is to say that the overwhelming material that has been written about siblings has not been about sibling relationships. Rather, writing on siblings has emphasised siblings as correlates, comparison groups, or focused on them in some other way as individuals. The material thus derived has either been based on a lack of knowledge of the quality of sibling relationships, or assumptions about them. Domestic violence and mental illness are examples where there is virtually no literature on sibling *relationships*. The material on siblings of children with a disability provides an example where the bulk of the material has been based on correlational studies, rather than focusing on assessing sibling interactions. It is only in the last twenty years that investigators have begun to say: what is the impact of X on the *quality* of the relationship between two siblings? and what impact do variations in the way siblings relate to each other have upon A, B and C? Therefore, in writing this book, there are numerous places where there is either no literature or the literature that is available does not tell us what we need to know. That is the challenge: to produce a book that will enable practitioners to reflect more deeply on this missing dimension of family work when there continue to be substantial gaps in our knowledge.

The book has three primary aims. First, it aims to explore the powerful images of sibling relationships that may be expected to contribute to our understanding of how brothers and sisters get on with each other. Secondly, it will look at the more theoretical and empirically derived understanding of sibling relationships that has emerged from psychology over the course of the twentieth century. Finally, it will attempt to relate our knowledge of sibling relationships to practice, so that professionals working with children and families will have a stronger knowledge base when it comes to assessing and planning interventions in families where there are brothers and sisters.

The structure of the book reflects the developing complexity of our understanding of sibling relationships. It describes early, polarised conceptions of sibling relationships as being good or bad. It then proceeds to consider early work done which locates sibling relationships within a context of a network of family relationships. This is followed by the development of typologies of sibling relationships based on the very limited range of factors: gender and birth order. After this, thinking about sibling relationship begins to become much more sophisticated, looking at those factors which influence the quality of sibling relationships, and those aspects of an individual's social and psychological development that may be influenced by his or her sibling relationships. Finally, the book looks at sibling relationships in situations of adversity. The chapter on family support considers the kind of situations that professionals face in daily practice: substance misuse within families, parents with a mental illness, siblings with a disability, and domestic violence. In themselves, these are very large fields, and each one could itself form the basis for an entire book. When looked at from the point of view of sibling relationships however, as we find, there is very little research and much of the material is extrapolated from what we know about sibling relationships in general and what we know about the relevant issue. The final two chapters deal with sibling relationships in child abuse and in situations of loss respectively.

In some cases it has been necessary to use language that might not be considered 'politically correct' (for example, 'handicap' or referring to a child as 'it'). What is considered to be acceptable language to describe different human conditions varies over time and across societies. Occasionally, this language, despite its unacceptability, has been retained to keep close to the material from which it is drawn, but it should not be seen as reflecting the preferred mode of expression of the author.

Case material, where used (for example in the Practice Notes), represents a synthesis of service using children and families which the author has worked with over a twenty-year period in social work practice. In some cases they may be drawn from research samples. All names have been changed and identifying information or descriptive details removed or varied to eliminate the possibility of identification.

I would like to acknowledge the support of my friend and colleague, Professor Sonia Jackson, without whose advice, mentoring and encouragement I am quite sure this book would never have appeared in print.

1 Sibling Relationships: The Big Picture

It often seems as though sibling ties could only represent either perfect alliance or insurmountable hatred. (Le Gall, 1998)

There is a polarisation in the way sibling relationships are seen. They are extremely complex and variable social relationships. They are sensitive to other intrafamilial relationships. They undergo considerable changes over the course of the lifespan. They provide an arena in which powerful positive features coexist with equally powerful negative ones.

However, there is a tendency to simplify the complexity of sibling relationships. On the one hand sibling relationships may be viewed as supportive and nurturant relationships, an alliance between equals. As equals, siblings share a world different from that shared with the parents. They may be the ones who protect us in school from bullies (whether we want them to or not). They may be the first ones with whom we will share our concerns, fears and anxieties. The very words, *sisterhood* and *brotherhood* suggest a form of camaraderie between unrelated people, as if to say, 'we are so close that we could be sisters' (or brothers). As noted by Cohen (1993, p. 98), 'The appeal for solidarity among women always asks for symbolic "sisterhood"'. The appeal for human relationships to transcend racial, ethnic and cultural differences is usually phrased in terms of 'brotherhood'.

On the other hand sibling relationships may be viewed as the first expressions of competitive relationships, competing in the first instance for the scarce resources of food and sustenance, and parental love, affection and approval. In such a view, the rivalrous feelings in young siblings are accompanied by an as yet undeveloped sense of restraint, and may result in expressions of hostility thankfully made ineffective because of the inability of combatants, through immaturity, to do any real damage. In the alliance view positive sibling relationships are the preparation for cooperative and supportive ventures in later life (such as friendship and family building). In the rivalry view, sibling relationships can be seen as the training ground for competing in school and, later, employment. Cohen (1993, p. 98) notes, in reference to nineteenth-century literature, 'sexual competition between sisters is inevitable in these books' citing from Spacks (1986, p. 141), 'Sex provides the arena of conflict in a society which defines a woman's worth by her marriage.' In many societies throughout history, primogeniture (the passing of inheritance to the first son), whilst perhaps creating order within society about wealth (and titles) passing across generations, also created conflict between brothers, often with murderous consequences.

Where do those powerful, yet extreme images of sibling relationships come from? An individual's views of sibling relationships may result from two broad types of influences. One is the influence of one's own family relationships. One's direct experience of sibling relationships, and the parental images of such relationships that the parent(s) have derived from their own sibling experience, are powerful influences on how we view siblings. Another influence could be the child's understanding of the nature of the current relationship between his or her parents and the parent's siblings (the child's aunts and uncles). Further back, deeply embedded influences can be derived from the sibling relationships each of the four grandparents had with their brothers and sisters.

The second source of images of sibling relationships is the way in which such relations are described to us. Where do these portrayals of sibling relationships come from? They derive from folklore, legends, myths, fairy tales and literature. The earlier sources are powerful because of their archetypal qualities; literature is powerful because, using fictional characters in fictional situations, it can convey real-life themes in a way that is vivid, detailed and applied, and several writers have noted this feature.

All of us have been exposed to images of sibling relationships from some, if not all, of these varied sources. They tend to portray relationships between brothers and sisters as characteristically good or evil (although they may change over time). Overlaying complexities in sibling relationships are rarely found. The simultaneous coexistence of prosocial and antagonistic relationships between brothers and sisters is uncommon. In those few cases where they are found, for example in the story of Joseph and his brothers (see next section), they are not described in terms of the alternating quality of sibling relationships within the same relationship over time. Therefore we can see sibling relationships as archetypes and schemas, as discourses – powerful internalised influences derived from underlying, pre-existing ways of seeing things and from the language we use to define and describe them.

A further theme in the polarisation of sibling relationships is one in which certain features of children's character are portrayed in relation to the sibling to provide contrast. At its most stark, this can be seen in contrasting children in terms of being good and bad. But there is a vast array of psychological dimensions along which children can be seen as different. It can be argued that in children's development there are processes at work that do not allow siblings to occupy the same psychological space in the minds of those who raise them, care for them, or know them. It is the differences between children that form the basis of thinking about them, not their similarities. If one is outgoing, the other is not; if one is intelligent, the other is less so. Even if both are seen as artistic, one will be more so. Kelsh and Quindlen (1998) express this well:

> In the movie *The Godfather* there are three of them: the smart thoughtful one, the stupid childish one, and the macho uncontrollable one. In *Little Women* there are four: the homebody, the writer, the artist, the child. And in Jane Austen's *Sense and Sensibility*, they make up the title. One thinks; the other feels. They are, therefore I am not. That is the crux of the sibling relationship. (p. 71)

Sulloway (1996) describes this process as siblings 'finding a niche', or 'niche picking':

> The term *contrasts effects* has been used to describe these kinds of systematic sibling differences. Although the phenomenon is now well documented, the psychological mechanisms that underlie it are only beginning to be understood. (p. 96, original italics)

He proceeds however to suggest that the function of this diversification process is as a strategy to increase 'parental investment':

> Siblings become different for the same reason that species do over time: divergence minimizes completion for scarce resources. (p. xv)

Mink and Ward (1993) develop the theme of images of sibling relationships in literature. In connection with sister relationships they note:

> the tradition of using sisters to present 'paired' behaviour, with one sister being 'good' in contrast to the 'bad' one. As a result neither sister is portrayed as an individual. (p. 7)

This differentiation difficulty could be said to be particularly true of twins, and perhaps less applicable where there is a wide age gap between siblings. Pingree (1993, p. 96) explores the issues of identity, and duality in twins in Eudora Welty's *The Golden Apples*, noting, 'their twinship continues again and again to define and confine who they are'. When twins are not allowed to occupy the same space, if one cannot be artistic (musical, intelligent, graceful, etc.), because the sibling is seen that way, then the influence can be confining indeed. Ainslie (1999) refers to 'the bifurcation of identity traits', a concept meaning that twin characters are polarised into traits such as male/female, active/passive, leader/follower, stronger/weaker, smarter/less smart. Twins are not allowed by their social environment to be the same.

Archetypes, schemas and discourses

Let us consider some of the images of sibling relationships to which we may have been exposed. The following material looks at four themes relating to the portrayal of sibling relationships in folklore, legends, myths, fairy tales and literature: 'Siblings as Allies', 'Siblings as Rivals', 'The Emphasis on Different-ness of Siblings', and 'All Brothers? All Sisters?'

Siblings as allies

Greek mythology provides us with two tales of sisters, the *Gorgons* – snake-haired monsters who could turn a person to stone with a single glance, and the *Graeae*, their guardians – three sisters, who between them had only a single tooth and a single eye which they shared. In the case of the Graeae, we encounter sibling interdependence, a theme we will revisit.

Bettelheim (1976) argues that the symbolism of sibling relationships in fairy tales refers to the child's need to transcend adult-dependent relations to move to placing greater reliance on relations with age-mates. The theme of sisterly devotion, endurance, courage and self-sacrifice is found in *The Wild Swans* by Hans Christian Andersen (Kingsland, 1985). Further positive images of sibling relationships come from the fairy tales, *Brother and Sister* and *Hansel and Gretel*. Bettelheim (1976) says *Hansel and Gretel*:

> is one of many fairy tales where two siblings cooperate in rescuing each other and succeed because of their combined efforts. These stories direct the child toward transcending his immature dependence on his parents and reaching the next higher stage of development: cherishing also the support of age mates. (p. 165)

In Sophocles' (BC 495–406) play, *Antigone*, the central plot is Antigone's defiance of the edict set down by the King (Creon), forbidding the burial of her brother, Polyneices, who lies dead outside the walls of Thebes. In her defence of operating in compliance with a higher law than that of mortals, Antigone notes that an adult sibling, unlike a husband or a child, cannot be replaced:

> If my husband had died, there would have been another man for me; I could have had a child from another husband if I had lost my first child. But with my mother and father both hidden away in Hades, no other brother could ever have come into being for me. (Mink and Ward, 1993, p. 1)

Here we see several elements of the sibling relationship that are significant. The theme of discretionary versus obligatory sibling relationships will be considered in the next section. We also see some of the elements of the impact of gender on sibling relationships. Antigone risks the wrath of the King to tend the body of her dead brother, Polyneices (with the help of her sister). Polyneices had been killed in battle by his brother. All the elements of the differences between sister–sister, sister–brother, and brother–brother relationships are contained in the play.

Sibling hero-worship is described in George Eliot's *The Mill on the Floss*. An analysis in terms of sibling relationships is provided by Waddell (1993). Eliot (Marian Evans) was the third of three surviving siblings of her father's second marriage (subsequent twins died in infancy), having an older sister and an older brother. The *Mill on the Floss*, her first great novel, was to a large extent autobiographical, reflecting in Maggie, the central character, and her brother, Tom Tulliver, the idolisation Eliot felt for her brother, Isaac. Waddell (1993) draws a comparison between Tom in the novel, and Isaac, the novelist's real-life brother. She maintains that both brothers took on the responsibility for the rest of the family, in the latter case assuming control through the management of finances. Both were extremely concerned with the appearance of social correctness. In the novel, Tom renounces his ruined sister (following what appeared to be a sexual liaison); in the biography Isaac ceased communications with George Eliot for twenty-three years, because she lived in a common-law marriage.

Again, we find some of the familiar themes that will be developed, based on the overlaying of birth order and gender onto sibling relationships. Tom adopts the 'big brother' role – a pseudo-father figure, in the absence of the father. Isaac did the same. Loyalty, devotion and selflessness characterise the portrayal of the female approach to sibling relationships, certainly to a greater extent than the male.

Two more recent novels from the end of the twentieth century, describe the experience of growing up as a black woman in Southern America in the early twentieth century. In both Maya Angelou's *I Know Why the Caged Bird Sings* (1969) and Alice Walker's *The Color Purple* (1983), growing up is vividly portrayed as harsh, brutal and oppressive. The more general descriptions of the way in which black people were oppressed in the American South, and the way in which women were controlled and dominated by men, are overlaid with vivid descriptions of individual circumstances that are particularly oppressive. For both, the sibling relationship provides support which enables the narrator to find a way in which to survive.

In *I Know Why the Caged Bird Sings*, the narrator Marguerite ('Ritie' or 'Maya') begins the tale with the description of her journey as a 3-year-old, in the company of her 4-year-old brother Bailey, from California to live with her grandmother in a rural Arkansas town. Many of the subsequent events in the book are related in terms of the two children being together, sharing experiences. They are able to induce bursts of giggling and laughter by mimicking people in their lives. They share a common language (Pig Latin), which Ritie incorrectly believes to be a language exclusive to her, her brother and her friends. They make secret pacts. They share moments of emotional upheaval, for example, believing their parents were dead. When Ritie is sexually abused, her brother is the one to whom she first reveals the truth – but first being assured that the abuser could not carry through on his threat to kill her brother. Her brother reassures her and she believes him – she trusts her brother would never lie to her. Then, following the abuse when she decides to stop talking to everyone, her brother is the only exception.

Her brother is a constant companion for her whilst other significant figures in her life change, so much so that even a separation for just a month is painful. In a world in which there are so many people to be distrusted – adults, white people – the one person who could be trusted was her brother.

But Angelou also describes the growing apart process that comes with growing up but in a manner suggesting diminishing companionship rather than diminishing affection. And when, at age 16, in San Francisco, Bailey is compelled to leave home abruptly under acrimonious circumstances, Maya comes to visit him in his new home, offering her assistance: 'I'm your sister, and whatever I can do, I'll do it.'

In Alice Walker's *The Color Purple*, the entire story is recounted through letters (an 'epistolary novel'), from Celie, the protagonist, in the first instance to God, and then subsequently, when her faith in God is undermined, to her sister Nettie. However, much of the sister's story is told through letters from Nettie to Celie. The novel therefore is entirely the correspondence of two sisters (although not exclusively with each other) who are separated throughout much of their lives. When Nettie leaves the home of Celie and her husband, she says to Celie that she will write to her, but over the many years that follow, Celie never receives a single letter from her. It transpires, however, that she has been writing regularly to Celie, whose husband has been intercepting the letters and hiding them.

Although there is no direct contact between the two sisters Celie and Nettie throughout most of their adult lives, it is a powerful, sustaining, relationship for Celie. In a confrontation with her husband she challenges him:

> You took my sister Nettie away from me, I say. And she was the only person love me in the world. (Walker, 1983, p. 170)

In the end the sisters are reunited after a lifetime apart.

A significant underlying theme in both of these books is the powerful sustaining influence of the sibling, in the first case a brother, in the second, a sister. They are presented as companions, as attachment figures when other relationships are disrupted, as confidantes (in both cases), and as people who love us.

Both of these books were bestsellers and were made into films (*I Know Why the Caged Bird Sings*, 1979, director: Fielder Cook; *The Color Purple*, 1985, director: Steven Spielberg) and these powerful positive images of sibling relationships have reached millions of people all over the world.

Siblings as rivals

There are a number of fairy tales in which the theme of one 'good' brother is described in contrast with the other brothers ('Lousy Jack and his Eleven Brothers': Philip, 1992; Grimm's 'The Golden Goose' and 'The Queen Bee': Rackham, 1973). The 'good' brother, usually one who is younger, and occasionally of limited intelligence (using epithets such as 'Blockhead' and 'Simpleton'), is invariably successful in obtaining what the other brothers want (wealth, the princess, etc.).

The subtext suggests that the brother's simplistic naiveté and good nature are factors contributing to his success. The older brothers are generally portrayed as being more competitive and mean-spirited towards the younger brother than vice versa.

Forsythe (1991) explores the meaning of 'brother stories' in the Old Testament (Genesis) from a psychoanalytic perspective. Genesis contains eleven descriptions of male sibling rivalry. The well-known phrase 'Am I my brother's keeper' comes from the biblical portrayal of the first sibling relationship, that between Cain and Abel. Cain, the farmer, became jealous of the favour accorded to his younger brother Abel, the shepherd, and killed him. This is the first of a number of significant biblical portrayals of fraternal jealousy and rivalry to the point of actual or attempted fratricide. The tale is told with significant variations, but retaining the central fratricide, in different cultures: Kabil and Habil (Palestine); Cain and Abel (Turkey); Abel and Cain (Italy); and The First Grave (Poland).

Also in the Old Testament, Jacob cheated his brother Esau out of his father's blessing by deceiving their father, Isaac, into believing that he was in fact Esau. When Esau learned of Jacob's deception, he wanted to kill him, forcing Jacob to flee, spending twenty years in exile before seeking reconciliation with Esau.

The story of Joseph and his brothers is perhaps the best-known biblical tale. He was the favourite of his father, Jacob. Jacob gave to Joseph a special multicoloured coat causing envy amongst his brothers. His brothers conspired to kill Joseph by throwing him into a well, but relented and instead sold him into slavery. In later years, the brothers went to Egypt during a time of famine to buy grain, only to find they were brought before Joseph, who had become a governor. They did not recognise him, but he recognised them, and despite what they had done to him, he forgave them.

These biblical narratives highlight a theme of fraternal enmity based on differential favour and primogeniture. The latter, however, does not invariably lead to rancour and discord between the brothers, as for example in the case of E'phraim and Manah'she (Genesis). Perhaps because of wealth passing from father to son, sister relations in the Old Testament are not given such prominence.

The Arthurian legend provides a somewhat more complex view of the sibling (sister–brother) relationship. It is interesting because it highlights several themes to be discussed here – how sibling relationships change over time and how they can contain conflicting features. There are many different versions of Arthur's story and consequently many different versions of his relationship with his half-sister, Morgan le Fey. The accounts agree, however, that Arthur and Morgan had the same mother (Irgraine) and different fathers. From the different accounts, the enmity between them may have been attributable in part to: (a) the relationship being one of half-siblings; (b) Arthur's father having killed Morgan's father; and (c) Irgraine having relinquished the care of Arthur to Morgan, so that Morgan was not only a sister, but also a mother-substitute. In legend, Morgan does what she can to see Arthur defeated:

> And ever as she myght she made warre on kynge Arthure, and all daungerous knyghtes she wytholdyth with her for to dystroy all thos knyghtes that kynge arthure lovyth. (Malory, p. 367, in Benko, 1993, p. 24)

In the end she succeeds in contributing to his death. But Benko (1993) highlights contrasting versions of this sibling relationship contained within the work of Malory (*Works*) and Bradley (*The Mists of Avalon*) (perhaps in part attributable to the differences between Malory being male and Bradley female). For Malory, the relationship is characterised by enmity between the innocent and good Arthur and the evil, wicked Morgan although overlaid with complexity. In the work of Bradley, there is perhaps more of a concession to the reconciliation that in both versions eventually came about, as Morgan conveyed the dying Arthur to Avalon (their common home).

Arthur refers to his earlier relationship with Morgan, in a time before they were enemies:

> God knowyth I have honoured hir and worshipped hir more than all my kyn, and more have I trusted hir than my wyff and all my kyn aftir. (Malory, p. 88, in Benko, 1993, p. 25)

As Benko (1993) states:

> The variations and continuities in Morgan's character and role and in Morgan and Arthur's sibling relationship between Malory's and Bradley's versions . . . speak to changes and continuity in the perception of sibling relationships and gender roles over time and by men and by women authors. (pp. 23–4)

These two features (changes over time; gender roles) are issues that will be addressed further. She concludes with:

> The differing yet similar literary portrayals of Morgan and Arthur ...
> suggest the existence of subconscious rivalries and loyalties which
> remain constant within families throughout history and suggest the ulti-
> mate significance of gender relationships between not only men and
> women in general but also brothers and sisters in particular. (p. 31)

The emphasis on different-ness of siblings

Some sources highlight how different siblings can be; some focus on
how differently they are treated. These are both themes that will be
developed in this book. We have already encountered tales in which
the different-ness between siblings is emphasised to highlight the
character of the hero, for example in 'Lousy Jack and his Eleven
Brothers', in 'The Golden Goose', in Arthur and Morgan's tale, and in
the Old Testament. In the story, 'The Green Lady' (Philip, 1992) (and
in 'The Old Witch') we find the theme of differences between the
character of two sisters a major focus: 'Now one of these girls was a
steady decent girl, and the other was a stuck-up, proud, conceited
piece' (p. 58). The girls successively make their way in the world, and
whereas the 'decent' girl makes her fortune (in service with the
eponymous green lady in the woods) and marries a prince, the other
tries to imitate her journey, but because of her character, at each
decision-point within the story makes a different, unkindly, choice
and, in contrast, comes to an unhappy end.

In 'The Frog Lover' (Philip, 1992) we find the theme of differences
between how natural children are treated in comparison with
stepchildren: 'There was a stepmother who was very unkind to her
stepdaughter and very kind to her own daughter; and used to send her
stepdaughter to do all the dirty work' (p. 95), a theme we find echoed
in 'Cinderella' and in 'Sweetheart Roland' (Rackham, 1973). In the
latter we have the following introduction:

> Once upon a time there was a woman who was a real Witch, and she had
> two daughters; one was ugly and wicked, but she loved her because she
> was her own daughter. The other was good and lovely, but she hated
> her for she was only her step-daughter. (p. 99)

All brothers? All sisters?

A number of sources emphasise the situation where the siblings are of
the same gender, either all male, or all female. *Pride and Prejudice*,

Little Women and *King Lear* feature varying numbers of sisters (five, four and three respectively). These are interesting both for their authors' perceptive accounts of the roles sisters take up in families and for the contrast they provide in relations between siblings.

Whereas in *Pride and Prejudice* and *Little Women* sisterly relations are characterised generally by warmth, in *King Lear* we see the less familiar theme of strong rivalry and conflict between sisters: Goneril, Regan and Cordelia, Lear's three daughters. However, we also see the more familiar theme of rivalry between brothers (Edmund and Edgar). And interestingly, the sisterly sibling rivalry is about the same type of issues frequently encountered in the literature in relation to male sibling rivalry: inheritance, the allocation between siblings of material goods, and the differential relationship (and treatment) by the parent of the siblings. Cordelia is portrayed as being the favourite; it is not surprising therefore that Goneril and Regan do not intercede on her behalf when Lear becomes enraged with her. They enjoy the consequent reversal of fortune and benefit materially from it as well.

This theme of the fidelity of the youngest daughter of daughters – only Cordelia being faithful, both Goneril and Regan proving themselves disloyal to their father – is reflected in other sources. In 'The Frog Sweetheart' (Philip, 1992) only the youngest daughter is prepared to accept the proposal of the frog in exchange for clear water from the well needed to save her father's life. In 'Cap O'Rushes' (Philip, 1992) a rich father asks his three daughters to express how much they love him – only the response of the youngest fails to please him.

What about brothers? Dostoevsky's *The Brothers Karamazov* looks at three brothers, Alyosha, Dimitry and Ivan, portraying their characters in very different ways (largely for literary purposes). Alyosha is the religious spiritual character; Ivan is the intellectual. There is a fourth, illegitimate brother, Smerdyakov, living in the home as a servant and valet. It is he who eventually kills the father, Fyodor. Although, for our purposes the novel does not contribute to the idea of the polarisation of sibling relationships into those characterised by 'positive/good' or 'negative/evil', it does contribute to the conception of differences between siblings within families (albeit perhaps deliberately exaggerated for literary purposes).

We have drawn on images of sibling relationships from folklore, legends, myths, fairy tales and literature to find evidence of support for the polarisation of the portrayal of sibling relationships as either relationships of alliance and support or of rivalry and conflict. We have found considerable material that supports the contention of such polarisation, but, in so doing, we have also begun to anticipate some of the other themes to arise in consideration of sibling relationships.

We have encountered the portrayal of difference, both in terms of the differentiation of character that is described amongst siblings, and in terms of the differential way in which siblings are treated. Themes in the sources examined suggest that simply to have a sibling may be a factor limiting who one is allowed to be. Gender becomes an important subtheme. Relationships between sisters are characteristically warmer; the relationship in which there is an older sister and a younger brother is likely to have the sister as the nurturant, caretaking individual. Relationships between brothers are more likely to be characteised by both rivalry and/or camaraderie (but this is not invariant). Older siblings are likely to use the power of their age differential in relation to younger children (either for good or otherwise). Finally, siblings are likely to be more positively characterised the more directly they are blood-linked. In other words full siblings are more likely to be characterised as warm, helpful, supportive and protective, whereas stepsiblings are likely to be characterised as mean, vindictive, competitive and rivalrous:

> The fairy tale replaces sibling relationships with relations between stepsiblings – perhaps a device to explain and make acceptable an animosity which one wishes would not exist among true siblings. (Bettelheim, 1976, p. 237)

These themes will be further developed.

Cross-cultural perspectives on sibling relationships

Cultural context is the second major theme of this chapter. I use the concept of 'culture' in its broadest sense (for example, including differences between ethnic groups within the same country, and social class differences).

Sibling relationships in a cross-cultural context: the meaning of 'sibling'

To begin with, there may be different cultural views of the meaning of 'sibling'. Graham (1999) for example notes:

> The notion of half-siblings ... does not exist within an African-centred worldview. (p. 261)

She notes that the family incorporates:

> the lineage both of the mother and the father, and also includes members who are not biologically related and an extensive network of cousins. (p. 261)

Prevatt-Goldstein (1999) notes:

> 'Sibling' is an academic term that does not easily fit into everyday experience. The language of 'sisterhood' and 'brotherhood' is more usual in black traditions and is used to cover a wide range of relationships. (p. 195)

This differing cultural definition of sibling relationship is also noted by Cicirelli (1994):

> In nonindustrialised societies, siblings may be defined by extension of the term to certain types of blood kin, or by classification on the basis of criteria other than genealogical criteria alone. (p. 9)

Some of the very intriguing groups of relations he describes as being defined as siblings are:

- children of both parents biological siblings (Cook Islands);
- children of the parent's cross-sex siblings (Solomon Islands);
- cousins of the same sex, parent's siblings of the same sex, and grandparents of the same sex (New Hebrides);
- children fostered in the same household (Kenya: Abaluya);
- children of the same village or tribe who are of the same age range (Kenya: Giriama).

He therefore highlights the necessity to understand the definition of 'sibling' in a particular cultural context when making comparisons across cultures.

Sibling relationships in a cross-cultural context: a comparison

To date, the most definitive work on sibling relationships in a cross-cultural perspective is that by Cicirelli (1994). He compared sibling relationships in nonindustrialised societies with those in industrialised societies. Some of these differences are set out in Table 1.1. Cicirelli (1994) also looks at the significance of gender in sibling relationships in a cross-cultural context. He notes that the order of closeness in

TABLE I.I A COMPARISON OF SIBLING RELATIONSHIPS IN
INDUSTRIALISED AND NONINDUSTRIALISED SOCIETIES

Nonindustrialised societies	Industrialised societies
Obligatory	Discretionary
Greater emphasis on sibling caretaking	Less emphasis on sibling caretaking (although it does occur)
Assume great importance throughout life	Assume less importance throughout life
Characterised by sibling solidarity	Although present, less characteristic
Larger numbers of siblings	Smaller numbers of siblings
Smaller spacing between siblings	Greater spacing between siblings

Source: From Cicirelli, 1994.

industrialised societies, going from closest to least close, is sister–sister, brother–sister or sister–brother, and finally brother–brother. He also notes that sisters assume a very important role for both brothers and sisters later in life. In nonindustrialised societies, on the other hand, the relationship between sisters in adult life is less important than the relationship between a sister and a brother (important for marital arrangements) and between brothers (very important for social and economic activities). A very important finding is that within nonindustrialised societies sibling relationships are considered to be obligatory, whereas in industrialised societies they are discretionary. It would seem that in an industrialised society you can choose just how much significance (or otherwise) you wish to attach to your relationships with your brothers or sisters.

It is interesting to compare Cicirelli's findings concerning adult sibling relationships in industrialised societies with those of Young and Willmot (1957). In their study of family and kinship relations in East London, adult sisters were found to have more frequent contact with sisters (52 per cent of those surveyed having contact in the previous week), whereas men having contact with sisters was 35 per cent, women having contacts with brothers was 42 per cent, and least of all was contact between brothers (27 per cent). They also found that, generally, the lower the social class, the more contact there was between siblings (which they attribute mostly to greater geographical distance being associated with higher social class). However, they also found that frequently upward social mobility on the part of a sibling led to loss of contact with the family.

One can speculate that a common factor operating between cultures (comparing industrialised with nonindustrialised societies) and within industrialised societies (although it is dangerous to generalise from one specific case) is that greater economic prosperity is associated with less significance attached to sibling relationships. This would be in accord with Cicirelli (1994), who notes that 'in nonindustrialised societies, sibling relationships are of fundamental importance in determining family functioning ... with sibling cooperation essential to attain marital and *economic goals*' (p. 16, my italics).

It may be, therefore, that economic necessity, to the point of promoting survival, is a factor that requires siblings to cooperate with each other, and that when this economic necessity is removed (through general prosperity, through individual upward mobility), sibling cooperative relationships are no longer as necessary for the promotion of survival and well-being. This hypothesis would account for a number of observations regarding sibling relations. It may also put into context why sibling caretaking is more common in nonindustrialised societies than in industrialised ones. In part it is because of sheer economic necessity (mothers as well as fathers must be enabled to contribute to the family's survival). In part it may be preparation for a closer sibling relationship that will be needed later in life.

Sibling relationships in a cross-cultural context: sibling caretaking

Sibling relationships vary around the world because relationships within families vary so dramatically across cultures and societies. It would be ethnocentric to presume that there is anything 'natural' or even statistically common about the way in which children are reared in Western societies. But the abhorrence of sibling caretaking in Western societies is one such presumption. Valsiner (2000) emphasises the ideological component of sibling caretaking:

> As a general rule all over the world, the primary organizers of the social environments of the young children (except for feeding) are older siblings, rather than the parents ... The exclusive role of the mother in early childcare (which was normatively prescribed by Bowlby ...) is a cultural-historical artefact of a number of sociological factors: nuclearization of the households, lower reproductive success of women, social

politics of keeping work out of the home – and women out of work. The focus on exclusive 'maternal responsibility' for early childhood is a cultural construct of an ideological nature. (p. 224)

An early study looking at the caretaking patterns of young children in six different cultures – New England, Mexico, Philippines, Okinawa, India and Kenya – found that New England mothers spent a greater proportion of their time with their infants than those in any of the other five societies (Minturn and Lambert, 1964). The factors that are associated with sibling caretaking are women having more work to do, mothers working away from the home, and the circumstances leading to the availability of alternative caretakers, such as place of residence, birth order and family size (Whiting and Whiting, 1975).

Sibling caretaking is widespread throughout the world (Weisner and Gallimore, 1977), and yet there has been little study of its 'ethnographic incidence'. They note the frequent reference to sibling caretaking in non-Western autobiographical accounts, and provide this interesting example of a boy from the Idakho in Western Kenya:

Because there was no older sister in the family, and my mother had to go off to work in the *shamba* [gardens] everyday, it wasn't long before I was obliged, though still a very young child myself, to become the day-to-day 'nurse' for my baby sister. For my mother to make me succeed in this function, she had to train me – to give me instructions and to see how well I carried them out. (Lijembe, 1967, pp. 4–5)

Weisner and Gallimore (1977) highlight several significant features of sibling caretaking for example that the caretaking sibling may be caught between conflicting demands of the parent and the sibling he or she is looking after, that the style of parenting of the sibling can be different from, or even opposite to, that adopted by the parent, and that the style of sibling caretaking changes as the child goes from infancy to childhood. They conclude:

There is certainly no evidence that children suffer when cared for in part by older children as opposed to their parents ... Child caretaking thus contributes to role flexibility for mothers and caretaker diversity and skills for children. (1977, p. 180)

It is important to remember that caretaking is not a homogenous entity, and, in addition to children receiving basic care from a sibling, there is a possibility that the type of care received from a sibling differs from the type of care received from a parent. In this sense, it could be argued that sibling caretaking contributes to a diversity of social interaction experience for the young child (Lasky, 1983).

Prevatt-Goldstein (1999) discusses the theme of responsibility (and reciprocity) in black sibling relationships, noting that sibling care-taking may have a different meaning in other families (asymmetrical parenting or co-parenting) from that in black families (providing a foundation for lifelong reciprocal relationships). This echoes a theme from Korbin (1980) who tries to distinguish sibling caretaking that is abusive from that which is not. As pointed out by Korbin (1980) 'in the United States, the notion of a child of eight, ten, or eleven caring for an even younger child has come to be regarded as abusive or neglectful' (p. 25). The caretaking child is seen as being abused (by having her childhood taken away), and the younger child is seen as being neglected, by being provided with a standard of care that is less than one would expect to be provided. However, amongst cultural groups where sibling caretaking is accepted, it is not only an expedient means to provide care for a young child so that mother can devote her time to either looking after even younger children or to subsistence, it is also a means of preparation of young people for the adult roles they will assume. It creates a sense of esteem for the young carer who is performing a vital role for the family. It promotes a sense of inter-dependence (rather than autonomy), which is valued in many non-Western cultures. For Korbin (1980) the key to ascertaining whether sibling caretaking is culturally beneficial or abusive lies in the context. Is it a role that is thrust unwillingly upon certain powerless members of a society in which childcare is devalued, and who would much rather be doing something else? Or, rather, in the context of a society which values the role of caring for children, and those who take on that role, is it something that the young person might look forward to eagerly, as representing a rite of passage, or status transition for the young person?

Clearly children's views, as caretakers and as cared-for, are impor-tant. An interesting study in Scotland (Kosonen, 1996b) looked at sib-ling caretaking in a study of 69 primary school-aged children. Sibling caretaking was found to be a common experience (for children in the 9–12 age group), which was 'viewed primarily positively both by the caretaking and looked after children' (p. 267).

What are we to conclude from these apparently conflicting views of sibling caretaking? At the very least it would seem that one should exercise extreme caution when concluding that caring for younger brothers and sisters will deprive the older sibling of their childhood. For rather than simply being a question of the extent of harm caused by being required to care for a younger sibling, it may be a question of trade-offs, positives and negatives in the experience, which, depending upon the context, may result in a net positive or a net negative for the older sibling.

We may also conclude that practitioners need to be very cautious about making judgements about the abusive nature of sibling care-taking, particularly when dealing with people from other cultures. There is an inherent danger of ethnocentrism when making a judge-ment of two-fold neglect in sibling caretaking when dealing with families in a situation where such caretaking is truly valued by the young person. This applies not only in relation to looking at cultural practices in other societies, but in relation to ethnic minority groups within a predominantly white society.

Sibling relationships in a cross-cultural context: a case study

An anthropological study of four brothers and sisters growing up in Mexico City in the post-World War II era was undertaken by Oscar Lewis (1964). It is presented as first-person narrative accounts of the five members of the family, Jesus Sanchez and his four children, Manuel, Roberto, Consuelo and Marta (see Figure 1.1).The study is not explicitly about sibling relationships; the focus is on the way members of the family have been affected by events in their lives. But

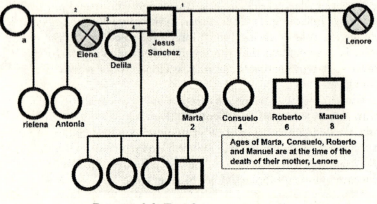

FIGURE 1.1 THE SANCHEZ FAMILY

there is a lot of material in the book about the various relationships between the brothers and sisters. And in these descriptions we find a number of the common themes about sibling relationships that are discussed here: stepfamily relationships, the incest taboo, the 'big brother' role, differential treatment, favouritism and disfavouritism within the family, jealousy, hostility and aggression.

The book is poignant in the descriptions of the lives of the four children who despite their efforts cannot seem to find happiness in their family. They talk of crying alone in misery, feeling rejected by, and not being able to gain approval from, their father, feeling rejected by the other siblings, not feeling respected by the younger siblings, and ambivalent anger towards their father because of his emotional and psychological investment in his subsequent children. Consider for example the following:

> Consuelo: 'I had nothing but bitterness all though my childhood and a feeling of being alone.' (p. 89)

But the children acknowledge that their father has continued to support them and despite their feeling rejected by him, continue to love him. For his part, Jesus Sanchez is a hard-working provider for his family who feels that his four children are a major disappointment to him, and he rarely fails to convey this to them. It is clear that he is fulfilling his duty towards his children, but in other ways, for example, emotionally, he does not seem to be engaged with them, particularly the boys. He describes himself:

> Jesus: 'I wasn't very affectionate with the children either. I don't know whether it was because I didn't get much affection in my childhood or because I was left to take care of them alone or because I was always worrying about money. I had to work very hard to get them food. I didn't have time for them.' (pp. 11–12)

As suggested, the family seems to have become unhinged with the death of the children's mother, Lenore, and the three older children describe the impact of this:

> Manuel: 'I didn't notice it so much then because while my mother was alive my *papa* still loved me ... If my mother had lived, things might have been different.' (p. 23)

And:

> Roberto: 'For me there was only one mother in all the world, and even though a hundred others came along and wanted to act like my mother, it was not the same thing.' (pp. 64–5)

And:

> Consuelo: 'I felt alone partly because of losing my mother and partly because of the way my brothers and sister treated me.' (p. 89)

Marta was seen as being too young to remember her mother.

The Sanchez Family is intriguing because in the face of adversity and hardship, the sibling relationships are strained to the point of aggression, enmity and even violence. As noted by Consuelo, 'What a bitter disappointment for me when the years passed and I only saw my family grow apart'. (p. 256)

It appears to go against the principal contention here, that sibling relationships can be a positive, resilience-promoting resource, in adversity and challenging circumstances. However, we begin to see another theme, which will be addressed later, that stress in families can also undermine the cohesiveness of sibling bonds. As we see in the Sanchez Family, however, there is an expectation that the children should pull together, and a lack of understanding why that does not happen. The following helps us to begin to understand:

> Manuel: 'Having lost our mother, we children should have been closer; we should have backed each other up. But we could never be like that because my father always stepped in between us boys and the girls.' (p. 28)

Differential treatment within the family, perhaps preceding the death of the mother, may, in part, contribute to the inability of siblings to support each other. This topic will be considered further in Chapter 4 (see Question 3).

Summary: sibling relationships – the big picture

This chapter has highlighted polarities and disparities in the way sibling relationships are seen: siblings as allies and siblings as rivals. There are contested views of sibling relationships. They may be seen as characteristically protective and supportive; they may be seen as competitive and rivalrous. They are rarely seen as both at the same time within the same relationship, and yet, as suggested here, this is exactly what they are. Sibling relationships are the place where we learn as we grow that love and hate, rivalry and support, envy and pride, resentment and caring and other conflicting emotions can exist in the same relationship, at the same time. Emotions about, and within, sibling relationships are usually portrayed as unequivocal and powerful, but their real strength may be that they are complex enough to contain features which, on the face of it, may appear incompatible and in conflict.

2 Sibling Relationships in the Family Context

We have to divide mother love with our brothers and sisters.
Our parents can help us cope with the loss of our dream of abso-
lute love. But they cannot make us believe that we haven't lost it.
(Judith Viorst, 1986, p. 96)

This chapter begins with a simple description of the family in terms of
the three family subsystems described in the family therapy literature.
Continuing from the previous chapter, it contends that sibling relationships are much more complex that they have perhaps been portrayed to be, arising within families which are themselves exceedingly
complex social units, and considers the factors that make such relationships so complex (size, influences of other relationships, levels of
influences). The chapter proceeds to consider the temporal dimension:
how sibling relationships change over time.

The complexity of sibling relationships and their social context, the family

The latter half of the twentieth century saw the integration of systems
thinking into understanding social relations, initially competing with,
and then perhaps taking over from earlier psychoanalytic models.
This was particularly seen, for example, in the development of groupwork and family therapy, both of whose origins were more strongly
influenced by psychoanalytic thinking, but which went on to become
much more systems-oriented. Kurt Lewin (1951) was a profound
influence on early systems thinking and theorising. His work came
after the Gestalt school of psychology, whose aphorism, 'the whole is
greater than the sum of the parts', indicated a focus on the holistic
within psychology that eschewed the reductionist approach. Lewin
was an acknowledged influence on Urie Bronfenbrenner who later
developed a model of child development based almost entirely on
systems thinking (Bronfenbrenner, 1979).

Minuchin (1974) developed a family systems model in which the family is understood as comprising three subsystems. These emerge as the family develops. The first, the spousal subsystem, is formed 'when two adults of the opposite sex join with the express purpose of forming a family' (p. 56). It is the social system formed by the inter-action between the two adults in the family. The second subsystem to emerge as the family develops is the parental subsystem. 'A new level of family formation is reached with the birth of the first child. The spousal subsystem in an intact family must now differentiate to perform the tasks of socializing a child without losing the mutual support that should characterize the spouse subsystem' (p. 57). At its simplest, with the first (or only) child in the family, this can be seen as two additional social systems, the system comprising the mother and child, and the system comprising the father and the child. Thus, in the family at this stage we have three systems, of two different types. The third subsystem, the sibling subsystem, is established with the birth of a second child. Then we have all three types of family subsystems and, in the simplest model, six interacting social systems: each parent with each child (four); the parents with each other (one); and the children with each other (one). Minuchin describes the sibling subsystem as 'the first laboratory in which children can experiment with peer rela-tionships. Within this context, children support, isolate, scapegoat, and learn from each other. In the sibling world children learn how to negotiate, cooperate, and compete' (p. 59).

Because the Minuchin terminology can be confusing (for example, parental subsystem could be mistakenly understood to mean the relationship between the parents), a different terminology to identify the three subsystems is used here:

Spousal subsystem = Parent/parent subsystem
Parental subsystem = Parent/child subsystem(s)
Sibling subsystem = Child/child subsystem(s)

These family subsystems are illustrated in Figure 2.1.

To begin with let us consider three factors contributing to the complexity of family systems arising from this model. First, note that the bi-directional arrows indicate the reciprocal nature of the influ-ences. This emphasises the child's active contribution to the process of interaction between him- or herself and the parent. It is also important to highlight that the influence between siblings is bi-directional no matter how young the younger of the two siblings.

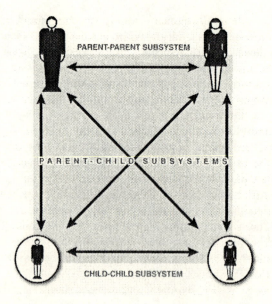

FIGURE 2.1 FAMILY SYSTEMS MODEL

Secondly, the order of complexity of relationships increases dramatically as the family grows in size with the addition of further children. As has been noted by Wedge and Mantle (1991) there is a dramatic increase in the number of sibling relationships as the number of siblings in a family increases, illustrated in Table 2.1. Bearing in mind that these are simply the number of *dyadic* sibling relationships within the family depending upon how many siblings there are, if one then adds the parents to the family, the number of intrafamilial dyadic

TABLE 2.1 NUMBER OF SIBLING RELATIONSHIPS

Siblings	Relationships
2	1
3	3
4	6
5	10
6	15
7	21

Source: Wedge and Mantle, 1991.

relationships again increases dramatically. Thus a family of two parents and four children would have fifteen dyadic relationships.

The third factor is the influence of relationships within the system. Relationships within the family influence other relationships within the family. Thus, understanding the family is not simply about looking at three isolated sets of relationships, but concerns itself as much with how one relationship influences another. There are those who suggest that looking at sibling relationships (and indeed family relationships more broadly) simply in terms of multiples of dyadic relationships is to oversimplify the complex dynamics within families and does not do justice to the complexity of levels of influences. In part, a reason for this critique derives from the very notion of systemic thinking – that the relationships between components of a system exert an influence that may be distinct from the influence exerted by the components of the system themselves.

Relationships as an influence is conveyed by Bronfenbrenner (1979) in his description of the 'mesosystem'. Without going too deeply into his social ecology model of human development, let us consider an example. Where a child in the family (which exerts an influence on his or her development) attends school (which also influences the child's development) then the quality and nature of the relationship between the school and the family will exert an influence on how the child develops which is distinct from both the influence of the family and the influence of the school. Let us consider, for example, two scenarios involving a 9-year-old boy with behavioural difficulties (both at home and at school). In one scenario, the parents seek help from the school, and together they work out a way of dealing with the child's behaviour, by implementing a programme of behavioural management both at home and school. The school values the parents' involvement in trying to address a difficulty they are having at school with the child, and the parents are glad that the school is taking an interest in helping to resolve a difficulty that is creating stress and tension in the home. In the second scenario, the school feels that the parents are to blame for the child's difficulty and also that the parents are attempting to pass the blame onto the school; the parents feel that the school is not doing what it could to get the behaviour under control, which they believe originates in a school context, and spreads over to home. The relationship between the parents and the school is one of tension, distrust and defensiveness – not a good basis for resolving the difficulties. In each case the nature of the relationship between the parents and the school is going to have an influence on how effectively the problem is addressed (and ultimately on how the child develops). In teaching and social work over the last twenty-five years, this understanding of the enhanced effectiveness of intervention when parents and professionals work together in a spirit of mutual cooperation has been promoted under the title of 'partnership'.

With intrafamily dynamics, therefore, one can suggest that not only do individuals within families influence each other, but also that relationships within families influence the individual family members, and further that relationships within families influence other relationships within families. As we have seen, the more siblings there are in a family, the more complex becomes the network of interrelationships within the family. With the arrival of the first child comes a second level of social interactions, that is an individual being influenced by the relationship between two others within the family. A father is influenced by the relationship between the mother and child; a mother is influenced by the relationship between the father and child; and very importantly, a child is influenced by the relationship between his parents. The addition of a second child creates a new level of intra-familial social interactions. Now relationships between two people can be influenced by relationships between two others. Significantly, the sibling relationship is influenced by: (a) the relationship between the two parents (b) the relationships between the father and each of the two children; and (c) the relationships between the mother and each of the two children. With four children in a family the network of social relationships begins to become very complicated indeed. Larger families become too complex to use diagrams.

A typology of three types of intrafamilial influences is proposed:

First order: individual ⇔ individual
Individuals influence, and are influenced by, other individuals

Second order: relationship ⇔ individual
The relationship between two individuals influences and is influenced by individuals in the family

Third order: relationship ⇔ relationship
The relationship between two individuals influences and is influenced by another relationship between two individuals within the family

An example of a first-order influence would be the relationship between a mother and her child or that between siblings. An example of a second-order intrafamilial relationship would be the influence exerted on the children (each and individually) by the marital relationship. Another example would be the impact that the relationship between the siblings (for example perhaps quarrelling and bickering) has upon the parents as individuals. Third-order influences (between relationships) can be seen in the kind of influence that the bickering between siblings has on the relationship between the parents. Another third-order influence is how the relationship between one parent and a child (for example differential treatment of some sort, such as favouritism or scapegoating) influences the relationship between siblings. These third-order influences are discussed more fully in Chapter 4.

Therefore, when trying to understand sibling relationships, it is perhaps important to adopt a position of humility in the face of the immense complexity of this social system called a 'family' within which such relationships arise. When one begins to consider second- and third-order influences within families, there are many questions arising about the nature of intrafamilial relationships involving siblings, for example:

- How does the relationship between the parents influence their individual relationships with the children? How does the relationship that the parents have with their children influence how they, the parents, get on with each other?
- How does the relationship between the parents influence how their children get on with each other? How does the relationship between the siblings influence how the parents get on with each other?
- How does the nature of the relationship that each of the parents have with the children influence how the children get on with each other? How does the nature of the sibling relationship influence how each of the parents get on with each of their children?

Figures 2.2 and 2.3 illustrate how much more complex family systems become as they go from being a three-person family to a four-person family. Who would have thought quite so much was going on in families with such a simple structure as two adults and two children? I will not even try to represent three, four, five or more children in the family; the illustrations would be of inordinate complexity.

And if that were not complex enough, this model simply focuses on a snapshot. At any one time, these processes are occurring within families. If one then adds a temporal component to it, so that influences can be chained over time, one gets questions like:

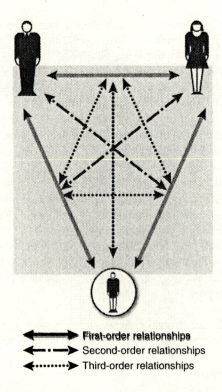

First-order relationships
Second-order relationships
Third-order relationships

FIGURE 2.2 RELATIONSHIPS IN A THREE-MEMBER FAMILY

How does the relationship between the parents influence the development of the children and their sibling relationship? How does that sibling relationship then influence both the parents and the other siblings? How do they (parents and other siblings) then influence the relationship between the parents?

One might ask the question, as illustrated in Figure 2.4, how does the quality of the relationship between siblings at one time influence the quality of the relationship at a later time? This process continues for as long as the family exists. This model is based on the assumption of two parents (or parent-figures) in the system, and at least two children (whether or not biologically related). At the time when family therapists were beginning to theorise about family systems, the traditional, two-parent, nuclear family was perhaps much more common than it is today, although it is likely that even then it may have been supposed to have more widespread applicability than

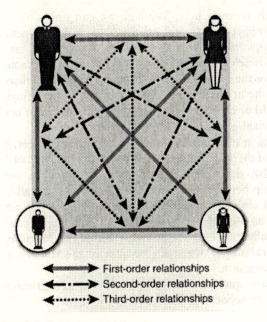

First-order relationships
Second-order relationships
Third-order relationships

FIGURE 2.3 RELATIONSHIPS IN A FOUR-MEMBER FAMILY

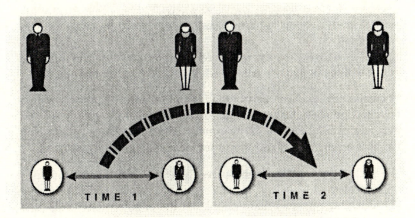

TIME 1   TIME 2

FIGURE 2.4 SIBLING RELATIONSHIPS OVER TIME

it in fact had. No such assumption of the normality of two-parent households is made here, although we can only consider the intra-familial impact of parental relationships as an influence on sibling relationships where there are in fact two parents (or two parent-figures). These two parents do not need to be in a common household in order for their relationship to be an influence, and there may be two adults in the household who are not in fact both biologically parents of the child or children. Likewise, the children do not need both to be the biological offspring of the two parents.

Looking at the three questions we considered earlier, it can be seen that two of them are more directly related to the issue of the influences on, and by, the sibling relationship. The question about how the relationship between the parents influences, and is influenced by, the individual children within the family is perhaps less relevant to our emphasis on the sibling relationships, although it: (a) can be seen as an indirect influence, and (b) probably forms the mainstay of thinking about intrafamilial dynamics, because of the relative neglect of the sibling dimension.

The two questions therefore can be disaggregated into four questions by separating out reciprocal influences:

Question 1: How does the relationship between the parents influence how their children get on with each other?
Question 2: How does the relationship between the siblings influence how the parents get on with each other?
Question 3: How does the nature of the relationship that each of the parents have with the children influence how the children get on with each other?
Question 4: How does the nature of the sibling relationship influence how each of the parents gets on with each of their children?

We will return to these questions in Chapters 3 and 4. For now we shall note the similarity between these four questions to be addressed, and five factors identified by Furman and Giverson (1995) as influencing the development of relationships between siblings. They are:

(1) the general nature of the parent's relationships with their two children;
(2) differences in the relationships that the children have with their parents;
(3) techniques adopted by the parents for disciplining the children or responding to specific sibling interactions;

(4) the means adopted by the parents specifically to influence the sibling relationships in one way or another, for example by promoting positive interactions or discouraging negative ones; and

(5) the quality of the relationship that the parents have with each other.

Stages in sibling relationships

We have already referred to the time dimension by considering how sequential influences within families make the already extremely complex snapshot of intrafamilial influences even more complicated. Now we consider the time changes more globally – over longer periods of time. Sibling relationships change over time. In general, to borrow an aphorism, they do tend to get worse before they get better, as individuals develop over the lifespan.

Stage One begins with the experience of becoming a sibling, a very significant stage in the development of sibling relationships and one about which much has been written. Stage Two considers the experience of growing up together during early childhood, middle childhood and pre-adolescence. In Stage Three, corresponding with adolescence, siblings begin psychologically, and before very long, physically, to separate from the family, and each other. This is frequently a time when sibling relationships are at their most strained. But in Stage Four there is a re-emergence of positive sibling bonds that frequently happens at certain times after siblings have left home – marriage, the birth of children, a sibling's divorce, the death of the parent(s). In the fifth stage, in later life, after both parents are deceased, sibling relationships frequently take on a renewed significance. Let us consider these stages in sequence.

Stage one: birth of a sibling

The humorous arrival of Baby Sinclair in the television series, *Dinosaurs*, captures this situation, as the baby hatches from the shell saying: 'I'm the baby, gotta love me. Come on. Gotta love me; I'm the baby'. The two teenage dinosaurs, Robbie and Charlene, react with humour and good-natured indulgence, which is not necessarily how younger children, or indeed teenagers, might actually react to the arrival of a new baby.

In fact, it is quite common for children in the family to have reactions to the arrival of a new sibling. Let us consider how children who are already established within the family might react and what might account for these reactions.

What kind of reactions?

Some children have very dramatic reactions to the arrival of a new sibling, but for most, the reactions are not extreme. In *The Piggle*, Donald Winnicott, the noted child psychiatrist (Winnicott, 1980), describes his work with a young girl. Here, in relation to their 2-year, 4 month-old daughter (at the time of referral), the parents seek Winnicott's assistance because of difficulties and great changes in her that largely seemed to stem from the time of the birth of her younger sister when she was 21 months old. As they noted in their letter, 'this and our anxiety about it seemed to bring about a great change in her' (p. 6). Another case suggests just how devastating the impact of a sibling arrival can be. In this case, the treatment of an 11-year-old boy had been necessitated because he had been traumatised at the age of $4\frac{1}{2}$ when a younger sibling was born (Weintraub, 1990). The fact that his mother became very depressed and was hospitalised for nearly a year following the sibling's birth made the situation worse. The case study describes how the therapist had overcome the threatened disruption to the therapy by continuing the therapy via the phone when she herself had to be confined to bed because of a threatened miscarriage, a situation that reawakened the early trauma for the young boy in treatment. Fortunately for most children, the extremes described here are not very common. The majority of older children do not require psychiatric treatment for the upset caused by the arrival of a baby brother or sister. Nevertheless, we should not underestimate the impact it has for the older child.

Interestingly, for some children there are positive changes associated with the arrival of a new baby. When looking at the security of a child's attachment, using Ainsworth's Strange Situation technique (a procedure to assess the quality of attachment between a child and his/her carer, see Chapter 7) before and after the birth of a sibling, it would seem that first, attachments are relatively unstable during this period, and secondly, and more surprisingly, nearly as many children go from having insecure attachments before the birth to having secure attachments after (26 per cent) as the other way round (32 per cent) (Touris *et al.*, 1995). The authors suggest that the transition from insecure to secure attachments may be a reflection of the total commitment of the mother's psychological resources to the impending arrival, leaving her little for the child who is already there. As they note:

> If the pregnant mother is preoccupied with her own physical and emotional state, she is less available to her firstborn infant, less responsive, less sensitive, and less adaptable. In such cases, the quality of the mother–infant interaction may improve after the birth of the sibling. (p. 296)

It can be very difficult to predict how the child might react to the arrival of a new sibling. Mendelson (1990) used his own personal experience of having two sons to attempt to understand the psychological impact. He approached the issue of transition to siblinghood using three theoretical perspectives: family systems theory; role acquisition theory (life transition); and a personal-narrative approach. He notes, 'Despite our increasing knowledge about children's reactions to a new brother or sister, it is still difficult to predict how a particular child will respond. It is, of course, easier to construct a coherent explanation afterwards' (p. 101).

Field and Reite (1984) found that during the time mothers were in hospital, children displayed increases in negative affect, heightened activity levels, increased heart rate, night walking and crying. Longer periods of deep sleep at this stage were seen as 'conservation withdrawal', although they could perhaps also be seen as a reaction to the heightened activity levels during the awake, but stressed, states. After the mothers' return, decreases were noted in positive affect, activity level, heart rate and active sleep (which suggested to the researchers that the children had been suffering from depression). Trause (1981), in a comparison of siblings who were allowed to visit mother and new arrival in hospital with those who were not, found that both groups, that is *all* siblings, showed significant increases in temper tantrums, excessive activity and sleep problems (benefits of visitation are discussed on page 45).

Most firstborn children (over 90 per cent found by Dunn and Kendrick, 1982) become 'more demanding' and 'more naughty' following the birth of a sibling. This behaviour can sometimes take the form of aggressive acts towards the child. Children are more jealous when the new child is of the opposite sex (which may be related to more attention given by mothers to a baby of a different sex). Griffin and de la Torre (1985) highlight common reactions of children to the birth of sibling: attention-seeking behaviour; direct aggression; denial and withdrawal; or maturity and independence. They suggest methods by which parents can ensure that normal jealous feelings are channelled in a healthy and harmless way.

The important thing about these disturbances to the older child's social and personal equilibrium is that they are not usually permanent. 'The birth of a sibling is associated with a significant increase in behaviour problems of the children, but these increases are temporary' (Baydar, Hyle and BrooksGunn, 1997).

Why these reactions?

What might account for the reactions that children have to the arrival of a new baby brother or sister? There are indeed a lot of things that happen before, during and after the birth that might contribute to it being a challenging period for the firstborn child. Before, there are transitions, changes happening all around the child, which, depending upon his age and understanding, the child may be able to relate to the forthcoming arrival. If he or she is very young, then it may be an experience of change without understanding. A new room may be being prepared, or indeed, if space is tight, modifications may be made to the firstborn child's room. The child's mother, who previously had been accessible to the child, may become less so, as the mother becomes more and more absorbed in her inner experience (the phrase 'primary maternal preoccupation' has been used to describe this inner directedness on the part of a mother during pregnancy). There may be deliberate strategies invoked by the parent to help their child adjust to the experience of having a new brother or sister. The parents may try to expose the child to young babies. They may begin to give the child less attention (or arrange for the child to be with others more), so that he or she can become accustomed to not having so much of the parent's time.

Because mothers are usually admitted to hospital for the delivery, there are separation issues. The film narrative of John, aged 17 months (Robertson and Robertson, 1989), is a good example of this. He was separated from his mother for nine days without contact with her, and the impact on his general development was dramatic. One can only speculate on the impact on his relationship with his younger sibling. Of course, current periods of confinement are much shorter, usually only several days for a first delivery. But separation from mother is not the only significant change at the time of confinement. The father may be spending time at home caring for the firstborn or the child may be spending more time with other carers (grandparents, family relatives, friends of the family, etc.).

With the arrival of the newcomer, the child is confronted with a very different set of family relations. As indicated earlier in this chapter, the complexity of the family network of relationships is increased dramatically in the transition from three to four (and even more so for four to five, five to six, etc.). The firstborn has to adjust to the new sibling, certainly. But more than that, he or she has to develop an understanding of:

- the mother's relationship with the new sibling;
- the father's relationship with the new sibling;
- the influence the newcomer may have on each parent and on their relationship with each other;
- how the parent's relationship to him- or herself has changed;
- how the parents cope with his or her relationship to the new arrival.

The birth of a sibling produces significant changes in the family environment (Baydar, Greek and BrooksGunn, 1997). The most fundamental changes for the child are in the quantity, quality and pattern of the nature of the interactions with both of the parents. Both parents spend less time with the firstborn child (Dunn and Kendrick, 1980; Kendrick and Dunn, 1980; Taylor and Kogan, 1973; R.B. Stewart *et al.*, 1987), although this reduction is likely to be more pronounced in the case of the mother, because of her higher base level of interaction to begin with. As pointed out by Mendelson (1990), the same amount of time that both parents each spent with the firstborn child is replaced by the amount of time they each spend with the two children; collectively, the same amount of time that was spent as a threesome, is afterwards spent as a foursome. It is common for fathers to spend more time with the firstborn around the time of the arrival of the baby. This may in many cases resemble a 'getting to know you' exercise, as fathers may take on responsibility for the care of the child (bathing, feeding, night-time routines) that they previously had left to the mother. The nature of the interaction with the parents changes as well. Many parents try to involve the firstborn in the care of the baby as a way of helping him or her to come to accept the new arrival; this is very different from the kinds of interactions before the baby's arrival, even if it does promote a sense of involvement. And of course, family routines are altered, usually in a less predictable way, until the baby settles into stable sleeping and feeding patterns (which vary from baby to baby). For the firstborn it is not just change, it is CHANGE.

As an example of some of these post-arrival changes, consider the work of Javaid and Kestenberg (1983). Coming from a psychodynamic perspective, they emphasise the mother's exclusive bonding to the new arrival. They consider the concept of 'entrancement': a state of mother's 'being in love' with the new child and a mutual estrangement between the mother and the previous child. Although this process creates guilt for the mother and may make the older child sad, it is seen as an adaptive process in that it allows the mother the psychological space to devote herself to the newborn at a time when the infant is most vulnerable, which in turn enhances her self-esteem as a mother. The older child in the family, who may feel hurt and angry, is compelled to develop other object relationships (for example with the father). These are temporary states of affairs, but when resolved, there is a more even distribution of both love and anger on the part of the mother towards both children.

Abarbanel (1983) looked at an unusual impact of the arrival of a second child, the revival of the mother's own sibling experiences. This highlights how dramatic the changes in the family can be. Two case studies are presented which focus on a mother's relationship with her female toddler at the time of having her second child. The revival of the mother's own sibling experience is said to affect her relationship with her toddler. The quality of her preparation of her daughter for the new arrival is also examined. Both the child's age and mother's spacing from her own siblings are said to have an impact on the mother–child experience during the second pregnancy. Both a negative case study and a positive one are provided. In the first, mother's unresolved sibling rivalry holds her back from being psychologically available to her toddler and this adversely affected the toddler's attitude towards the newborn child. In the more positive case, the revival of mother's sibling experience helped her to prepare her daughter to anticipate the new baby with pleasure.

What helps with a child's adjustment to the arrival of a sibling?

Dunn (1995), in her guide to parents on coping with the transition from one child to two, emphasises that age gap does not have the significance that perhaps it was thought to have. More important are the temperamental and psychological differences between the two children. In this sense, she is providing the kind of advice that many have found helpful when advising parents on the task of parenting: expect children to be different!

Clearly, the support of the parents is vital. Interestingly, Gottlieb and Mendelson (1990), in their consideration of how firstborn girls adjust to the arrival of, and get involved with, a new sibling, found that the level of distress of the girls was related to support from the mothers before the sibling's birth, and to support from the father, afterwards. It is very intriguing to speculate why this gender pattern emerged. Sibling involvement with the newborn was associated with types of parental support, especially during the postnatal period.

The way in which children prepare, or are prepared by parents, for the arrival of the new child seems to be important – but it is not necessarily clear why it is important. How to handle the arrival of the second child is a major source of anxiety for parents, and there is no shortage of books and internet sites available to fill the gap for suggestions as to how to handle this very tricky process. However, there is no particular evidence to suggest that parental preparation of the child – for example, by talking with the child about the forth-coming baby or reading books to the child about children arriving in families – whilst reassuring to parents that they are doing what they should be doing in relation to their child, is actually effective. Con-sider, for example, the following from Dunn (1995) when addressing the issue of preparing the firstborn:

> There are no hard and fast answers to these questions – so much depends on the individual child and her parents. Various 'experts' have taken a strong position of how to 'prepare' a child for the birth of a sibling, some advocating lengthy discussions and lots of books, while others claim that it makes no difference. The fact is, there is no good hard evi-dence for either position. This is partly because almost all children get some preparation for the arrival . . . So we really have no basis for judging how a child would react to a baby without any preparation. (pp. 33–4)

Nevertheless, given our contention of the complexity of interactions within the family, if it makes the parents happy to do something in relation to the child, then there may be positive spin-off effects in terms of how the child feels.

On the other hand, there is some indication that the way children get on with their new baby brother or sister is related to their play, specifically, how much they play, what kind of play they are involved in, and with whom they play. Field and Reite (1984) studied the behavioural and physiological responses of the sixteen children before, during and after mother's confinement. They found that increases in fantasy play across these periods were seen as active coping with the two types of stress: that arising from the maternal separation and that from the arrival of a new sibling.

Kramer, in association with colleagues (Kramer and Gottman, 1992; Kramer and Schaefer-Hernan, 1994), looked at how children adjust to becoming a sibling for the first time, comparing those children who adjusted well with those who did not. They looked at children before and after the birth of their first sibling. Children who interacted more positively with their siblings, were the ones who before the birth: (a) played longer; (b) engaged in fantasy play that was thematically relevant to becoming a sibling; and (c) had better peer relations than low-sibling acceptance children. Apart from anything else, these findings remind us how important play is for the child. It has very significant implications, and should not be trivialised by adults as inconsequential. For the child, the anticipatory work of pretending what life will be like when the baby arrives is very serious, even if it may not appear so to the adult. Donald Winnicott suggested that children who cannot play cannot be helped therapeutically, and therefore the first step in therapy with such a child is to help them to begin to be able to play. But here we have a situation in which the child instinctively 'knows' that play (that is thematically relevant) is useful to him or her. This important principle of the therapeutic value of play, and of the child's instinctive drive to use play therapeutically to resolve conflicts and address issues, is at the heart of non-directive play therapy. It follows that parental encouragement of their child to play (in a way that is thematically relevant to the forthcoming changes) can contribute to the child's post-arrival adjustment. For example, reading age-appropriate books about becoming a sibling may be informative, but they may also stimulate the child's own imaginative and therapeutic processes; it may promote the child's ability to engage in thematically relevant play.

Another issue that has been considered as possibly having an effect on the child's adjustment is the presence of the sibling at the birth, a practice begun in California in the late 1970s. DelGuidice (1986) studied the differences in sibling rivalry within a group of children of 22 parents (16 children present; 12 not present). Eight specific behaviours were looked at: reverts to behaviour outgrown, throws temper tantrums, physically interacts with baby, takes toys from baby, states dislike for baby, has nightmares, has sleeping problems and physically interacts harshly with parents. The results showed no significant difference between the two groups for any of the eight behaviours. Judy Dunn (1995) also looks at this issue and considers that there is no evidence for benefit either way, but advises against it. She notes a body of professional opinion against the practice for a variety of reasons. One of these reasons is boredom, and she notes an account provided by one child who indicated that he would rather have watched TV!

Visitation as an aid to the firstborn's adjustment

As indicated, part of the difficulty for children at the time of the arrival of the birth of a sibling is the separation from the primary carer, usually the mother. Field and Reite (1984) looked at children's responses to separation from mother during mother's confinement. However, this study did not look at the mediating effects of visitation (and of course visitation to the hospital not only involves contact with the new sibling, but also with the mother whom the child might well be missing). In this case children (16 children aged 22–60 months) were deprived of contact from their mothers for the duration of hospitalisation. It is distressing to think that as late as 1984, children were still not being allowed to visit parents in hospital in view of all the evidence emerging from the Robertsons at least twenty years before (Robertson and Robertson, 1989). It might be pointed out that around the same time as this study, Shuler and Reich (1982) noted that many institutions were seen to be changing to a more liberalised policy about sibling visitations to hospitalised children.

Contact between firstborn and mother, and lots of it, during this period of time may offset the negative impact of the separation for the child, but it may bring other difficulties. Most women (84 per cent according to Mackey and Miller, 1992) would choose to have older children visit, and believe that both mothers and children derive benefit from the visits. The downside, however, can be the emotional reactions of the mothers and siblings, the lack of control between siblings and infants and inconvenient location for the visit.

Several studies have highlighted how visiting benefits children. Trause (1981) looked at the issue of siblings being allowed to visit newborn siblings in hospital to see if there were any effects. The reactions of 14 firstborn children (aged $1-3\frac{1}{2}$ years old) to 'routine' 2–6 day separations associated with maternal childbirth were compared with the reactions of 17 siblings who were allowed to visit their mothers in hospital for about one hour per day. Siblings who were allowed to visit were initially much more responsive to their mothers and to their new siblings. Maloney et al. (1983) randomly assigned

57 siblings to one of two groups, a visitation group and a non-visitation group, and found after a two-week follow-up, that the visitation group showed improvement in over-activity behaviour and family adjustment and 28 per cent derived psychological benefit from the visit; they enjoyed their visits and wished to return.

Stage two: growing up together

We will consider in more depth the nature of sibling relationships in childhood in the next chapter. This section focuses on how such relationships change during early childhood, middle childhood and early adolescence. As noted by Dunn and McGuire (1992), research in this area has largely focused on *early* childhood, usually over very short periods of time. In the early years of life the youngest child undergoes a reorientation from the parent to the sibling(s). There is markedly more interaction with the brothers and sisters and significantly less with the mother from about toddlerhood (Dunn and Creps, 1996). Further, it is around this age or a little later, (between the ages of 3 and 4) that older siblings start taking much more of an interest in their younger siblings and begin to communicate more with them. As the younger siblings become more capable, more cognitively sophisticated and physically able, they become better playmates. As noted by Dunn and McGuire (1992, p. 69), 'By the age of 4 years, children's relationships with older siblings are apparently of more significance in sociocognitive development than they were 1 year earlier.' It is a period when more positive aspects of the relationship begin to develop, and a relative stability of those positive features emerges. For example, Stillwell and Dunn (1985) in a longitudinal study looked at the issue of continuity of sibling aggression and friendliness. They followed up 25 6-year-old children who had been observed at home when they were 2–3 years old with their infant siblings to ascertain if aggression or friendliness in the relationship continued over time. They found considerable stability over the period of time, and significant direct correlations between positive features of the sibling relationship at Time 1 and Time 2.

It should also be noted that there are variations in stability between older and younger siblings. The friendliness of older siblings towards younger children is likely to remain relatively stable over time, but the behaviour of the younger sibling towards the older child is much less stable (Abramovitch, *et al.* 1986; Stillwell and Dunn, 1985). This may be accounted for simply by the fact that children's characteristics and personality become much more set as they become older; older children will have had that much more experience to contribute to the type of person they have become than younger siblings, and are therefore, arguably, less susceptible to change, more generally, than younger siblings.

It is also a period of time when the level of aggression begins to diminish. Martin and Ross (1995) looked at how sibling aggression developed over a two-year period between firstborns (3.6–4.9 years) and secondborns (1.9–2.6 years). They recorded aggression levels, and, as might be expected, older siblings were more aggressive than younger siblings although the difference reduced over the two years. Of interest though is that there was an association between the level of aggression of the older child at the beginning of the two years, and the level of aggression of the younger child at the end – that is, the more aggressive the older child was at the beginning, the more aggressive the younger sibling was at the end of the two years. This is probably the result of modelling – the younger child learning to be aggressive from the aggressive behaviour of the older child.

Pepler *et al.* (1982) found the interaction patterns remained quite stable over an 18-month period in early childhood. Older siblings tended to initiate prosocial and agonistic (combative) behaviour whilst the younger siblings tended to imitate more. They also found that for the mixed-sex pairs, the amount of aggression increased while imitation decreased over time.

Stability of aggression over time in early childhood was also found by Dunn and Munn (1986), who noted that by the age of 24 months one begins to see relatively mature behaviour such as conciliation, teasing, reference to social rules, and justification. Sibling aggression, however, at this stage was found to be correlated with earlier sibling aggression.

Changes in aggression and conflict in the sibling relationship during this stage are also related to the levels of conflict between parents and children. For example, Volling and Belsky (1992), in their longitudinal home-observation study, found aggression and conflict in the sibling relationship to be related to high levels of conflict between the mother and both children, to over-controlling mothering and to an insecure infant–mother attachment. Prosocial sibling interaction on the other hand was associated with facilitative and affectionate fathering.

Also, as the younger sibling gets older the relationship between the child and older sibling becomes much more egalitarian. It is unclear whether this is because both children are becoming less dominant, or whether it is because the younger sibling is able to exert more influence. Factors such as the child's temperament, the level of positivity in the relationship between the parent and children, differential negativity in the relationship that the parent(s) has with the children, and the level of conflict between the parents, all combine to influence the quality of the relationship between siblings (Brody, Stoneman and McCoy, 1994), which may prove quite consistent over time between middle childhood and early adolescence.

Dunn, Slomkowski, Beardsall and Rende (1994) looked at adjustment difficulties in relationships between two groups of siblings (the younger group's average age of 3, and the older group's average age of 5), and followed them up after 5 and 7 years. Adjustment difficulties were measured using the dimensions of internalising behaviour (fear, inhibition and over-controlled behaviour) and externalising behaviour (aggressive, antisocial and under-controlled behaviour). They found positive relations to be more significant than negative relations in association with adjustment difficulties. Specifically, they found 'hostile, critical comments about the sibling and descriptions of fighting with the sibling were *not* related to adjustment problems two years later – rather it was the lack of friendly behaviour and warm feelings towards the sibling that showed links with the later adjustment measures'. This study is particularly significant in the study of sibling relationships. It suggests that both hostility/fighting and friendliness/warmth may be present in a sibling relationship and if so, the presence or absence of friendliness and warmth may be more indicative of how that sibling relationship will develop than the presence or absence of hostility and/or fighting.

Dunn (1996) looked at the significance of life events, socioeconomic status and gender as mediating variables influencing the extent of change in the quality of the sibling relationship from middle childhood and early adolescence. She also looked at the subjective perceptions of the family members as to what they thought contributed to changes over time in sibling relationships.

Stage three: sibling relationships in adolescence

Let us begin our consideration of sibling relationships in adolescence by looking backwards to those same relationships in early childhood. Dunn, Slomkowski and Beardsall (1994) asked how much sibling relationships change as children grow up (from early childhood to adolescence). They found:

considerable continuity in the siblings' positive and negative behaviour
toward one another over the 7 to 8 years between the early childhood
and early adolescence periods (p. 321)

Steinmetz (1977) noted that the nature of conflicts between siblings
changed as children grew older. When younger, conflicts tended to
be about possessions (learning to share toys; etc). Older children,
however, tended to have conflicts with siblings about space. As the
importance of having a space of one's own emerges with the onset of
adolescence, invasion of that space becomes an issue worthy of an
energetic defence. Parents may be able to understand this emerging
need and accommodate it; younger siblings may not.

Le Gall (1998) looks at how sibling relationships change in the
transition from childhood to early adulthood. She notes the work of
one researcher who, when posing the question: 'Is there any person in
your family or family-in-law that you would rather avoid?', found a
positive response from over one-quarter of respondents (26 per cent),
and, of those, most talked about a member of the same generation.
However, Le Gall (1998) also discusses the more positive side of
sibling relationships:

> Naturally, there are frictions, oppositions, rivalries and jealousies. But,
> in general, all our participants talk a lot more about the affection they
> have for their siblings than about any hostility they may feel. 'I adore my
> little sister.' Except for a few cases, when they mention a disagreement
> with a younger brother or sister it is most often trivial. (p. 92)

What seems to reconcile these apparently conflicting perceptions is the
transition from being a teenager to becoming a young adult. Le Gall
summarises:

> taking all things together, conflicts between brothers and sisters take
> real shape during adulthood. In other words, whether or not there had
> been any disagreements during childhood or adolescence, significant dif-
> ferences emerge or reach full proportions when siblings, as adults, are
> equipped with fully developed reasoning powers ... we believe that sib-
> ling quarrels are more likely to develop and become manifest during
> adult age. (pp. 93–4)

Dunn and McGuire (1992, citing Buhrmester and Furman, 1987)
comment:

> The changes in adolescence in patterns of warmth parallel those found for perceptions of relationships with parents, and probably reflect increasing involvement with peers outside the home. (p. 69)

This may account for the finding by Buhrmester and Furman (1987) that, within the adolescent period, older children (around the age of 17) describe less conflict with siblings than younger adolescents do. It is possibly related to the increased amount of time that older adolescents spend away from the home, and the ability to avoid irritating conflicts with younger siblings simply by removing oneself. There is also less companionship between siblings between the ages of 8 and 17, although this is not necessarily accompanied by a reduction in intimacy and affection (Buhrmester and Furman, 1987). It may also reflect the fact that the older sibling is less of an interest for the younger sibling as the latter gets older and enters adolescence him- or herself, placing greater emphasis on peer relationships. Although children at both ends of the adolescent spectrum may still live in the same home, by this stage they live in different worlds. Nevertheless, it needs to be acknowledged that researchers appear to describe different, and contradictory, findings about the nature of the relationships between siblings in the period of adolescence and the transition to adulthood. Buhrmester (1992) describes the different pathways of peer and sibling relationships in the adolescent period:

> the developmental paths of sibling and peer relationships diverge during early adolescence when dependency on peers sharply rises and dependency on sibling wanes. This divergence comes during the time when youths are experiencing puberty and striving to construct autonomous identities outside the family. Friends become soulmates in this enterprise, whereas siblings are often left behind with the family. (p. 29)

Stage four: sibling relationships in adulthood

Sibling relationships change over a longer time period. Over a short period of time, their basic underlying nature may remain fundamentally the same, as we saw when we looked at continuities of sibling relationships in young children. However, in the longer term, they do change considerably. If measuring children's sibling relationship at two points in time is likely to produce similarities, then asking adults about their sibling relationships as a child is likely to produce responses suggesting considerable change. Or, if the underlying character is the same, the way it shows itself, or indeed what the siblings can do about it, may have changed over the years. Frequently sibling relationships change around the time of life-stage transitions, for example when one or other of the siblings leaves home or when either or both of the parents die. Le Gall (1998) notes, 'in ways similar to other family ties, sibling ties recompose over time and are therefore open to change' (p. 94).

Merrell (1995), in her consideration of how sibling connections influence adult relationships, observes:

> From birth to death, the sibling relationship undergoes an amazing amount of change and development, all because the players involved continue to evolve and grow. It is hardly possible for a relationship to remain the same over a period that can be as long as eighty years or even longer. The volatile emotional quality of a single relationship can look like a cardiac patient's EKG reading. (p. 16)

Stocker *et al.* (1997) have attempted to analyse adult sibling relationships using the same dimensions from research into childhood sibling relationships (see Stocker, 1994): warmth, conflict and rivalry. They developed the Adult Sibling Relationship Questionnaire and found differences on these dimensions to be associated with variations in family structure, the amount of contact between siblings and sibling mental health. Bank and Kahn (1997) draw on twenty years of clinical experience to explore, among a wide range of other issues, how sibling relationships change (or don't) over time. The following is an extract concerning continuities:

> Why would anyone allow oneself to be rebuffed, rebuked, abused, or humiliated by a brother or a sister over months, or even years, when one is free not to associate with one's sibling? Whenever conflict between siblings persists over time, both participants obtain secret and powerful gratifications from the struggle. These satisfactions are not immediately apparent, but they can be determined by a thoroughgoing study of the siblings' previous emotional experiences with one another ... This hypothesis can be useful when we search with our patients for answers to such questions as: 'Why do I keep reaching out to my sister, only to have her kick me around and ignore me?' 'How come I keep acting like a sucker with my brother?' (p. 227)

On the other hand, however, they note the very positive sibling bonds in adulthood with this powerful quote:

Having a reasonably affectionate relationship in adulthood with a brother or a sister is so common, statistically, that we might consider such a relationship a birthright. (p. xxiii)

Stage five: sibling relationships in later life

Finally, let us consider sibling relationships later in life. Cicirelli (1995) in particular has extended the focus on sibling relationships to later in adult life, by integrating his own empirical studies into the relationships of adult siblings with research into childhood sibling relationships. In looking at the issue of family caregiving for elderly and disabled adults (1992) he looks at the role of siblings as 'secondary caregivers'. As might be expected, he found that brothers spend fewer hours per week as secondary caregivers than sisters, although in sibling networks where there are no sisters it was found that brothers provided as many hours' care as sisters did in other families. In his study he found the following patterns of adult sibling relations in providing care:

TABLE 2.2 ADULT CAREGIVING SHARED AMONG SIBLINGS

Proportion of care provided	%
Principal caregivers provide all the care; siblings provide none	5
Principal caregivers provide over 50 per cent of care; siblings divide the remainder	55
Respondent provides more care than siblings but no one provides more than half	19
Approximately equal distribution of caregiving load between respondent and siblings	21

Source: Cicirelli, 1992.

Although Cicirelli's (1992) study is extremely useful in looking at adult patterns of sibling relations around a particular task, it is a here-and-now focus and says nothing about how those sibling relationships have changed over time or been influenced by the types of sibling patterns laid down as children. This is what we really want to know.

Gold (1989) interviewed 60 men and women over the age of 65 in a retrospective study of their sibling relationships during their life. They were then followed up with a postal survey two years later asking the same questions as the survey and 54 responses out of the initial 60 were returned. It was found that only two dimensions of the sibling relationships remained stable, closeness and contact. The other dimensions (envy, resentment, instrumental and emotional support, acceptance/approval, psychological involvement) had all changed, and in some cases significantly. From this they conclude that sibling relationships in later life are neither consistently static nor dynamic.

TABLE 2.3 SIBLING RELATIONSHIPS THROUGHOUT THE LIFESPAN

Stage	Characteristics
Birth	Displacement issues; upheaval within social environment; period of instability; potentially, but not usually, dramatic consequences for firstborn which are mostly not long-standing
Early childhood	As young baby grows to toddlerhood, becomes more oriented towards older sibling(s); older siblings responds more positively towards younger sibling; playmate. Aggression reduces. But 'playmates' may bicker and squabble . . . frequently
Middle childhood / Early adolescence	Very variable relationships. Presence or absence of warmth a significant factor
Adolescence	Potentially the low point of sibling relationships. Physical distance may preclude contact. Avoidance of interaction
Adulthood	Without the pressure of living together and without competition for the same emotional needs to be met within families, siblings are freed to re-find their relationship. Many of the patterns set down in childhood may continue. New ones may be established
Later life	With parents deceased, siblings remain as the last living co-relations. Siblings may be involved in joint arrangements for the care of ageing parents

Summary: sibling relationships in the family context

This chapter has drawn on family systems theory to highlight the complexity of relationships within a family and to note increasing complexity as the family grows from being without children, to having one child, two children and multiple children. I have developed the idea of first-order, second-order and third-order relationships within families to describe relationships between individuals, between an individual and a relationship, and between relationships to illustrate the growing complexity of the family as it develops. This provides a context for considering how sibling relationships change over time.

The salient points of sibling relationships throughout one's life are summarised in Table 2.3. It should be remembered, however, that the correlates of the quality of sibling relationships, which are examined in Chapter 4, are many, and therefore they are dependent on much more than simply the stage of life one has reached.

3 Changing Understandings of Sibling Relationships: Theory and Research

> Siblings can serve as playmates, companions, agents of socialization, advocates with the peer group, and allies in dealing with parents, as well as models of both positive and negative behaviour. (Brody and Stoneman, 1994)

There are three sections in this chapter. The first section looks at the early understanding of sibling relationships arising from psychoanalysis. The second section considers the early attempts by family therapists and psychologists to understand sibling relations, albeit in rather global terms. The third section looks at the developments within psychology over the last twenty years, during which there has been a period of renewed interest in sibling relationships, exploring their complexities in much greater depth than hitherto.

In the study of sibling relationships, theorising has preceded research. Generally, this is a risky undertaking. Without research, explanations of sibling relationships are likely to be based on preconceptions, misconceptions and half-science. This is not to dismiss completely the earlier theorising about sibling relationships, but one must be aware if its limitations.

Psychoanalytic understanding of sibling relationships

Freud

Early thinking on sibling relationships tended to emphasise the impact of having a sibling on the parent–child relationship, or on the ability of the individual to resolve certain intra-psychic conflicts before progressing to the next stage of development. Freud (1856–1939) in his extensive writings on the development of the individual actually said very little about sibling relationships, but what he said was influential. We consider here two aspects of Freud's thinking about sibling relationships: (1) the sibling as a displacement in the relationship with the mother; and (2) the sibling as a rival in the Oedipal complex.

In relation to the first theme, consider the following:

> A child who has been put into second place by the birth of a brother or sister, and who is now for the first time almost isolated from his mother, does not easily forgive her this loss of place; feelings which in an adult would be described as greatly embittered arise in him and are often the basis of a permanent estrangement. (Freud, 1917, p. 334)

This is powerful material, setting the scene for generations of psychoanalysts afterwards to reflect upon.

He suggested that the birth of sibling produces a potential opponent in the child's bid to gain power during the emotional chaos of the Oedipal conflict. In the Oedipal situation, it is posited that the child of about 4 years of age, during the 'phallic' stage of development, wishes to destroy the father and possess the mother. Because of the unacceptability of these desires and because the father is too powerful to be destroyed, these wishes and longings become repressed but remain in the unconscious.

For both of these issues, displacement of mother's attention, and the Oedipal situation, the significance of rivalry and jealousy in sibling relationships in psychoanalysis may be reflections of their personal significance for Freud. According to Jouvenot (1997), Freud's experiences with jealousy included both sibling and professional rivalries, which wielded a power over him all his life.

Adler

Much of the psychoanalytic thinking about siblings can be attributed to Adler (1870–1937), a psychoanalytic theorist primarily known for his development of the concept of the 'complex' (for example, the 'inferiority complex'), and for the concept of the 'life style', but who was also an early theorist on the nature of sibling relations (Adler, 1958). He suggested that the arrival of a new child in the family is a very traumatic event for children who are already in the family and who have already so to speak, 'staked their turf'. The term 'dethronement' developed by Adler denotes the experience of the young child going from being the centre of attention (especially when combined with psychoanalytic notions of omnipotence and magical thinking) to being an 'also ran'. The term 'dethronement' conveys both the subjective experience of losing pride of place and familial disorientation.

Levy

Levy has been a powerful influence on bringing awareness of siblings to a wider audience. He was a leader in the American Child Mental Health Movement, and the originator of the concept of 'sibling rivalry'. The beginning of systematic observation of siblings began in the 1930s with Levy's work (1934, 1937, 1943). Sibling rivalry is seen to be a powerful influence in families, varying according to gender and birth order.

Levy's method was to use a standardised play technique involving dolls in a scenario designed to evoke feelings of sibling rivalry, and categorise the child's play. He took the actual aggressive act, or incident, as relayed through the play, and analysed it in accordance with psychoanalytic concepts (for example, escape, denial, projection, regression). The emphasis on the standardisation, which for a psycho-analytic approach was relatively novel, can be seen in the following:

> The sibling rivalry (SR) experiments offer certain special advantages in the study of hostility patterns. The children are placed in identical situations in the play of the older child and the new baby at the mother's breast. The same play material and the same technics in encouraging and stimulating activity are used. Each child brings his particular experience and personality configuration to bear on a standardized play situation. (Levy, 1943, p. 441)

The following describes the methodology:

> When the play is started in the usual manner, the child is told that the mother has to feed the baby. Clay breasts are put on the mother-doll, the baby is placed in position and encircled by the mother's arms, whereupon the mother is seated in a chair and a doll representing brother or sister is placed near the chair. The child is then told, 'Now, this is the game. The brother comes and sees a new baby at the mother's breast. He sees it for the first time. Now what does he do?' (Levy, 1937)

This methodology may be open to the same criticisms that later came of Piaget's work, that children do not understand what the experimenter is getting at, and so provide responses on the basis of what they think the experimenter wants to hear. In an adult-centric world, it is not too difficult to imagine that children will be motivated to give the adult what he or she wants, especially if the child is quite young (e.g. primary school age). Evidence for this possibility comes from the following extract from Levy:

> The inhibition of the impulse may take the form of assumed stupidity like, 'I don't know what you mean. I don't know what you want.' (Levy, 1941)

Here, Levy suggests that the 'assumed' stupidity is a defence against the expression of hostility towards the baby which the child knows is what the child-doll would do/want. By current standards of research methodology, there is certainly an element of looking for what you hope to find, or 'leading' the child to the behaviour that you want him or her to provide. Ignoring the scenario, or providing a non-hostile response may be less likely because of the experimental instructions. On the other hand, Levy does indicate that children do not invariably respond aggressively, for example describing the 'very strong maternal protective attitude' of girls between the ages of 8 and 10. However, most children do respond with some type of aggressive response:

> In regard to sibling rivalry, however, the aggressive response to the new baby is so typical that it is safe to say it is a common feature of family life ... In reviewing the patterns ... of children ranging from two to thirteen years, it is most useful to conceive of the act as an ongoing social process, a dynamic unit of behavior, with various influences brought to bear upon it in every phase. The completed primitive performance is an act in which the child attacks the baby doll and destroys it by biting it, tearing it with his fingers, or crushing it with his feet. If the experiment is repeated, there is, in most of the instances at ages three, four and five, a fulfilment of hostile activity of this type. In others there are varying approaches to this end-point, easily observed and measured. In the beginning of the act when, presumably, the impulse to attack is felt, one observes, varying forms of inhibitions to the impulse, so that the act does not come out. (Levy, 1941, p. 359)

Levy goes on to describe the various psychoanalytic concepts used to understand how the older child stops him- or herself from acting (repression, superego injunctions). Thus, Levy attempted to gain a level of scientific credibility for the near universal existence of 'sibling rivalry'.

Later psychoanalytic reflections on sibling relations

Earlier psychoanalysts located the desire to destroy the newcomer within the individual, and considered that like the unseeable, unknowable conflicts surrounding the Oedipal complex, this desire must be addressed and dealt with in a way that allows the child to progress. At the same time it must be dealt with in a way that precludes the forbidden subjects from coming into consciousness. One hates, one must learn to accept it, and one must move on. But there is no suggestion that these rivalrous feelings are beneficial. Neubauer (1982), however, looked at the positive contributions to the child's development of the emotions of rivalry, envy and jealousy that arise in the normal course of sibling relationships. One positive contribution is an increased alertness that facilitates comparisons and thereby promotes the differentiation of object and self (object relations theory). Psychoanalytic models that are based exclusively on the dyadic mother–child relationship, ignoring the role of father, other caretakers and siblings, neglect this aspect. Neubauer (1983) considers the role of sibling position and the impact of envy and jealousy on the sibling relationship, emphasising that these factors change continuously during a child's development, which may affect personality organisation and character formation. Differences in how rivalry, jealousy and envy develop over time are seen as related to whether the child is an older or younger sibling. Two areas in which these three features, as shaped by the sibling's experience, play a role are: (a) siblings' potential effects on character formation; and (b) influence on object choice.

Provence and Solnit (1983) discuss observations of a $4\frac{1}{2}$-year-old boy and his $2\frac{1}{2}$-year-old sister to demonstrate positive sibling influences. They contend that the capacity of siblings with an age gap of about two years – i.e. close to each other in developmental stages – to form a positive relationship is not sufficiently emphasised. They suggest that this is the case because parents frequently focus on the rivalry, envy and jealousy which are seen as normative in the sibling relationship, rather than on their 'predominant friendliness, loyalty to each other, and ability to form a united front in response to an external threat or discomfort'. They note that the sibling experience provides frequent and ongoing opportunities for children to develop a capacity for empathy.

Another positive aspect of the sibling relationship is that it provides an early experience for the child of separating and becoming an individual. A case study by Leichtman (1985) considered how a girl's relationship with her 22-month older brother shaped her emerging identity and object relationships in her first $3\frac{1}{2}$ years. A developmental model is put forth. In infancy, the siblings are significant figures in their own right. During the second year, the influence of the sibling increases. In the third year, the older sibling influences the younger sibling's consolidation of identity. Finally, in the preschool period, for the younger sibling, separating and individuating from older siblings is an important developmental task.

Sibling relationships – neglected in the psychodynamic literature – are seen as having an important influence on psychodynamic concepts such as the development of internalised object relationships, organising principles and transference phenomena. Fueloep (1995) describes the evolution of psychoanalytic approaches to competition (Freud's penis envy; Klein's pre-Oedipal envy). He highlights its origins in almost universal experiences of sibling rivalry, and notes differences between constructive and destructive manifestations.

Akhtar and Kramer (1999) describe four stages in the development of psychoanalysis. The fourth, and current, stage is concerned with the impact of other significant people:

> a growing interest in moving beyond the parental objects is discernible. Analysts are beginning to investigate the role of grandparents and siblings in the growth and development of the child. (p. 4).

They proceed to describe factors that affect the sibling relationship: parental availability, the relationship between the parents, the parental behaviour toward the children, social siblings (referring to biologically non-related children living together as brothers and sisters), twins and twinning, the sex of the siblings, the age difference between the siblings, and a sibling having a special status.

Although latter psychoanalytic thinking has focused on other aspects of sibling relationships, rivalry has dominated psychoanalytic views of child development. Therefore, it is particularly interesting to consider the work of Stearns (1988) who examined the rise of the concept of jealous rivalry among siblings in the twentieth century. It is suggested that the twentieth century saw important new dimensions in what Americans came to believe (wrongly, according to Stearns) was a tragically inherent part of family life. The author contends that understanding this construction of sibling rivalry would help to understand the operation of jealousy in a wider context. From this perspective, there is an argument to be made that perhaps the Freudians and post-Freudians did not discover sibling rivalry ... they created it. This would perhaps be over-statement, and to support such a contention one would need more historical evidence and possibly more anthropological evidence of the absence of such rivalry in other cultures. Certainly, as indicated in Chapter 1, notions of rivalry between siblings, particularly brothers, are embedded in the mythology and biblical stories of the Western world. In view of the archetypal nature of sibling relationships, and the bifurcation of the social construction of sibling relationships into good and evil ones, this may perhaps be overstatement, but it is an idea with some merit. It is well to remember that psychoanalysis, as a way of understanding the human psyche, has been pervasive and influential within the social sciences. It has not only introduced concepts for understanding sibling relationships, but has defined discourses in relation to them.

Family therapists and the early psychology of sibling relationships

Clinicians working with families quickly appreciated the significance of sibling relationships in terms of both normal development and psychopathology. Minuchin and Fishman (1981) suggest that siblings form a child's first peer group, and note that in large families there may be a variety of subsystems of siblings according to developmental stages. The issue of how siblings form subgroups within a large family of five, six, seven or more siblings (for example on the basis of similarity of age, gender, common interest, etc.) is a very intriguing one about which there is very little written.

Minuchin and Fishman (1981) comment that family therapists have tended to under-utilise the sibling context, and describe a number of means to address this, including meeting with siblings alone. Greenbaum (1965) adopted this approach, and advocated the use of joint sibling interview in pairs as a diagnostic method for children referred to a child guidance clinic. Guidelines for sibling selection and methods of interview were then suggested.

Bell (1961) looks at sibling interactions as a later stage in family work, and describes three circumstances under which sibling relations arise in family treatment; (a) remarks directed to siblings rather than to parents (early in therapy); (b) parents complain about sibling strife; and (c) as a separate stage of treatment (following exploration of father–mother interaction). In giving case material to illustrate the sibling emphasis, he then proceeds to consider issues such as jealousy (on the part of a daughter because the two brothers are favoured) and resentment (at being asked to play; at being bossed).

Framo (1965) asks the question, 'How can children from the same family be so different?' as a way of addressing questions raised by both professionals and families about why pathological family dynamics have a differential effect on children of the family, i.e. why are some children unaffected whilst others are not. Examining research into families he found that when looked at in more depth, the 'well' siblings in families were not so well after all. Of course, this doesn't attack the premise of the question: why should we expect children to be the same just because they grow up in the same family? This is a very intriguing aspect of families to which I return when I describe the work of recent theorists on non-shared environmental influences (Chapter 4, Question 2).

Koch (1960) interviewed 360 children (ages 5 and 6) to look at the impact of gender, ordinal position and age gap ('formal character-istics') on how much time siblings spent together, how much they enjoyed their play with siblings, the amount of jealousy, the areas of conflict, and their perception of the extent to which parents treated them differently. One of her findings was that a pair of brothers seemed to produce more quarrelling than any other combination of siblings.

Toman/McGoldrick

Until recently, psychological thinking about siblings was dominated by birth order, gender, and age gap/family size – 'formal' or 'status' factors. Toman (1994) has been a leading theorist in the development of this approach. He suggested that important personality character-istics are determined by the child's family configuration, i.e. the net-work of sibling relationships. The model is based on the idea that people take up family roles based on birth order and gender and these roles carry over into relationships outside the family. He developed ten detailed personality profiles based upon sibling positions, summarised in Table 3.1. Toman considers that these profiles can predict how one will get on with friends and marital partners. The premise is that one's sibling position fits with (or doesn't) that of the sibling position of one's partner or friend. He discusses this in terms of complementarity and non-complementarity of the two profiles. He describes this in his 'duplication theorem':

TABLE 3.1 TOMAN'S BASIC TYPES OF SIBLING POSITIONS

Sibling position type	Characteristics
Oldest brother of brothers	Loves to lead and assume responsibility for other persons, particularly for men. He tries to take care of them and sometimes even to boss them around; identifies with persons in positions of authority and power
Youngest brother of brothers	Likes to lean on other people, particularly on men. He wants to have friends, to have men appreciate and respect him, and to be understood by them; willing to accept responsibilities but does not want to be in top command
Oldest brother of sisters	A ladies' man; appreciates women, regardless of whether they are colleagues and fellow-workers, lovers or spouses. He does not refuse a leadership role when offered, but he will not seek it out; he is not a man's man
Youngest brother of sisters	A great one with the ladies; they seem to love him and be anxious to care for him. They want to keep house for him, to handle his files or his suits, to cook for him, etc. He has been more important to his parents than were his sisters. He can take charge of others and assume responsibilities of leadership
Male only child	More used to dealing with considerably older people; wants to live under the view of older people, including persons in authority and power; wants to be loved, supported and helped more than others
Oldest sister of sisters	Likes to take care of things and give orders. She wants to know what is going on around her. She wants people to report to her, to be up to date and in control. She derives her claim to authority and leadership from another person with authority, usually an older man
Youngest sister of sisters	Loves change and excitement. She is vivacious, impulsive, even erratic, and easy to challenge. She finds herself in competition with girls and women, and men too, more often than other girls do. She is attractive but also moody and capricious
Oldest sister of brothers	Independent and strong in an unobtrusive way. She loves to take care of men and does not insist on . . . recognition of the fact. She wants men to be satisfied with whatever they have to do. The men in her charge are her main concern but she does treat them like little boys . . . she likes to appear superior
Youngest sister of brothers	Attracts men more pervasively as a rule, than other girls or women can. She does it quietly, though . . . Often she is all that a man would conventionally wish of a woman: she is feminine, friendly, warm, sympathetic, sensitive and usually tactful. She can give in without being obsequious or servile. She is a good pal . . .
Female only child	Depends on the care and attention of relatively older persons . . . wants her superiors, her colleagues and her friends to be what her parents were for her . . . she impresses others as a do-gooder with latent or manifest claims for preferential treatment . . . fellow-workers, particularly the female ones tend to find her egotistical

Source: Toman, 1994.

other things being equal, new social relationships are more enduring and successful, the more they resemble the earlier and earliest (intrafamilial) social relationships of the persons involved. (Toman, 1994, p. 78)

He provides an example:

A husband, for example, might be the oldest brother of two sisters. This would imply that he has learned to lead girls, to feel responsible for them, to protect them and to help them. Depending on his wife's sibling position, she may be able to accept her husband's role easily or only with difficulty. No troubles are likely if she is the younger sister of brothers. In that case she would have learned to let boys take responsibility, to submit to their leadership as well as to be protected and spoiled. We could argue that these two partners complement each other by their age ranks. He is the oldest and she is the youngest. Moreover, both of them have been accustomed to life with a peer of the opposite sex in their original families. Their relationship with each other is similar to earlier relationships they have had. (pp. 79–80)

Bowen (1978), an early pioneer of the systemic approach in family therapy, found his clinical work consistent with Toman's theory and profiles. He perhaps overstates the case when he suggests that 'no single piece of data is more important than knowing the sibling position of people in the present and past generation' (p. 385). Wilson and Edington (1982) are amongst those who attribute lifelong consequences (e.g. attitudes, relationships) to birth order (cited in Wedge and Mantle, 1991).

McGoldrick and Gerson (1985) stress sibling relationships in their eco-map orientation to the family. The emphasis they put on the importance of the sibling constellation derives largely from the work of Toman (1994). They observe that although the issue of sibling constellation has long been discussed in the literature, there has not been agreement about its role in development. They note that ethnic groups vary in the role that sibling position plays in the family. Referring to Bank and Kahn (1997), they note that under adverse situations siblings may become each other's main protector and resource. Table 3.2 sets out some of their observations regarding birth-order impact in families. Substantial consideration is devoted exclusively to birth order by Sulloway (1996) who computerised and analysed more than a half-million biographical data points from over ten thousand biographies as evidence to substantiate his contention that latter-born children are the radical thinkers, the ones to defy convention, who live

TABLE 3.2 IMPACT OF BIRTH ORDER

Older sibling	Younger sibling	Only child
Over-responsible, conscientious and parental	Childlike and carefree	More socially independent; less oriented toward peer relationships
Feel special; responsible for maintaining family welfare	Often 'baby' of the family	More adult-like in behaviour at an earlier age
Sometimes resent younger siblings	May be used to having others take care of him	Perhaps more anxious as a result of attentiveness and protectiveness of parents
Great things often expected (firstborn)	May feel more carefree; less burdened by family responsibility	Mix characteristics of both younger and older children but more like older
Sometimes suffers under pressure to excel	Often less respect for authority and convention	Often close attachments to parents throughout their lives
Examples: John Adams, John Quincy Adams	Example: George Bernard Shaw	Example: Indira Gandhi

Source: McGoldrick and Gerson, 1985.

lives that are less ordinary and who are prepared to rebel against established thinking

In addition to individual profiles derived from sibling position, McGoldrick and Gerson (1985) comment as well on how other relationships may be affected by the sibling relationship background of an individual. Two oldest children who marry may have difficulty due to the lack of complementarity in their expected roles. Both may compete for power in the relationship, as in the case of the Roosevelts. On the other hand, two youngest children may compete for 'juniority' as in the case of Elizabeth Taylor and Richard Burton – Burton was the second youngest in a large family, and the authors note that often in large families a few of the younger children will have characteristics of the youngest.

McGoldrick and Gerson (1985) identify factors influencing one's sibling constellation:

1. Gender
2. Distance in age between siblings (age gap)
3. The timing of each sibling's birth in the family history
4. The child's characteristics
5. The family's 'programme' for the child
6. Parental attitudes and biases regarding sex differences
7. The child's sibling position in relation to that of the parent.

Although they set out the influences of sibling constellation factors derived from Toman's work, they are careful to provide a caution as to its use:

> It is important not to take the hypothesis about sibling constellation too literally. Many people fit the characterisations, but many do not ... In fact, the empirical research on sibling constellation is at best inconclusive. (McGoldrick and Gerson, 1985, p. 61)

This leads us to criticisms of Toman's work. First, deriving from the cautionary note of McGoldrick and Gerson above, noting the lack of empirical support and the non-fit of many people, the profiles resemble too much, in terms of language style, a horoscope. Instead of 'oldest brother of brothers' one could read 'Capricorn' or some such equivalent, and it would probably be very difficult, stylistically, to tell the difference. Indeed, this unfortunate analogy is added to by Toman's extension of the model into prospective partners. Again it sounds a bit too much like 'Virgos are not good partners for Scorpios'. But Toman (1994), himself, is mindful of the limitation of the approach:

> single characteristics of a family constellation such as 'oldest sister of brothers' or 'male only child' ... at best only explain 10% to 20% of the variance of a person's long-term social behavior ... Eighty to ninety percent, and even more, of the influence on behavior and social preference comes from other sources, such as education, ethnic or religious background, physical appearance or special talents, etc. (p. 263)

Both Lamb (1982) and Dunn (1984) have been critical of this type of approach, Lamb because of its emphasis on the circumstances of the sibling relationships rather than on the processes that mediate sibling relationships, and Dunn because it is too simplistic in view of the complexities of sibling relationships. Stocker, Dunn and Plomin (1989), in one study of the influence of various factors on quality of the sibling relationship (maternal behaviour, children's temperament, age and family structure variables), concluded:

> Family structure variables were less important in accounting for variance in sibling relationships than were the other groups of predictors. (p. 715)

Daniels, Dunn, Furstenberg and Plomin (1985) found that family constellation variables explained as little as 1–2 per cent of the variance between the experiences of siblings, commenting:

> Clearly the influences within the family on an individual's development are far more complicated than a focus on these constellation variables alone would suggest. (p. 772)

To be clear, the variables that Toman has identified in his family constellation model are useful ones, and certainly worthy of the attention that they have received in empirical research into factors that influence the quality of the sibling relationship. It is simply that exaggerated claims should not be made about the extent of their influence.

Finally, family constellation variables and the model are not focused on the quality of the sibling relationship; rather, they focus on what a particular type of sibling configuration does to the individual. There is, by implication, material in the model about sibling relationships but the emphasis is on the individual.

Recent psychology of sibling relationships

The fundamental principle underlying research into sibling relationships in the last twenty years is that sibling relations are extremely complex and, therefore, simplistic concepts do not do justice to the rich tapestry of intricate subtleties contained within them. To really begin to understand sibling relationships one has to get down to the detail. There is little value, for example, in taking a single dimension, such as sibling rivalry, and assessing the sibling relationship to see whether it has more of it or less. There are a number of questions that arise from our knowledge of the highly complex nature of sibling relationships. What are the important dimensions of sibling relationships? What factors influence how siblings relate to each other? What conditions or potentiators operate in connection with those factors, i.e. when do they work and what makes them work? How do interaction effects influence the quality of the sibling relationship (for example through the operation of mediating variables)? This level of research questioning means that it is necessary to abandon the horoscope model of sibling relations; it is necessary to abandon simplistic understandings based on birth order, gender, age gap, etc. (although those factors have some significance), to achieve a fuller understanding.

Leaving these two schools of thought (psychoanalytic school, and the family constellation model) will entail a transition from a more clinically based understanding of sibling relationships to an empirical understanding based on experimentation and methodical observation, a more firmly grounded understanding. The emphasis in this empirical work has been on the *quality* of sibling relationships, as both an independent (input) and dependent (outcome) variable.

Therefore we ask three questions: what is meant by the quality of sibling relationships? What factors influence the quality of sibling relationships? How does the sibling relationship influence the development of the individual? Acknowledgement must be made of the work of Judy Dunn, in both the USA (Pennsylvania and Colorado) and the UK (Cambridge), not only for her contribution to our much fuller current understanding of sibling relationships, but also for the extent to which she has successfully been a publicist for the significance of sibling relationships in human development. A good place to begin is with the following extract from Dunn, Slomkowski, Beardsall and Rende (1994):

> The relationships between siblings are, for instance, emotionally powerful, and their interactions frequent and uninhibited throughout early and middle childhood (Boer and Dunn, 1992). Individual differences between sibling pairs in friendliness and hostility in early childhood are also striking: some children spend their early years with a sibling who is friendly, supportive and affectionate, others, with one who is constantly disparaging, aggressive or hostile. (pp. 491–2)

The emphasis on an empirical understanding of sibling relationships has also had some spin-offs for understanding the individual development of the child. Children grow and develop in a social environment, and yet much of earlier theorising about child development has ignored that. For example, a considerable modification of the Piagetian approach to understanding how children's cognition develops was the emphasis put on the social context of that development by Vygotsky. Similarly, Dunn has demonstrated, for example, how focusing on sibling relationships has reframed our thinking about children's cognitive and social development. Children can be seen to engage in much more advanced social interactions involving considerable cognitive ability when they are observed with siblings rather than when the child's cognitive abilities are assessed in isolation (Dunn, 1984). Specifically, she has noted that when using observational methodology (watching children's interactions with others), children are able to display much more sophisticated developmental processes than they had been considered capable of when being assessed using more individualised task approaches. For example, children are clearly less egocentric at an earlier age, when seen negotiating with older siblings about issues that matter to them, rather than when they are sat in a chair at a table with an object on it and asked to report what the teddy bear sitting in another chair sees on the table (a typical Piagetian task).

Let us now consider the three questions earlier posed. As will be clear, our contention here, drawing on contemporary literature, is that in contrast to the earlier polarised understanding of sibling relationships as essentially good or evil, such relationships are immensely complex and as varied in their nature, as different from each other, as people are. That should hardly be surprising. If people are so very different from each other, why should the relationships they have with each other be any less different. But making sense of it requires us to find dimensions, measurements, scales and the like. Before we can understand how factors influence the quality of the sibling relationship we must clarify what are the aspects of these relationships that we can measure and understand. Using experimental terminology, before we can explore the independent variables, we must be clear about the dependent variables, that is, the outcome measures, or the ways in which sibling relationships are different from each other.

What is meant by the quality of sibling relationships?

There is a lot of research using siblings that is not about the nature of the relationship between siblings but rather about the influence that one sibling exerts on the other. Buhrmester (1992) describes the situation found by him and Furman in the mid-1980s:

> In fact, most of the literature on 'sibling relationships' did not examine sibling relationships at all, but rather examined whether constellation variables like birth order and age-spacing were related to assessments of individual personality. (p. 30)

Very frequently, siblings are used as control groups for comparison, where the subject child has some feature, characteristic or behaviour of interest to researchers (delinquency, substance abuse, behaviour disorder). The question in this kind of research is something like: what does the difference between the delinquent child (as an example) and the non-delinquent sibling tell us about the nature of the causes of delinquency? It is as helpful to identify the reasons why one individual does not become delinquent (substance misusing, etc.), as it is to identify why another individual does. However, methodologically, one does wonder if the researchers are using siblings as control groups as a convenience sample, because, in fact, there is little basis for making any presumption of equality of other factors based on growing up on the same family. As I will discuss later (see Chapter 4, Question 2), children growing up in the same family are indeed frequently found, in many ways, not to be very similar.

But this research into siblings rarely looks at the quality of the sibling relationship. That is why, for example, when we come to consider the nature of the relationship between a child and his or her sibling with a disability we can assert, despite the relatively large body of literature, that there is still very little written about the impact of the disability on the actual nature of the sibling relationship. Most of the research has tended to focus on the impact of a child's disability on the sibling as an individual, that is, 'How does the disability of a child influence the development of his or her sibling?', not 'How does the disability of a child influence the relationship between the child and his or her sibling(s)?' Dunn (1984) notes, for example, that research has not focused on the qualities of sibling relationships. The intimacy and affection that a child shows towards his or her siblings are probably very important as indicators of sibling relationship quality as well as being an influence on the sibling relationship.

This is a vital issue when considering sibling relationships. It is too simplistic to suggest, as sometimes may appear to be the case, that because siblings squabble and bicker or perhaps 'don't get on', this one dimension of the sibling relationship is, or should be, definitive. Dunn and Kendrick (1982), studying the transition to siblinghood, note that siblings appear to upset one another as frequently as they comfort each other.

Let us consider attributes of the sibling relationship that researchers have considered. Table 3.3 provides examples of research into the sibling relationships. The columns on the right indicate independent (input/experimental) variables and dependent (outcome) variables. Presently, our focus is on output variables because researchers use these dimensions to measure sibling relationships. Most output variables can be subsumed under 'positive interactions' and 'negative interactions' (Table 3.4).

In addition, Dunn (1984) describes sibling relationships as capable of being affectionate, conflict-ridden, jealous and domineering. Later, Dunn (1988a) describes intimacy, competitiveness, ambivalence and emotional understanding as further qualities of sibling relationships. Clearly a number of these qualities of sibling relationships have some degree of overlap. Under the heading of positive sibling relationship might be included positive activities, positive affective climate, positive behaviour and positive sibling interactions. These are clearly not the same, even if they are similar in some respects. Similarities and differences between concepts used to describe (and measure) sibling relationships is an important theme.

The Department of Health's *Sibling Relationship Checklist* (Department of Health, 1991), developed by the Bridge Consultancy, was intended as a tool to aid practitioners in the assessment of the sibling relationships in families. It focused on a number of factors that might characterise these relationships (and which might be expected to vary from one sibling relationship to another). Examples are:

- Defending or protecting behaviour
- Offers or accepts comfort (two items)
- Teaches or helps sibling
- Initiates or responds to play (two items)
- Shows affection
- Misses sibling when apart
- Resolves conflict through age-appropriate reasoning
- Annoys, teases or irritates
- Shows hostility or aggression
- Blames sibling (or attempts to get him or her into trouble)
- Behaviour sabotages efforts to meet other sibling's needs.

TABLE 3.3 EXAMPLES OF INDEPENDENT AND DEPENDENT VARIABLES USED IN STUDYING THE QUALITY OF SIBLING RELATIONSHIPS

Researchers	Year	Independent variable(s)	Dependent variable(s)
Lamb	1978	Parental presence, sibling age	Interactions between sibling (generally, and in comparison with child/parent interactions)
Abramovitch et al.	1979	Sex, age, age gap	Agonistic (combative, aggressive) and prosocial behaviour, imitation
Hetherington	1987	Divorce and remarriage	Involvement, warmth/empathy, rivalry, conflict/aggression, avoidance, coercive power/control, positive power/control
Dale	1989	With whom playing (mother, sibling)	Cooperative pretend play
Stocker et al.	1989	Maternal behaviour, child's temperament, age and family structure	Positive and negative; competition, cooperation and control
Brody et al.	1992	Mother's and father's behaviour; differential treatment	Sibling relationship variables
Kramer and Gottman	1992	Quality of peer play, fantasy play, conflict management	Positive activities, positive affective climate, negative activities, negative affective climate (all broken down further into specifics
Raffaelli	1992	Age–gender constellation of dyad	Sibling conflict

Volling and Belsky	1992	Mother–child, father–child, parental relationship; infant–mother attachment	Sibling conflict and cooperation; prosocial sibling interaction
Brody et al.	1994	Temperament, interparental conflict, positivity in parent–child relationships, differential positivity in parent–sibling relationship	Negative and positive relationship qualities
Dunn et al.	1994	Behaviour of other sibling, life events, gender and gender composition, socioeconomic status	Positive and negative behaviour, warmth, rivalry, intimacy
Dunn et al.	1994	Earlier sibling relationship quality	Later adjustment difficulties
Kramer and Schaefer-Hernan	1994	Fantasy play with a friend before birth of sibling	Positive sibling interaction (%), length of fantasy play, social quality
Stocker (and Stocker and McHale, 1992)	1994	Friendships, maternal warmth, adjustment measures	Warmth, rivalry, hostility
Brody et al.	1996	Sibling temperament as a mediator of a) parent–child relationship quality, and b) family problem-solving behaviour	Sibling relationship quality
Dunn and Creps	1996	Age; compare mother–child, with sibling child	Frequency and quality of sibling interaction
Kowal and Kramer	1997	Child perception of parental differential treatment	Child's appraisal of sibling relationship
Brody	1998	Children's characteristics; family processes	Sibling relationship quality (prosocial and conflicted interactions)

TABLE 3.3 (CONTINUED)

Researchers	Year	Independent variable(s)	Dependent variable(s)
Erel et al.	1998	Marital relationship, mother–child relationships	Sibling positive behaviour; sibling negative behaviour
Rinaldi and Howe	1998	Sibling conflict strategy (destructive or constructive)	Siblings' affective relationship quality (negativism, warmth)
Brody et al.	1999	Parental psychological functioning	Harmony and conflict in sibling relationships
Dunbar	1999	Differential treatment (as indicated by parents and by siblings)	Companionship, antagonism, prosocial behaviour, arguing/fighting, competitive behaviour, admiration of sibling, affection, rivalry
Dunn et al.	1999	Mother–partner affection and hostility, and parent–child negativity, indices of social adversity at time I	Positivity and negativity in sibling relationship
Rushton et al.	1999	Placement variables	Warmth, conflict, rivalry
Stoneman et al.	1999	High residential mobility	Warmth/harmony and conflict
Kojima	2000	Maternal regulating behaviour (three types)	Positive and negative behaviours towards sibling
Reese-Weber	2000	Conflict resolution skills (interparental, parent–adolescent)	Adolescent sibling conflict resolution skills
Howe et al.	2001	Sibling style; maternal style at time I	Agonism; cooperation

TABLE 3.4 POSITIVE AND NEGATIVE SIBLING STUDY
OUTPUT VARIABLES

Positive	Negative	Neutral (or both)
Admiration	Aggression	Child's appraisal of sibling relationship
Affection	Agonistic (aggressive) behaviour	Frequency and quality of sibling interaction
Companionship	Antagonism	Imitation
Conflict resolution skills	Arguing /fighting	Involvement
Cooperation	Avoidance	Length of fantasy play
Cooperative pretend play	Coercive power / control	
Empathy	Competitive behaviour	
Harmony	Conflict	
Positive activities	Hostility	
Positive affective climate	Negative activities	
Positive behaviour	Negative affective climate	
Positive power / control	Negative behaviour	
Positive relationship qualities	Negative relationship qualities	
Positive sibling interaction	Negativism	
Positivity	Negativity	
Prosocial behaviour	Rivalry	
Prosocial sibling interaction	Sibling conflict	
Warmth		

For each of these qualities, the parent (or carer) rates the behaviour as occurring often, sometimes, or never and, very importantly, they are asked to give examples of the behaviour. The checklist focuses on inter-actions in terms of sharing, differences between the siblings, reciprocity and mutual modelling. Whilst perhaps of heuristic value, the *Sibling Checklist* has not had the rigorous testing in terms of reliability and validity indicators that a number of other methods have.

In recent years, psychological testing methods have been developed to assess the quality of sibling relationships. Furman and Buhrmester (1985) developed one of the earlier measures, the *Sibling Relationship Questionnaire*. Beginning with interviews with children they identified twelve features of sibling relationships described by many researchers: intimacy, prosocial behaviour, companionship, similarity, nurturance (both ways), admiration (both ways), affection, dominance (both ways), quarrelling, antagonism, competition and parental partiality. Using a statistical factor analytic technique they found four factors: warmth/closeness, relative status/power, conflict and rivalry.

The *Sibling Relationship Inventory* (Stocker and McHale, 1992) has also been developed and used by researchers to explore sibling relationships. This is a twenty-item questionnaire used in interview/testing with a child old enough to answer questions and make judgements about the ratings attached to aspects of his or her relationships with brothers and sisters. It is targeted at children aged 6–12 years. It requires the child to make judgements about the frequency of different types of behaviours using two types of Likert-style frequency indicators. The first type, Scale A, is:

1. Almost never, less than once a week (AN)
2. Occasionally, once a week (OC)
3. Sometimes, several times a week (S)
4. Pretty often, once a day (PO)
5. Always, several times a day (AL)

applied to questions 1–9, including examples such as:

2. Brothers and sisters sometimes cause trouble or start fights or arguments with one another, even if they love each other a lot. How often would you say that you start fights or cause trouble for TS? ['TS' refers to 'target sibling'].
4. Some children share secrets with their brothers and sisters and other children don't. How much do you share secrets with TS?

7. What about doing nice things like helping or doing favours for TS? How often do you do these kinds of things?

Scale B has a slightly different set of measures:

1. Hardly ever (HE)
2. Occasionally (OC)
3. Sometimes (S)
4. Pretty often (PO)
5. Always (A)

applied to questions 10–20, including examples such as:

10. Most children are affectionate with their brother or sister some-times even though they fight at other times. How often are you physically affectionate with TS (such as by hugging, kissing, hold-ing hands)?
17. Some children feel jealous or upset at times about the attention or affection their father gives to their brother or sister. How often do you feel sort of jealous about how your father treats TS?

The twenty questions break down into four groups (five items each) addressing different aspects of sibling relationships, rivalry, hostility, affection and relative power/status. The last item was found not to be statistically useful, and did not replicate findings of previous research (Furman and Buhrmester, 1985).

These three factors, warmth (or affection), rivalry and hostility, have proved to be very significant in contemporary thinking about sibling relationships and are frequently used as outcome measures. They are seen as independent ('orthogonal') dimensions, which means there can be high levels of rivalry with low levels of hostility and vice versa. The presence of warmth does not necessarily mean the absence of either rivalry or hostility. One can have a warm sibling relationship but still have rivalry in it. Warmth and hostility can coexist in the same relationship. The level of one is not determined, or indeed even necessarily influenced by, the level of the others. This is a very impor-tant consideration in the understanding of sibling relationships. One implication, for example, is that it is not sufficient to look at the level of hostility or rivalry in a relationship, and if high, presume that the level of warmth is low.

TABLE 3.5 MEASURES OF SIBLING RELATIONSHIPS AND SIBLING RELATIONSHIP FACTORS

Authors	Year	Measurement tool	Target group	Method	Description
Koch	1960	Unnamed: formal attributes	5–6-year-old children	Interview in context of conversation	The nature of the relationship between children as indicated by the children themselves
Schaefer and Edgerton	1981	Sibling Inventory of Behaviour (SIB)	Children	Parental ratings	–
Stillwell and Dunn	1985	Unnamed	Average age 6 years	Open ended interview	Coded into per cent positive and per cent negative comments
Furman and Buhrmester	1985	Sibling Relationship Questionnaire (SRQ)	School-aged children; preadolescent	Open-ended interview followed by questionnaire	12 qualities of sibling relationships reduced onto four factors: warmth/closeness, relative status/power, conflict and rivalry
Daniels and Plomin	1985	Sibling Inventory of Differential Experience	Adolescent and young adult	Questionnaire (completed by post)	4 scales: subjective indicators of differential sibling interaction, differential parental treatment, differential peer characteristics, events specific to each sibling
Hetherington	1987	Sibling Relationships Inventory	Adults and children in middle childhood	Form completion	7 scales
Stocker and McHale	1992	Sibling Relationship Interview	6–12-year-old children	Interview; 5-point Likert scale	20 items, 3 of the 4 scales used having high validity

Author	Year	Name	Age group	Type	Description
Lanthier and Stocker	1992	Adult Sibling Relationship Questionnaire (ASRQ)	Early adulthood and older	Questionnaire	81 items; 14 scales; 3 factors (warmth, conflict, rivalry)
Fish et al.	1995	Sibling Need Involvement Profile	Siblings of children with a disability	8-page questionnaire	Helps parents and professionals identify what siblings know and how they feel about their brother or sister's disability.
Stein and Albro	1997	Sibling Conflict Interview	–	A series of open ended questions	–
Slomkowski et al.	1997	Social Interaction Between Siblings (SIBS) Interview	6–11-year-olds	Interview	Assessment of sibling influences on antisocial behaviour
Stocker et al.	1997	Adult Sibling Relationship Questionnaire (ASRQ	Adult	Questionnaire	81 items in 14 scales: intimacy, affection, emotional support, instrumental support, knowledge, similarity, admiration, acceptance, dominance, competition, antagonism, quarrelling, maternal rivalry, paternal rivalry (underlying factors: warmth, rivalry and conflict)
Riggio	2000	The Lifespan Sibling Relationship Scale (LSRS)	Adult	Questionnaire	48 items in six subscales exploring beliefs about and attitudes towards relationship with a sibling as a child and as an adult

A fundamental contention being put forth here is that the quality of the relationship between brothers and sisters may be more significantly determined by the presence, or absence, of warmth than by the presence or absence of hostility and jealousy.

Reiss *et al.* (1994, p. 81) note that 'moderate levels of conflict are endemic in sibling relationships ... However, evidence suggests that these patterns of conflict are generally mixed with more positive feelings and behavior, including care taking'. Since expressions of hostility are widely present in sibling relationships it may be a poorer indicator of the nature of the relationship, and predictor of the future relationship, between two siblings than the presence or absence of warmth, which may vary more between sibling relationships and therefore may be more indicative. In other words, one can suggest that below a threshold of being abusive, ordinary sibling squabbling, bickering and fighting may not be as indicative of the relationship as whether or not, in between the bickering and fighting there are indications of warmth.

A sample of measures used to assess sibling relationships is set out in Table 3.5. It is useful now to consider how the methodology of researching sibling relationships has developed and expanded over the years. Helen Koch (1960), although adopting a more formalised approach than had previously been undertaken, made efforts to have the interview questions put whilst the children were engaged in play with toy figures, and integrated the questioning into a conversational approach. Dunn, in her many years of studying sibling relationships, has used a range of methodologies in three large-scale projects (Cambridge, Pennsylvania and Colorado). Much of her work and that of her colleagues has been undertaken through observational and interview methods. Observational methods entail watching siblings interact and then rating for particular characteristics, for example positive and negative aspects of the relationship in the earlier stages of the research, or for more sophisticated features, i.e. justification, emotional understanding, warmth, affection, etc., in subsequent research. Other researchers, studying older children, adolescents and young adults, have developed methods that rely on the subject's ability to complete the questionnaires. The 'Sibling Relationship Interview' (Stocker and McHale, 1992) relies on a simple methodology, but requires the researcher to take the child through the questions and answers. In that sense it resembles a structured interview more than a questionnaire. 'The Sibling Checklist' (Department of Health, 1991) relies on parents and/or carers completing questions about their children's sibling relationships.

Summary: changing understandings of sibling relationships – theory and research

This chapter has looked at how our understanding of sibling relationships has grown over the last century, describing three stages in its evolution: the psychoanalytic stage, the family systems theory stage and finally the empirical psychological stage. In the first stage we have seen the emphasis on the early negative aspects of sibling relationships, rivalry and jealousy, fitting into the psychoanalytic framework of feelings that must be repressed because they are unacceptable. Rivalry within the Oedipal complex and 'dethronment' derives from Freudian and post-Freudian theorising and was the basis of the work of David Levy who tried to measure it in play situations involving dolls. The location of sibling relationships within a wider family context led to the family systems approach. Thus the notion of subsystems within families and the family constellation based on birth order and gender came to be fundamental concepts. However, particularly for family constellation approaches, there is a tendency to exaggerate how much knowledge can be derived from the limited cluster of factors (gender and birth order) which locate one within the family constellation. The final stage, the empirical psychological stage, looks at the more sophisticated understanding that researchers are trying to achieve by focusing on the concept of 'sibling relationship quality' and the various factors that influence it, and are affected by it. As a preliminary step we have identified the various measures and tools that researchers have used to look at sibling relationships. The next chapter looks at findings from empirical research.

4 The Quality of Sibling Relationships

It doesn't seem to matter how much time has elapsed or how far we've traveled. Our brothers and sisters bring us face to face with our former selves and remind us how intricately bound up we are in each other's lives. (Jane Mersky Leder, 1991)

In the last twenty years sibling research has expanded dramatically. We continue to have research that focuses on the siblings as comparisons with target subjects, and research that focuses on siblings' impact on the individual, but we also have a considerable growth in empirical research that looks at the quality of sibling relationships as an independent (input) variable and a dependent (outcome) variable. Clearly a single chapter cannot do justice to such a substantial body of literature.

We now turn our attention to seven major issues in sibling relationships – some of the 'big questions' in the field of sibling research. The first five of these are about the impact of various factors on the sibling relationship. The next two consider the impact of sibling relationships on other factors, thereby emphasising the reciprocal nature of the influence of sibling relationships.

Let us begin with the first five questions:

1. Do sibling relationships compensate for, or are they congruent with, the relationships that children have with their parent(s)?
2. Why are children who are brought up in the same family so different from each other?
3. What is the effect of treating children in the family differently?
4. How does the relationship between the parents impact on the relationship between the siblings?
5. Should parent(s) intervene or not in squabbles between siblings?

Question 1: Do sibling relationships compensate for, or are they congruent with, the kinds of relationships that children have with their parent(s)?

Before the empirical focus on sibling relationships (beginning in the 1980s), family workers suggested that the relationship between siblings in a family will become stronger where there are weaknesses in the relationships between the parents and the children – the 'compensating siblings hypothesis' (Boer *et al.*, 1992). The children turn towards each other to meet those social and care needs not met by the parents. This is quite a plausible contention. It fits in well with current understanding of factors contributing to resilience in children in the face of adversity; other means of offsetting the impact of potentially damaging influences are found. Within the family, what better opportunities would there be for children's attachment needs, care needs, needs for social interaction and needs for stimulation to be met, if the parents are not able to meet them, than through siblings? However, the opposite contention also seems extremely plausible. This would be that positive interactions between parents and their children foster positive interactions between the children. This contention – the congruence hypothesis – is consistent with social learning theory, and in particular, modelling. The parents provide a model for social interaction, and for how children should be treated within the family by the way in which they interact with the children. To summarise, the compensatory hypothesis suggests that deficiencies in the parent–child relationship can be made up for by strengths in the child–child relationships, whereas, the congruence hypothesis suggests that strength in the parent–child relationship will promote strength in the child–child relationship.

Part of the evidence for the compensation hypothesis comes from the early research into large families undertaken by Bossard and Boll (1956) who note that when

> parents are tired and weighted down with cares and responsibilities, they may not have the time, inclination, energy, or affectional resources to satisfy the respective emotional needs of their children. In such cases, it is natural for children to turn to other persons; and often this means other siblings. (p. 156)

Likewise, Bank and Kahn (1997) in their consideration of 'The Parental Vacuum' note:

the more available parents are both emotionally and physically, the less intense is the attachment between siblings. As parents are absent either emotionally or physically, the siblings may be forced to reach out for one another. (p. 123)

But they then go on to provide examples of how, in extreme circumstances, the opposite may apply, and children may adopt a survival strategy in which they look after their own needs individually leading to competition and conflict, rather than adopt cooperative strategies. This would appear, for example to be the case with the Sanchez children (Lewis, 1964).

Boer *et al.* (1992) describe three examples of research addressing this issue (Bryant and Crockenberg, 1980; Dunn and Kendrick, 1982; Hetherington, 1988) and in each of these three studies evidence was found supporting both a compensatory model and a congruence model! In summary, as noted by Boer *et al.* (1992) some evidence supports a compensatory model of sibling relationship and parent–child relationships (if one is bad, the other is good), other evidence supports a congruence model (both are good; both are bad), and still other evidence suggests that whether the link between the two is compensatory or congruent may depend on other factors, for example, as described by Dunn (1988b), individual differences between children and the child's developmental stage.

Question 2: Why are children who are brought up in the same family so different from each other?

Children are more alike genetically (with 50 per cent of genetic material in common) than they are like either of their parents, or indeed like anyone else in the world. With such genetic similarity, and an experience of being brought up by the same parents (although this is not always the case), the question arises: why are they so dissimilar? This is a very long-standing question. Indeed, Weill (1928) and Winnicott (1965) both, on the basis of clinical work with children and families, posed the question. Weill (1928) observed, 'Not only the occasional child, but every child has stood in his own individual, dynamic relation to his parents, his brothers and sisters to the general family situation' (p.4). Winnicott (1965) notes, for example:

We hear it said that it is strange that children can be so different from each other when they have the same parents and are brought up in the same house and in the same home. This leaves out ... the way that each child fits specifically, or fails to fit, into a certain imaginative and emotional setting, a setting which can never be the same twice, even when everything else in the physical environment remains constant. (p. 43)

Dunn (1988a) notes:

an important theme in current research on siblings is a concern with the question of why siblings develop to be so different from one another. (p. 125)

At its most extreme, the dramatic impact of this is emphasised in the following:

Upper middle-class brothers who attend the same school and whose parents take them to the same plays, sporting events, music lessons, and therapists, and use similar child rearing practices on them are little more similar in personality measures than they are to working class or farm boys, whose lives are totally different ... It is evident that most of the variance in personality arises in the environmental differences among siblings, not in the differences among families. (Scarr and Grajek, 1982, p. 361)

These extracts hint why children might be so different growing up in the same environment – because the environments are not really that similar. Thinking about this leads to considering just how different are the social environments of different children in the same family. Daniels and Plomin (1985), for example, note:

environmental influences relevant to psychological development largely operate in such a way as to make siblings in the same family different from, rather than similar to, each other. (p. 747)

They draw on the conceptual work of Rowe and Plomin (1981) to investigate the sources of differences, such as sibling interaction, parental treatment, extrafamilial network influences and unusual circumstances, for example accidents or bereavements, that affect family members differently.

We need to have, therefore, a clear understanding of 'nonshared' influences. Plomin *et al.* (1994) describe them:

Environmental influences that affect development are not shared by family members. That is, whatever they are, these environmental influences are experienced differently by members of the same family. Environmental influences of this type are called nonshared in the sense that they are not shared by family members. (p. 2)

It is intriguing to note that the origin of this type of thinking about influences on human development, as described by Plomin *et al.* (1994), was a sudden insight reflecting a type of reversal of figure-ground in the process of looking at genetic influences on human development. When positioned in the nature–nurture debate, non-shared influences can be seen as a bifurcation of the nurture end of the scale into those environmental influences which make individuals alike (shared influences) and those which make individuals different (non-shared influences).

As expressed by Hetherington *et al.* (1994):

One of the most notable findings in contemporary behaviour genetics is that *children growing up in the same family are not very similar* . . . These findings suggest that in order to understand individual differences between siblings it is necessary to examine not only the shared experiences but also the differences in experiences of children growing up in the same family. (p. vii, my italics)

What makes the social environment of one child different from another in the same family? Let us consider a few influences. First, unless both the children are the same sex (a 50 per cent likelihood with two children), then whereas one will be growing up with a male sibling, the other will be growing up with a female sibling; similarly, for more than two siblings, there are similarities *and* differences of the gender configurations of the siblings unless they are all of the same sex. For example, with a brother and two sisters, each sister will have a sister and brother, but the brother will have two sisters. Secondly, this applies as well to ordinal position. Unless the children are twins (or multiples), then one sibling will be growing up with an older sibling, the other will be growing up with a younger sibling. The social environment of growing up with a younger sibling is not the same as the social environment of growing up with an older sibling.

A third source of intrafamilial environmental difference is the significance of the child's gender for the parents. The meaning of a son for a father may be different from the meaning of a son for the mother, and likewise for daughters. In a society where sex is gendered, and sex roles are rather rigidly defined, the social environment will be pulling male and female children in very different directions. This is true despite attempts by parents to raise their children in a non-sexist manner (Carmichael, 1977; Greenberg, 1978; Statham, 1986). Fourthly, families go through life courses and the family which has a child and then four years later another may be considerably different in many ways at those two times – for example, where they live, their relative prosperity or lack of it, the employment of one or other parent, the social network and support available to the family. Fifthly, when so many more families are reconstituted, siblings may have two, one or no parents in common with each other. One may consider the extent to which children in a family unit may be treated differently by a parent who is a biological parent and one who is not. Finally, the health of the parents (or indeed any previously born siblings) may have changed between the births of siblings. This is not an exhaustive consideration, but it certainly is enough to emphasise ways in which children in the same family experience different social environments.

Parents are not the only, perhaps not even the major, influence on how children develop. But they are a significant influence, and differential treatment by parents (point five above) is an issue that has been substantially considered in the literature. McGuire and Dunn (1994) suggest three questions to tease out non-shared environmental influences:

(1) How differently are siblings treated by their mothers when they are the same age?
(2) Are there links between such differential experiences and children's social competence, behaviour problems and personality?
(3) Do the links between maternal differential treatment and children's outcomes persist over time?

Brody and Stoneman (1994) attempt to 'examine an important source of nonshared family experience, parental differential treatment, in terms of its associations with sibling relationship quality' (p. 129).

Question 3: What is the effect of treating children in the family differently?

There are at least three ways that parental differential treatment can be understood. First, in the sense that it is probably most frequently intended, children in the family may be consistently treated differently by the parents (and perhaps even by the siblings) so that some children are put into favoured family roles and others put into less favoured roles. Another type of parental differential treatment is where the two parents are not consistent in their approach to the children, but relate differently to the children in the family. Frequently one has a situation where one child identifies with one parent (often the parent of the opposite sex) and the other child with the other parent – 'split parent identification' (Schachter, 1982). Also, there may be congruence or incongruence in the type of differential treatment within families (that is mother and father showing different patterns of differential treatment). Most families are congruent in the differential treatment of children, but where there are incongruencies, these tend to be more about the affective treatment (level of emotional warmth) rather than differential discipline (McHale *et al.*, 1995). Parental accounts of differential *enjoyment* are related to differential favouritism, but not to their accounts of differential *discipline* (Volling and Elins, 1998). Incongruent differential treatment by parents (that is, parents having different favoured children) is associated with a higher level of marital distress (McHale *et al.*, 1995; Volling and Elins, 1998). Harmony between siblings and between parents occurred when fathers disciplined the older sibling more and mothers disciplined the children equally (Volling and Elins, 1998). On the other hand, Brody and Stoneman (1994) found differential treatment of siblings by fathers to be a determinant of sibling relationship quality – if father treated siblings very differently, there was likely to be more negative behaviour between them. An interesting aspect of the congruence of differential treatment is that between parents and children (see Dunbar, 1999, below p. 91).

A third type of differential treatment reflects how parenting may change over time. It is useful, where there is more than one child, to look at whether there is consistency between how a younger child is treated at a specific age, and the way the older child was treated *at the same age*. In other words, how similarly or dissimilarly do parents treat different children in the family when they reach the same age? It is quite common to hear older children in families complain that they have 'broken in' the parents for the younger ones, so that they can enjoy the benefit of more privileges, freedoms, etc. Likewise, parents may sombrely reflect that by the time they are getting really good at parenting through the experience of having raised a number, and learning from their mistakes, they have reached the stage of giving up having any more.

The astute reader may well anticipate where this is going. Being relatively powerless in the realm of adult affairs, children have a very keenly developed sense of injustice, especially if that injustice comes from within the family. As noted by Sulloway (1996):

> No social injustice is felt more deeply than that suffered within one's own family. (p. xv)

For many children, the important thing is how they are treated *now* that counts. The justification that when an older sibling was the same age they used to have the same bedtime, receive the same amount of pocket money, and had the same prohibitions and injunctions appears to carry little weight with younger siblings. It is still likely to be perceived as differential and unfair treatment. And there is good reason to believe that it is the perception of differential treatment that is significant rather than whether or not the treatment is actually different (Daniels, Dunn, Fursternberg and Plomin, 1985; Dunn and Plomin, 1990).

Dunn, Plomin and Nettles (1985) considered how similarly or differently mothers behaved towards two children at two different points in time (when the youngest at time 2 became the same age as the oldest had been at time 1, i.e. 12 months). They concluded 'mothers behaved very similarly towards their two siblings at the same age in infancy ... differential maternal treatment of children of the same age in infancy is unlikely to be a major source of the marked individual differences that have been observed within pairs of siblings' (p. 1,188). However, their sample was exclusively middle-class parents (including some adoptive families for comparison of genetic influences), and it is arguable that perhaps such families may experience more stability over such a relatively short period of time than a wider cross-section of families.

The major emphasis here will be on the first type of differential treatment, children in the family being treated differently by parents (and in some cases by siblings as well), or where the children perceive there to be such differential treatment. It is the subjective experience of differential treatment that has particular significance within the family, more so than any objective indicator.

There are many reasons why parents might treat children in the same family differently. In fact, it would be impossible for two children in a family to experience an identical environment (even if the parents were making extraordinary efforts to treat siblings identically). The issue of differential treatment is not one of *whether* some children are treated preferentially, or with disfavour, whilst others are not, but rather to what extent and how it is perceived. It could not be successfully argued that some families treat children differently and others don't; that argument would be unsustainable. In refutation, it could simply be argued that there is no such thing as any two children in any family being treated exactly alike. As noted by Brody and Stoneman (1994, p. 140), 'it is impossible for parents to treat their children completely equally; even if it were possible, it would not be desirable'. But towards one end of the scale would be less differential treatment between children, whilst at the other would be the extreme behaviour of scapegoating.

Age is often a basis for differential treatment in families. In a number of studies, more positive behaviour is consistently directed towards the younger sibling (Brody, Stoneman and McCoy, 1992a; Brody, Stoneman and McCoy, 1992b; Bryant and Crockenburg, 1980; Stocker, Dunn and Plomin, 1989). Mothers are also 'more responsive, verbal, controlling, and emotionally expressive with their young children' (Brody and Stoneman, 1994, p. 130, referring to the work of Brody, Stoneman and Burke, 1987a, and Bryant and Crockenburg, 1980). There is more parental interaction with younger children than with older children; this is consistently demonstrated (Brody, Stoneman and Burke, 1987a; Brody, Stoneman and McCoy, 1992a; Brody, Stoneman and McCoy, 1992b; Bryant and Crockenberg, 1980; Stocker, Dunn and Plomin, 1989), and may simply reflect what every parent knows – younger children need more from parents. Based on higher dependency needs, higher care needs, less sophisticated physical and cognitive development, younger children have greater needs for parental involvement than older children ... and get it. As noted by Brody and Stoneman (1994) this is not favouritism, it is simply a fact of life.

Nevertheless, it is probably the extent to which the perceived differential treatment is felt to be unfair that is associated with negative qualities in the sibling relationships rather than the extent of differential treatment (actual, or perceived). Differential treatment that is felt to be justified is less harmful to sibling relationships. Using the Sibling Inventory of Differential Experience (Daniels and Plomin, 1985; Plomin and Daniels, 1987), as well as interviews, Kowal and Kramer (1997) found that only one third of young adolescents (11–13 years) reported any differences in the way they and younger siblings were treated, and of those, three-quarters considered the differential treatment to be justified. Age, personal attributes, needs, relationship with parents or strategic behaviours were factors identified by the young people that made them different from their siblings and therefore justified the parental differential treatment of them. Children who perceived their parent's differential treatment to be justified, however, were judged to have more positive sibling relationships.

Do children and parents agree about intrafamilial parental differential treatment? As might be expected, when both children and parents are asked about differential treatment, some differences emerge. Dunbar (1999) suggests very high levels of incongruence between siblings and parents in terms of how they view the amount of differential treatment within the family. Siblings considered there to be more differential treatment than the parents did. Also, children rated the quality of their sibling relationships higher than the parents did. We can speculate that this may be because children are learning to accommodate hostility and warmth in the same relationships, whereas parents are over-influenced by bickering and squabbling in their evaluation of sibling relationships.

It is not only parents who may treat children in the family differently. Children may collaborate with parents, or in some cases rebel against differential (that is preferential) treatment. Le Gall (1998) provides an example of sibling coalitions that can form because of differential treatment:

> My younger sister, Marion, can be irritating at times, specially the way she takes my parents for a ride. At meal times she is very difficult to handle ... And Marion, if she doesn't eat it, uh, my mom cooks up something else for her.

> In this example, the conflict is related ... to differential treatment of the siblings by their parents. Sometimes this creates a collective sibling opposition, but one that affects her, who for all of them remains the 'little Benjamin,' only indirectly. 'Often, Mathieu [the brother] and I ally against Dad and Mom, for the way they're raising Marion.' (p. 92, original italics)

The reference to 'Benjamin' is a biblical one, the preferred son of sons.

But what do we know about the impact of parental differential treatment on the sibling relationship? Children as individuals are affected by differential treatment, and that which influences individuals in a relationship will affect the relationship. Behavioural problems of children are associated with differential treatment, and the magnitude of the difference between siblings in terms of behaviour problems was found to be associated with the extent of the differential treatment by the mother (Stocker, 1993, p. 485). Differences in emotional adjustment of adolescent siblings in the same family are also related to differences in parental treatment as perceived by both adolescents and parents (Daniels, Dunn, Furstenberg and Plomin, 1985). Younger children are more vulnerable to differential treatment in families (McHale *et al.*, 1995). Brody *et al.* (1998) looked at 'favouritism' and 'disfavouritism', and found that 65 per cent of 127 young adults and their siblings reported favouritism in their families and 24 per cent reported disfavouritism. Disfavouritism was related to lower family cohesion, higher family disengagement and higher family conflict.

Evidence for a general weakening of the sibling relationships where there is differential treatment comes from Brody, Stoneman and Burke (1987a). They found that when the younger child was maternally favoured, siblings talked less with each other and there was less inter-action of both positive and negative types. They simply had less to do with each other. Brody and Stoneman (1994) found that overall mothers direct more positive behaviours to both their children than fathers do and there was little difference between mothers and fathers in terms of differential treatment of children; both parents directed more of their interactions towards the younger sibling than towards the older. But they also found that 'differential treatment, particularly from fathers was associated with negative sibling behaviour' (p. 134). They attributed this to low levels of contact between fathers and their children compared to high levels of contact between mothers and children. Thus, differential treatment by father may be more signifi-cant because interaction with father is less common. On the other hand, they found that:

> School-age siblings whose fathers treated them impartially during problem-solving discussion, whose families are generally harmonious even when discussing problems, and whose parents consider their family relationships to be generally close, were less likely to develop conflicted relationships ... fathers' unequal treatment of siblings ... was especially significant to sibling conflict. (p. 138)

Dunn (1988a) notes:

> differential behaviour shown by parents towards siblings is clearly implicated in conflict frequency. Consistent evidence that differential maternal behavior is related to the quality of the siblings' relationship is reported in every study that has included assessment of maternal behaviour to both siblings. (p. 122)

She notes that this finding applies to families following divorce, to families with children who have a disability and to families who have a child with cancer. The link between sibling conflict behaviour and maternal differential treatment is particularly strong in families experiencing stress. Of course it should not be assumed that the stress leads to differential treatment, which leads to sibling conflict. It could be that family stress leads to a sibling conflict, which in turn leads to differential treatment. We know that sibling conflict is a major source of stress for families, and so it could even be that sibling conflict leads to family stress, which in turn leads to differential treatment. This issue of reverse cause and effect when looking at the influence of differential treatment is discussed by Daniels, Dunn, Furstenberg and Plomin (1985) and by Brody and Stoneman (1994). The latter observe:

> The cross-sectional designs used in these studies however, do not allow the conclusion that parental differential treatment causes difficult sibling relationships; parents may treat their children differently in response to the behaviours the siblings have enacted throughout their lives. (p. 130)

One of the striking features of the Sanchez Family (Lewis, 1964) previously described is the high level of perceived differential treatment (in the case of Roberto, almost to the point of scapegoating), which contributes to the high levels of conflict between the siblings and to the high levels of unhappiness for the children. But there seems to be significant disagreement between the children about who is favoured and who isn't. Consuelo is described as being favoured, but clearly doesn't feel herself to be. Consider, the following extracts:

> Roberto: 'My father favored the women. He had always taken better care of them and it seemed that he loved my sisters more.' (p. 71)

> Consuelo [in relation to Antonia, a step-sister]: 'I only know that my father loved her more. I began to doubt that I was really his daughter', and later, 'I couldn't explain why my father hated me.' She adds, referring to her sister and two brothers, 'I was never as close to them as they were to each other.' (p. 108)

> Marta: 'I felt that I was my father's favorite ... My papa treated us girls like royalty.' (p. 135)

> Manuel: 'But Antonia continued to be my father's favorite.' (p. 176)

To some extent, these differences can be accounted for because different children become favoured at different times, as the family progresses through the family life-cycle. But Roberto seems to have come in for particular disfavour on the part of the father, the reason why eventually becoming clear:

> Manuel: 'My *papá* never did like very dark people and it was probably on account of Roberto's dark skin that my father disliked him.' (pp. 23–24)

> Marta: 'When Roberto was born dark, my *papá* didn't like him because he thought my brother was not his son.' (p. 140)

And the unfairness of this, as perceived by Roberto, was described by Consuelo: 'Yes, *papacito*, you don't love me because I am dark, because my hide is black. That's why none of you love me ... but my soul is white!' (p. 111).

Such extreme examples apart, parents can be very aware, however, of the dangers of differential parenting, and can explicitly set a corrective agenda based on their own experiences of being parented. Kramer and Baron (1995), for example, looked at intergenerational linkages of sibling relationships. They examined how experiences with one's own siblings, when growing up, influence one's approach to sibling relationships as a parent. Mothers who described having negative sibling histories were most likely to have children who were more positive in their interactions with each other. These mothers specifically tried to reduce the amount of differential treatment of their own children.

In summarising, therefore, differential parental treatment that is based on the appreciation that children have different needs at different stages, and that as they grow they require less intervention from their parents compared with younger siblings, is simply part of ordinary development (Brody and Stoneman, 1994). It may be difficult for some older children to understand, but whilst parents may have to make efforts to help older siblings appreciate this, equalising the interaction so that the older child is given the same level and quality of interaction as the younger child is simply not an option. But this differentiation is based almost exclusively on age and the different needs of children at different ages. The younger child now is being treated in the same way as the older child was when he or she was that age. This is essentially fair (at least from an adult point of view). This is not preference or favouritism.

However, it may be very difficult for parents not to have some preferences in relation to their children. But the important process of ensuring that every child feels valued as an individual is one that parents should strive for. It is when this process is abandoned, and children are deliberately and disproportionately singled out for preferential ('holy cow') or non-preferential ('scapegoat') treatment, that difficulties may arise. Siblings look for justice, fairness and equality in the way family members are treated. When it doesn't happen, a strong feeling of anger may result, which will eventually come out in behaviour.

Question 4: How does the relationship between the parents impact on the relationship between the siblings?

Stress in families, of the kind described in the next three chapters may produce disharmony in the parental relationship. It is useful to consider how the parental relationship influences the relationships between siblings in the family. These effects may be direct, or they may be mediated by the relationship the parents have with the children as individuals. Stress and disharmony in the parental relationship affects the children as individuals and the parent–child relationships. Therefore, it would be very surprising indeed if the sibling relationship were not itself affected as well. Dunn (1993) observes:

> Most research supports the idea that good marital relationships are associated with good parent–child relationships, while difficulties in parent–child relations are more common in families with poor marriages. (p. 76)

Jenkins (1992, p. 130) notes 'marital disharmony is associated with increased emotional and behavioural disturbance in children. Conners (2000) found that a strong alliance between parents about issues of parenting, and a positive marital relationship were associated with lower levels of sibling conflict. In their controlled situation of giving families problems of sibling relationships to solve as a family, Brody, Stoneman, McCoy and Forehand (1992) found that family harmony during discussions about sibling problems was associated with lower levels of conflict between siblings. Brody, Stoneman and Burke (1987b), in their study of primary school-age children, found that the best predictor of the younger siblings' prosocial behaviour was a low level of conflict between parents.

However, a simple cause-and-effect mechanism, as illustrated in Figure 4.1, may not reflect the complicated processes underlying the

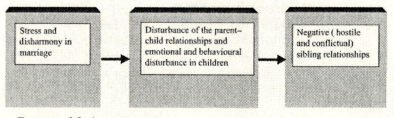

FIGURE 4.1 A LINEAR MODEL OF THE IMPACT OF MARITAL STRESS
AND DISHARMONY ON SIBLING RELATIONSHIPS

impact of stress and disharmony between parents on sibling relationships. One of the findings about relationships between relationships in
families is that the patterns are frequently clearer in families experiencing stress of some sort. Under ordinary circumstances, families
without stressful circumstances frequently show less clear-cut patterns
of influences.

The question arising from the work of Bank and Kahn (1997) is
whether, in the face of parental disharmony and stress, the sibling
relationship can provide a protective environment, shielding the children from the impact. Jenkins (1992) looked at sibling relationships in
disharmonious homes, and her work is worth describing in some detail
here. Although her main focus was on sibling relationships, the
outcome variables she looked at mostly were children's symptomatology, and she looked at sibling relationships as a moderating influence
on that. She looked at 139 families (a sub-sample from a previous,
larger study) divided into those with harmonious marital relationships
and those where the relationships were disharmonious. The closeness
of a sibling relationship was indicated by the siblings' spending time
together, showing signs of comforting each other and being supportive
during times of family difficulties. A poor relationship was indicated
by the presence of both high levels of hostility and lack of any indicators of warmth or closeness. She found:

> having a very close sibling relationship does act protectively for children
> who are experiencing the stress of parental disharmony, whereas the
> quality of the sibling relationship has little effect on children who are
> living in harmonious homes. (p. 132)

and

> Parent–child relationships were important for the quality of chil-
> dren's adjustment irrespective of whether they were in a harmonious or

disharmonious home, whereas sibling relationships acted in a compensatory way only when the children were in a disharmonious home. (p. 133)

She also found that marital disharmony was very destructive of the sibling relationship. In summing, she notes:

Children who live in disharmonious homes are more likely to develop hostile and aggressive relationships with their siblings than children living in harmonious homes. It is also clear, however, that if children do develop a close and supportive relationship with their sibling, this can offer some protection against the development of psychological disturbance. (p. 135)

This is in accord with Brody and Stoneman's (1994) finding that both negative sibling behaviour and Sibling Relationship Quality (SRQ) conflict scores were positively related to interparental conflict (p. 137). Marital conflicts increase children's aggression, their enmeshment in parental disputes and inter-sibling aggression (Cummings, 1994). Parental conflict simply doesn't do any good for sibling relationships at all.

Jenkins (1992) leads us to a way of thinking about the buffering effect of positive sibling relationships in situations of adversity that we shall encounter again in Part 2. Yes, strong positive sibling relationships can buffer against the worst effects of harsh social circumstances in the family, but sibling relationships are also undermined by those very circumstances. Therefore, their role can be pivotal for professionals who are looking to promote children's resilience to adversity in situations of abuse, separations, etc.

Question 5: Should parent(s) intervene or not in squabbles between siblings?

Deciding whether to intervene when siblings are squabbling is for the parent a case of balancing two conflicting sets of prescriptions. The case *against* intervention is that children need to learn to resolve conflicts without the need for outside intervention. They need to learn negotiation strategies: how to get their own needs met whilst learning to accommodate the needs of others. Dunn and McGuire (1992, pp. 90–91) look at the developmental significance of conflict between children. Some good *can* come out of it. To begin with, conflict promotes cognitive and moral development. The study of excuses and justifications has highlighted the nature of children's social and cognitive development as they are revealed through conflicts. Different strategies for dealing with conflicts with different people are also revealed (friends, non-friends, siblings, parents). Therefore, conflict and conflict strategies can be seen as indicators of relationships and how they are changing. Some relationships (e.g. siblings) are tolerant of conflict, but others (friendship) are less so. Some of the different strategies for dealing with conflict in sibling relationships are 'teasing, conciliation, social role playing, skills of cooperation' (Dunn and McGuire, 1992, p. 91).

If parents intervene too readily in sibling squabbles, then the children may never develop the abilities to find solutions to conflicts. They may need to learn, as well, that not everything is fair, and that there are times when one may have to accept injustice as inevitable when it comes from factors beyond one's control. Another argument against intervention is based on the understanding of sibling conflicts as attention-seeking behaviour. From this perspective, intervention will have the effect of increasing sibling conflict behaviour rather than reducing it, because it invites parental attention. From such a position, the best thing would be to treat sibling conflict like tantrum behaviour ... ignore it.

The case *for* intervention is first that, if unrestrained, younger children will succumb to the will of older siblings. Younger siblings may become less willing to assert their rights because they can expect to be forced by an older sibling to comply. This situation can easily cross the threshold into abusive behaviour if the older sibling does not learn that there are limits to what may be imposed on younger siblings, and that there is an authority in place to enforce those limits. In their consideration of the development of aggressive and antisocial behaviour within families, Bullock and Dishion (2002) indicate that 'Parents who do not attend to and manage sibling play may inadvertently allow conflicts to be solved by means of coercion.'

Where parents *are* willing to intervene, younger siblings are more willing to defend their property and rights, because they can count on the intervention of the parent to support their case if it is legitimate. They learn that there are rules that govern social interchange, and it is not simply a question of might makes right. People are expected to conform to social rules of behaviour. If they do not because of ignorance, then they must be taught the rules; if they do not because of defiance, then sanctions are necessary.

Most parents will adopt a line somewhere in between. They will not intervene in every altercation between the children. Indeed if they did, then they could expect to spend a lot of time sorting out squabbles. Children have on average nearly five fights with siblings every day (Prochaska and Prochaska, 1985). Dunn and Munn (1986) found that young children have 'conflict incidents' with older siblings very frequently: 8 per hour at 18 months of age, 7.6 per hour at 24 months. Parents can expend a lot of time if they intervene in every conflict. Neither will parents ignore every dispute. Parents have an internal threshold of intervention, a rough guide (noise level, sound of household articles crashing, interpretation of the motivation of the sibling eliciting parental intervention, etc.). But where should this threshold be set? Parental values regarding autonomy and gender constellation have also been found to affect parental intervention (McHale *et al.*, 2000). For example:

> mothers are more concerned than fathers are about younger girls' vulnerability in the context of fights with older, and presumably larger and stronger, boys. (p. 757)

The beginning of parental intervention in sibling squabbling is when the parent becomes aware of it, and despite widespread cultural norm against 'tattling' or telling tales, most children do. Younger children tattle mainly to enlist parent support to resolve conflicts, whereas older siblings tattle both in the context of sibling conflict, but also merely to inform their parents. Physical aggression and property damage are the two main issues that siblings tattle about, and these transgressions usually solicit parental punishment (den-Bak and Ross, 1996).

Once a parent is aware, what is he or she to do? Should she intervene? Is it best to let the children get on with it and sort themselves out? Findings from the literature disagree on this. Felson and Russo (1988) looked at the impact of parental punishment on sibling aggression. They noted that powerful third-party intervention tends to support the weaker party in conflict situations, and that this could unintentionally encourage aggression. They interviewed schoolchildren (4th–7th grade) and their parents about sibling aggression. Parents were more likely to punish older siblings for fighting and they were more likely to punish boys for fighting with their sisters. This tendency to punish the more powerful sibling resulted in more frequent aggression. They also found that sibling aggression was more frequent when the sibling age gap was three years or less, and was more likely between same-sex siblings. Girls were found able to be just as aggressive as boys.

Non-intervention in sibling disputes may have harmful consequences (Bennett, 1990). Not intervening when siblings are fighting may allow one child to establish dominance, and, although the fighting may therefore stop, the defeated child learns helplessness similar to the type of learned helplessness that some have argued develops as a result of domestic violence. The author suggests alternatives to non-intervention: treating the fighting as antisocial improper behaviour, imposing appropriate punishment and teaching the siblings prosocial behaviour.

Ross *et al.* (1994) examined how parents intervened in sibling conflicts between 2- and 4-year-old children in 40 families. Parents intervened 45 per cent of the time and directed their interventions to the child who had violated their sibling's rights or welfare. Parents generally supported rules for family interaction, but not all rules received the same level of support. Children could get away with tattling (telling tales), bossing, lying and excluding siblings, but there was stronger enforcement of violations of rules concerning aggression and sharing.

Baskett (1985) looked at consequences the child was most likely to experience in response to particular social situations and found certain patterns or behavioural chains. For example, crying led to comforting, but whining did not, and non-compliance led to progressively increasing disapproval and commands. Several important findings for our purposes were: (a) teasing a parent increased the likelihood of unpleasant consequences whereas siblings were more likely to laugh; and (b) physical aggression was more likely to anger parents than siblings, but when this increased, siblings would become more angry, whilst parents would maintain a more even level of response as before. This might be because parents feel a greater responsibility for how the child will develop, and thereby are concerned about the future, whereas a sibling, without such concerns, is more likely to respond on the level of immediate discomfort caused by the younger child's behaviour.

Around the time younger siblings are about 2 years of age, sibling aggression is correlated to maternal involvement. In families where mothers became involved with a large number of the sibling conflicts, the conflicts were longer and more likely to invoke physical aggression (Dunn and Munn, 1986). Dunn and Munn (1986) also noted that a maternal style of discussing rules and feelings helped to facilitate relatively mature forms of behaviour in conflict. Faber and Mazlish (1987) also place an emphasis on discussion, but acknowledge that parents must intervene to stop the aggression if the level of hostility and anger become unacceptable. They emphasise discussion, describing feelings, attending to the injured party rather than the aggressor, helping the children to develop skills of negotiating their way through conflicts and a range of measures intended to help parents feel there is something they can do.

Should parents intervene or not? The finding that parents intervene in about half of the incidents suggests that parents are adopting a common sense approach ... it depends on how extreme the situation is. Once a parent has decided to intervene, the question then becomes: what is the best approach to adopt? Teaching prosocial skills appears to promote more mature approaches to conflict-resolution between siblings.

What impact does sibling relationship quality have on other significant relationships?

Sibling relationship quality is not only an outcome of many factors, but is a cause of others. There are two particular questions of interest. First, how does the sibling relationship influence the development of the individual? Secondly, how does the sibling relationship link with current and future significant relationships outside the family (for example peer relationships)?

Question 6: How does the sibling relationship influence the development of the individual?

In fact, much of the early theorising about siblings addressed this question. The earlier material of Walter Toman (1994) was an attempt to look at how individuals were influenced to become the individuals they do because of the kinds of siblings (older/younger, male/female) they have. However, with the renewed emphasis on psychological aspects of sibling relationships over the last two decades, sibling status variables have proved themselves to be inadequate to deliver the kind of deeper understanding of sibling influences required and we look more to wide variations in the quality of the sibling relationship to provide answers. As noted by Dunn and McGuire (1992, p. 68), 'there is an especially wide range of differences in sibling relationships in emotional quality, from affectionate to very hostile and aggressive'.

Question 6a: How do siblings contribute to one's positive development?

To begin with, older brothers and sisters are effective teachers of their younger siblings, not only didactically (Cicirelli, 1972), but in other ways as well. Siblings have long been observed to be a rich source of pretend play, involving fantasy and imagination. There are types of play that only appear when young children play with older siblings, and do not appear in play with their mothers (Dale, 1989). For example:

> one type (without replica objects, and involving pretending with role identities/enactment, locations and psychological states) only appeared in games with the sibling. (p. 756)

One can imagine the situation in which, for reciprocal benefit, the older child is 'teaching' the younger child to play the types of games in which the older child can exercise his or her imagination and fantasy, and through the process promoting the ability of the younger sibling to do the same. Dale (1989) draws back from inferring this causality. The significance of the play without replica objects characterising sibling play, (and not maternal play) is not clear, but it is different, and that is important. Dunn (1988a) notes that siblings play a causal role in the development of a child's cooperative fantasy play.

Dunn has explored sibling influences in the development of children's social understanding and understanding of causality (Dunn and Munn, 1987; Dunn, Brown and Beardsall, 1991; Dunn, Brown, Slomkowski, Tesla and Youngblade, 1991; Dunn and Brown, 1993). More cooperative relationships in early discourses with older siblings were found to be associated with better social understanding (Dunn, Brown and Beardsall, 1991; Dunn, Brown, Slomkowski, Tesla and Youngblade, 1991; Dunn and Munn, 1987).

By about the age of 3 years, children had learned to use justifications in their disputes with both mothers and siblings. Justifications occurred in about one third of the disputes and tended to be based on their own feelings, their understanding of the consequences of actions, and, most interestingly, on an understanding of social rules (Dunn and Munn, 1987). The understanding of consequences of actions suggests that it is not only emotional and social understanding that can be facilitated by siblings; cognitive development is also assisted. The equal status of siblings combined with the frequency and intensity of their disagreements are seen to contribute to the development of their causal understanding and reasoning (Dunn and Brown, 1993).

Siblings also contribute to one's sense of emotional adjustment; warmth in sibling relationships and friendships is associated with less loneliness, fewer behaviour conduct problems and higher self-worth (Stocker, 1994). Rivalry in sibling relationships is related to higher levels of loneliness and depressive mood and lower levels of self-worth.

Question 6b: How do siblings contribute to the development of undesirable attributes?

Our focus here is on relatively ordinary harmful outcomes. Consideration of the damaging effects of abuse by siblings will be addressed in Chapter 5. It is important as well to again be cautious about causality when considering the links between sibling influence and negative attributes. As noted by Dunn (1992), both the negative sibling relationship and the negative attribute could be the result of the operation of a third factor, e.g. a more general disturbance.

There is a fairly substantial body of literature which demonstrates that actual psychopathology in a child is developmentally harmful for that child's siblings. Harmful outcomes for younger siblings include: increased psychopathology, difficulty maintaining social relationships, rejection of siblings as role models, and atypical role symmetry – where younger, unaffected siblings assume roles characteristic of older children in the family (Deal and MacLean, 1995).

Delinquency in adolescence may be influenced by the quality of earlier sibling relationships. There are two models put forth for this influence. In one, siblings are seen as 'key pathogens' in the process of becoming deviant (Patterson, 1984). In this behavioural model, through modelling processes, siblings learn about negatively reinforced parent–child interchanges and hostile-coercive interchanges with parents and then replicate those behavioural interchanges with each other. An alternative model however, focuses on the role of more positive sibling interactions as a facilitator of delinquency, suggesting that siblings may support each other in delinquency, and even engage in delinquent acts together ('partners in crime') (Carey, 1992; Rowe, 1985; Rowe and Gulley, 1992). Two of these three studies, however, focused on twins. Social interaction between siblings as a risk factor for the development of delinquent activity in adolescence (both models) is supported by Slomkowski and colleagues (Slomkowski et al., 1997; Slomkowski et al., 2001).

The link between sibling aggression and aggressive behaviour more generally has been substantiated (Beardsall, 1987; Brody *et al.*, 1987a; Dunn and Munn, 1986). When children are on the receiving end of aggression from siblings, they are much more likely to show aggressive behaviour. Dunn (1988a) indicates that siblings play a causal role in the development of a child's aggressive behaviour and in their style of conflict behaviour. Severe problems in a sibling relationship are indicative of other problems, but it is only for aggressive behaviour that this causal connection has been established.

Question 7: How does the sibling relationship link with current and future significant relationships outside the family (for example peer relationships)?

Dunn and McGuire (1992) distinguish between peer relationships (characterised by peer popularity and status) and friendships, and compare both with sibling relationships. The sibling relationship (and to some extent friendships) is marked by a higher degree of intimacy and dyadic interchange than peer relationships. Children choose their friends but not their peers, although that probably only applies as children get older. For very young children, the non-family associations that children have are probably the children of the friends of their parents, and reflect very little, if any, choice based on common interests, personality attractions, etc. that may come to influence choice of friends later.

Children's sibling relationships are commonly seen as preparation for the kinds of relationships they will establish with peers and friends outside the family. It is a transposition of a relationship essentially between equals from one context (the family) to another (the community). The expectation of linkages between sibling relationships and other relationships derive from three different theoretical sources, and although the routes differ, they all lead to the same conclusion: there are links between the various relationships (Dunn and McGuire, 1992). The three models are social learning, attachment theory and personality theory.

The process deriving from social learning theory is based on a generalisation of social relationships. Children learn to relate in certain ways to certain people, and then encounter new situations. In those new situations do they learn new ways to relate to people, because of the situation being new, or do they bring with them their now characteristic ways of relating to people, and apply them in the new situation? Is it the novelty of the new situation that influences the pattern of social behaviour, or is it the psychological/social attributes brought from the past that will determine how the individual responds and interacts. The model suggests there will be carry-over.

The second model suggesting a linkage between sibling and peer/ friendship relations is attachment theory (considered further in Chapter 7). Here the child develops an internal working model of social relationships derived from his/her primary social relationship – attachment to a primary carer(s) or caregiver(s). Sibling relationships are seen as a prototype or a blueprint for subsequent relationships. These are then modelled on that first relationship as a template. The third model, that of personality development, suggests that personality characteristics of the child (developed, in part, in response to previous social experiences) elicit certain typical patterns of responses from others. It is therefore a part of the child's psychological make-up that contributes to the similarities in different social settings.

Let us consider the evidence for the way in which sibling relationships link to other relationships. As we might expect, the picture is more difficult than the above models might imply – some behaviours do carry over; some do not. Findings from research are frequently inconsistent in this area, thereby suggesting again that simplistic answers derived from theoretical considerations may not provide the answers (Dunn and McGuire, 1992). A rather consistent finding, however, is the link between sibling aggression and peer aggression. Boys who are aggressive in their relationships with siblings tend to be aggressive with their peers, and are very likely to be socially excluded for that reason (MacKinnon-Lewis et al., 1997). If one looks at how similar or different the behaviour of very young children is in the home setting compared with the preschool setting, there is little correlation except for specific types of behaviour. Children who are more aggressive towards siblings (and children who are more often onlookers or unoccupied at home) show similar behaviour with peers (Berndt and Bulleit, 1985).

A very important question to ask about the link between peer and sibling relationships is whether they are additive or compensatory in terms of a child's psychological adjustment (East and Rook, 1992; Stocker, 1994). This has similarities with the previous discussion of family relationships being compensatory or congruent (see p. 83). If the links between sibling and peer relationships are additive, then in effect, the more problems one has in one's relationships, the worse the overall adjustment. Inversely, the more good relationships one has in different social situations, the better the overall adjustment. In the compensatory model, relationships that are deficient in one area of social interactions (for example with siblings) may be compensated for by better relationships in other areas (for example with peers) thus offsetting the impact of the poor relationships on the child's personal psychological adjustment. Although children who are isolated in their peer relationships derive very little social support from school friends, they can derive high levels of support in their favourite sibling relationship at home (East and Rook, 1992). In such cases, the support from the sibling is also associated with lower levels of socio-emotional difficulties. Clearly in this situation, sibling relationships can compensate for other less satisfactory social relationships. A compensatory link was also found in the links between a 7-year-old's home and school relationships – poor sibling relationships could be offset by positive peer relationships and vice versa (Stocker, 1994).

Another intriguing aspect of the linkage between sibling and peer relationships is whether they are gender sensitive. It has been found, for example, that girls who are neglected by their peers have positive sibling relationships (East, 1989) and girls were found to be more affectionate towards their peers than towards siblings (Vandell et al., 1990) but, in both cases, no such associations were found for boys. One may speculate that this may be because girls are socialised into stronger social relationships in the first place, whereas for boys there is considerably less emphasis in their upbringing on the development and sustaining of social ties. The evidence on gender stereotyping of prosocial behaviour is consistent with this. There is enduring sexual stereotyping regarding prosocial behaviour (Durkin, 1995). It is also consistent with the observation that 'females may have a stronger need for, and may be more competent at, exchanges involving intimate disclosure' (Buhrmester, 1992, p. 25).

As indicated, a number of researchers have found consistency in children's relationships with peers and siblings. Volling et al. (1997) found 'consistency of individual differences in relationship quality across friend and sibling dyads'. Mendelson et al. (1994, p. 416) found that 'popular kindergartners tended to feel positively about and to identify with a sibling; and, if they had an older sibling, the sibling tended to report high companionship'. Closeness in friendship for 3–5-year-olds was found to be associated with friendlier sibling relationships with younger siblings (Kramer, 1990).

Of course there is the possibility that both sibling relationships and peer relationships are influenced by other common factors. This would contribute to any commonality found in both sets of relationships. Marital conflict, for example, was found to be associated with both problematic sibling relationships and problematic peer relationships (Stocker and Youngblade, 1999).

But there are times when, looking at boys and girls together, no relationships are found between children's sibling relationships and their peer relationships (Abramovitch *et al.*, 1986; Stocker and Dunn, 1990). Stocker and Dunn (1990), for example, note:

> Children's sibling relationships were not associated with peer relationships; however, there were some links between children's relationships with siblings and with friends. (p. 227)

They found that children who have very positive friendships were quite competitive and controlling with the siblings; closeness in friendships was associated with hostility in sibling relationships. This could be reflective of a compensatory process between sibling and friendship relationships previously discussed.

Buhrmester (1992) has looked at both sibling and peer relationships as they develop into adolescence and considers that they have distinctive developmental courses (siblings' relationships, for example, containing very high levels of conflict). Sibling relationships also become 'more egalitarian and less asymmetrical' (p. 34) as the children progress into adolescence – but also less intense. The intensity that characterised the sibling relationships seems to be transferred to friends, peers and others.

Summary: the quality of sibling relationships

This chapter has looked at the empirical psychological understanding of sibling relationship quality. It has looked at factors that influence the quality of the relationship between siblings, and at how sibling relationships influence how we develop and relate to others. The chapter focused on seven questions, derived from the current literature on sibling relationships.

It began with a consideration of the relationship between sibling relationships and those relationships that children have with their parents – are they compensatory or congruent? Is lack of warmth in the relationship between a child and a parent made up for by warmth with a sibling? Is there likely to be lack of warmth in both? We found evidence in support of both possibilities, and also a suggestion that *whether* the relationship is compensatory or congruent may depend on other factors.

We then looked at why children in the same family are so different from each other, suggesting that perhaps the difficulty lies in the assumption that children growing up in the 'same' family are, in fact, experiencing an identical social environment. For a variety of reasons, children in the 'same' family actually experience very different social environments. This led to a consideration of the effects of treating children differently within the family. The subjective experience of a child being treated as a 'holy cow', or as a 'scapegoat', can leave children in the family dealing with a very strong sense of unfairness. The next question focused on the marital relationship and the impact that has on how siblings get along. It is not surprising that stronger marital relationships are associated with more positive sibling relationships, but the mechanisms for this association are not necessarily simple. It was also noted that whilst the harm of stress within families on the children can be reduced by supportive sibling relationships, those sibling relationships can be undermined by family stress. The fifth question looked at parental intervention in squabbles between siblings. Most parents attempt to find a balance between over- and under-intervention, thus protecting, when necessary, the more vulnerable sibling in disputes, but at the same time allowing children, whenever possible, to learn how to develop conflict resolution strategies.

Finally, the chapter looked at how we are affected by the nature of the relationship we have with our brothers and sisters, both in terms of the kind of person we turn out to be and in terms of the relationships that we have with others outside the family. Again, compensatory *vs.* congruent models were considered. It was found that some behaviours (for example, aggression) seem to be congruent (that is, present in relationships with both siblings and peers), but others were not.

PART II

Issues for Practice

Introduction

> When parents are frightening, abandoning, or invisible, siblings
> are not minor players in the family drama; they are the stars: the
> villains and the heroes who play a significant role in the child's
> life-and-death struggles for attachment, separateness and iden-
> tity. (Bank, 1992, p. 145)

A child being 'in need' has become the defining focus of all intervention
on the part of social services departments in the UK to provide child
and family support services. Although other agencies (for example
health and education) have a broader remit for the provision of universal services (education for all children; preventive child health services),
they are also concerned with more vulnerable children and work
collaboratively with the social services to provide focused and targeted
services in accordance with section 17 of the Children Act 1989. The
Children Act 1989 is very explicit in its assertion that services to benefit
children in need do not need to be targeted directly at the children, but
may be directed at the families of children in need. The principle behind
this is that helping parents is tantamount to helping their child(ren).
This is based on a conception of the influences on children being largely
parental. There is very little emphasis in the Act on the significance
of sibling relationships, with the exception of the presumption that
siblings who are being looked after by the local authority will be
placed together (section 27(3)(b)).

We recognise here an interesting anomaly when thinking about the
sibling relationships of children in adverse circumstances. Early theorising about sibling relationships was based on work with individuals

and families in adverse circumstances (psychoanalysis, family therapy) but was not empirical and was firmly based in research methodology. More recent theorising about sibling relationships has been empirical and research-based, but has not given much consideration to sibling relationships in families where there are adverse circumstances. The emphasis has been on sibling relationships in very ordinary families. Most of the descriptions of the samples upon which the recent psychological approaches have been based describe the families as coming from middle-class sections of the population. Neither of these take us very far in trying to understand sibling relationships in families where there is a child with a disability, families of children in need, families where there is a mentally ill or substance-abusing parent, families that are breaking up and reconstituting (either through separation/divorce, or care episodes for the children) and families where there is abuse or domestic violence. As we saw in the last chapter, it is very frequently the case that the patterns of intrafamilial interrelationship influences are much clearer in situations where the family is under stress (Dunn, 1993; Jenkins, 1992). We have already noted Dunn's (1988a) observation that differential treatment and family emotional climate factors assume an increased significance in families under stress.

Part II looks at these issues. There are two concurrent processes at work in relation to sibling relationships when families and the family members encounter difficulties or adverse circumstances. First, the protective quality of positive features of sibling relationships, to the extent that they are present, can provide a buffering effect on the impact of such circumstances. They may be a source of support for the children in such families; they may even be resilience promoting. It has been found, for example, that where families have had a large number of negative life events, the presence of an older sibling at home has been associated with less emotional and behavioural problems in the younger sibling (Sandler, 1980) – but note that there is no such association between older sibling presence and level of emotional and behavioural problems in families without high levels of negative life events. Likewise, Kosonen (1996b) looked at the emotional support and help provided by siblings, by asking two questions: When you are worried about something, who do you tell first? and When you need help with something you cannot do, who do you ask? Two of her findings are very relevant. She found that children would first turn to their mothers, but then to their older siblings for support (even before their fathers). She also found that for those children who were isolated, sibling support was particularly crucial. Consider:

> Nearly one third of the children who had no one else to turn to for support confided in their older siblings and nearly half of the isolated children mentioned their older siblings as their *only* source of help. (p. 271 my italics)

The second process however, for families in adversity, is the undermining of individuals in the family (creating stresses, reducing confidence and frequently causing behavioural difficulties) and undermining the sibling relationship. These two processes are countervailing, and the resultant ability of the sibling relationship to provide a buffering effect against the adverse family circumstances may depend upon the ability of the relationship to be maintained, and be positive, in the face of undermining influences. It is a contest of the two. The following example highlights some of these countervailing processes:

> high support from a favourite sibling was associated with better adjustment among isolated children on select outcomes. Despite the somewhat ameliorating role of siblings for isolated children, isolated children with high sibling support remained less well adjusted than did average children. (East and Rook, 1992, p. 163)

We should also take note that different types of adversities may have different impacts. There may be some in which siblings pull together, and others which create sibling conflict. Consider the following, for example:

> in the face of the adversities that these families experienced, the children grew closer, with friendly, affectionate behaviour being positively related to such adversities experienced ... The majority of children described the support that their siblings gave them in the face of problems such as difficulties with other children at school, maternal illness, or accidents and illnesses that they themselves had suffered ... This pattern differs from that described for families suffering from marital disharmony or difficult step-parent relationships, in which an increased level of sibling conflict has been reported. (Dunn, Slomkowski and Beardsall, 1994, p. 322)

It is interesting to note that the high level of sibling conflict in the Sanchez Family (Lewis, 1964) described earlier, is indeed associated with high levels of conflict between the stepparents and the children in the family. Roberto links his mutually antagonistic relationship with his young stepmother to the onset of difficulties between him and his sister, Consuelo.

An emphasis on sibling relationships within situations of family adversity should enable the practitioner to focus on a potential ally in achieving positive outcomes for children and families as a result of intervention. A neglect of it may be a missed opportunity.

5 Family Support and Sibling Relationships

This chapter looks at children living in families experiencing difficulties and requiring family support. It will consider the circumstances of children in four different situations which may categorise them as being in need:

(1) children of substance-abusing families
(2) children of mentally ill parents
(3) children with disabilities, and
(4) children living with domestic violence.

For each of these the emphasis will be, where there is material available, on what is known about the impact of the adverse circumstances on sibling relationships. In fact, of these four groups, the only one that has a substantial literature attached to it is children with disabilities, where the impact of a child's disability on the child's non-disabled siblings has been extensively reported. In such situations, there are known to be positive impacts as well as negative ones.

In each of these four situations, the discussion involves, to a greater or lesser degree, extrapolating from what is known about the impacts of these circumstances on individual children to how they might impact on the sibling relationships. There are also other observations about sibling relationships that are useful to note, even where there is no information available about the impact of the specific circumstances on the sibling relationship.

Children of substance-abusing families: drugs and alcohol

There is some literature that looks at the influence of siblings on an individual's usage of drugs and alcohol. Let us consider first drugs, then alcohol. From examining family histories, it was found that brothers and sisters of cocaine users are highly vulnerable to using drugs themselves (Luthar and Rounsaville, 1993). The direction of influence is likely to be from older to younger siblings (Penning and Barnes, 1982; Huberty and Huberty, 1986; Needle *et al.*, 1986; Gfroerer, 1987; Brook *et al.*, 1990). These studies are considered briefly below.

The link is sufficiently strong that sibling usage of drugs is a particularly important predictor of drug usage (Penning and Barnes, 1982; Needle *et al.*, 1986; Gfroerer, 1987). Young people are more likely to use drugs if an older sibling used marihuana (Gfroerer, 1987). Indeed, older siblings frequently supply drugs to, and use drugs with, a younger sibling. Parental drug usage plays little role compared with peer and sibling influences (Needle *et al.*, 1986; Brook *et al.*, 1990). Gfroerer (1987) pointed to social learning and imitation of older adults as being contributory factors in a young person's drug usage. Brook *et al.* (1990) found that older siblings and peers have a greater influence on drug usage than parents. Older brothers exerted an influence even if they: (a) advocated its use but did not model its usage; or (b) modelled its usage but did not advocate its usage. However, it was also found that where parents were drug users, an older brother who did not use drugs could offset the negative influence of the parents. This suggests that older brother's influence was more significant, one way or the other (usage or non-usage), than the parents. And if both older brothers and peers served as models for non-use, then younger brothers were least likely to engage in drug usage. In terms of drug usage at least, therefore, the relatively greater influence of siblings (in this case older siblings) over parents has been demonstrated. This finding that older siblings influence the drug-taking behaviour of younger siblings is important because the influence is exerted in two ways. Where parents are drug using, an older non-using sibling will exert an influence towards non-usage; where parents are not drug using, an older sibling using drugs will exert an influence towards usage.

Similarly, with alcohol, a younger sibling's use of alcohol is associated with their perception of the older sibling's drinking (D'Amico and Fromme, 1997). The role of vicarious learning of younger siblings from older siblings is a factor influencing adolescents' perceptions of health risk behaviour. D'Amico and Fromme developed a prevention strategy that acknowledges the significance of older sibling modelling. Likewise, Conger and Rueter (1996) comment on the 'usually neglected role of siblings in family influences on drinking behaviour'. In their model, sibling and parental influences 'legitimize, encourage, or fail to inhibit association with friends who will act as models and, perhaps, as sources of social pressure to drink'. Luthar and Rounsaville (1993) found that cocaine usage was associated with sibling alcoholism.

Rhea *et al.* (1993) looked at the reliability of sibling reports of parental drinking behaviour, i.e. the extent to which siblings' reports matched. They used both objective measures (e.g. two or more drunk-driving arrests) and subjective measures (e.g. parent only happy when drinking). As might be expected, the objective measures were more reliable than the subjective measures. They found a generally good concordance between siblings of their reports on their parent's drinking behaviour, but a significant gender difference emerged. They found that male siblings were more in agreement about their mother's drinking behaviour whereas female siblings were more in agreement about their father's drinking behaviour. Although this study tells us little about the impact of parental drinking on sibling relationships, it does tell us that gender is a basis of sibling agreement about parental behaviour.

The theme of collusion between siblings in engaging in deviant behaviour more generally, is addressed by Bullock and Dishion (2002, p. 143) who observe 'the sibling subsystem can form a unique context within families that potentially promotes or detracts from the socialization goals of caregivers'. They go on to note, 'Sibling collusion is a process by which siblings in a family form coalitions of deviance that potentially undermine parents' socialization efforts'. This may be a part of the explanation for the power of siblings to influence in terms of deviant behaviour. They suggest that siblings establish mutuality in terms of deliberately undermining the influence of parents and breaking family rules.

Practice Note 5.1   Children of substance-abusing families: drugs and alcohol

Mr and Mrs Pole have been married for three years, and have one son, Paul (aged 17 months). Dora Pole was married before and has three children, Jeanette (15), Sophie (12) and John (10) from that marriage. A contributory factor in the breakdown of Dora's first marriage was her misuse of alcohol. Her husband left her when the children were 7, 4 and 2 years of age. He felt that he was trying to hold down a demanding job and look after the needs of the children at the same time, because his wife was frequently incapable of looking after them because of her alcohol use. Following the marriage breakdown, the local authority looked after the three children. Mrs Pole went to a rehabilitation programme, and eventually the children were returned to her care after having been looked after for approximately ten months. The three children were looked after together, in a foster family, for the whole of the ten months.

During their time of being looked after, the children were very close to each other. Jeanette didn't make many friends, although she had friendly enough interactions with the other children at the school. She just seemed to be happy spending time with her younger sister and brother. In particular, she took delight and pride in helping the foster carer to look after John. The two young children very much look up to their older sister. John was very clingy towards Jeanette when they first arrived at the foster carer's home.

Mrs Pole remained in reasonable control of the alcohol difficulties until recently, when Mr Pole approached the local social services indicating that his wife seems to be returning to her previous pattern of alcohol usage and he is very concerned for all the children, but especially the youngest. When he returns home from work, he finds that Paul has not been fed all day, until the older children return home from school, at which time, Jeanette changes his nappy and gets food for him. She will then begin to prepare the evening meal for when Mr Pole arrives home from work. Mrs Pole begins drinking early in the morning, as soon as the children have gone to school, and drinks to an extent where she passes out and is like that when the children return. Paul remains in his cot all day. Mr Pole is obviously concerned about the neglect of Paul during the day, but equally expresses concern about the three older children. He has noticed that their relationship is not as warm as it used to be. In particular he notices that Jeanette, although she doesn't complain about the situation she finds herself in, is more irritable with Sophie and John. He is also concerned that she is not able to get on with her GCSE coursework, at a crucial time in her education. For her part, Jeanette does not complain about the role she has been put into in relation to Paul; she seems to just get on with it.

Consider:

1. In what ways might the particular difficulties (Mrs Pole's alcohol abuse) influence the nature of the relationship between the siblings? How might the two middle children's sibling relationships be affected as well by the family circumstances?
2. How should the worker attempt to understand the sibling relationships within the family? What methods or techniques might be used?

Children of parents with a mental illness

The impact of parental mental illness on sibling relationships is an area where there is no literature at all. There is a small body of literature that looks at the effect of having a sibling with a mental illness, either as adult siblings or as children (Kahn and Lewis, 1988; Judge, 1994; Greenberg Kim and Grenley, 1997; Marsh and Dickens, 1997; Jeon and Madjar, 1998; Marsh, 1998), which raises similar, but not identical, issues to those that arise in connection with siblings of a child with a disability, which are considered in the next section.

There has begun to develop, in recent years, a body of literature on the impact of parental mental illness on children, *as individuals*. The impact of parental mental illness on sibling relationships is clearly an area that could benefit from some research. With the advent of the UK government's *Framework for the Assessment of Children in Need and Their Families* (Department of Health *et al.*, 2000), there has been a considerable emphasis in government policy, from a child protection perspective, on tuning into the needs of children growing up in a home where there is a parent with a mental illness (Cleaver *et al.*, 1999). The importance of linking child-oriented child welfare services with adult-oriented mental health services has received considerable emphasis but has continued to be a challenge. Although the majority of patients in receipt of adult mental health services are likely to be parents (Oates, 1997), it is easy for the child(ren) not to be considered by the services – the so-called 'not noticed child' (Hindle, 1998). It requires liaison machinery, and a willingness to overcome interagency barriers (different attitudes, knowledge bases, orientations, etc.) to ensure that a seamless service is provided. What is required is a service in which mental health services take into consideration the needs of the children in families, and in which children's services are sensitive to the needs of parents with a mental disorder. The need for collaboration between children's services and adult services is vital (Falkov, 1996; Stormont *et al.*, 1997; Blanch *et al.*, 1998; Hindle, 1998; Sanders *et al.*, 1999). An important theme in child protection work, for example, is that, whilst the child's needs may be at the forefront of the intervention, parental needs are not to be dismissed, and indeed most often the best way to help the child is to support the parent(s).

We therefore must start with the impact of parental mental illness on the children as individuals. What do we know about this issue and this area of practice? I shall consider the different types of mental disorder, the increased likelihood of parent–child separation as a result of the mental illness, the risk to children's development (including fatality), the link between parental mental illness and other forms of social disadvantage, and the impact on the child of being put in a position where he or she must provide some level of care for the parent. Consideration of these five themes will put us in a better position to consider the implication for sibling relationships.

To begin with, we can expect there to be different impacts on children depending upon the nature of the parent's mental illness. There is a considerable difference between the parent suffering from strong delusions of persecution whose link with reality is tenuous and variable, and the parent suffering from anxiety or depression, but who nevertheless manages not to lose touch with what is real. Indeed, at the mild end of the spectrum of mental disorder, it is sometimes noted by organisations involved with mental health services just how common the less florid types of mental disorder are. At the other end of the spectrum however, bipolar disorders and schizophrenia in parents can be particularly concerning, and warrant careful consideration by practitioners. We might expect there to be different impacts according to type of mental illness, but is this borne out? Research tells us to be very cautious about drawing such a conclusion. There are no clear-cut patterns of child impact outcomes associated with type of parental mental illness (Sameroff *et al.* 1983; Cantwell and Baker, 1984). As noted by Rutter and Quinton (1987), 'many of the disturbances seen in the offspring are not specific to the type of parental psychiatric condition'. When we consider below the consequences for the child's development, we shall see that some of the best outcomes for children come where we would least expect them.

Depressed parents, psychotic parents, and parents with a range of neurotic disorders were considered by Cassell and Coleman (1995). They note that depression is likely to produce worse outcomes for children when it 'affects all aspects of family life, when relationships are unreliable or when the parent's hopelessness and lack of energy lead to neglect' (p. 171). Where the parent is psychotic, greater risk to the child is associated with the child somehow being part of the delusional system of the parent.

A second area for consideration is the impact of separation between parents and children, an issue considered more substantially in Chapter 7. In the case of parents with a mental illness, separation can occur because in many cases severe mental illness leads to hospitalisation, and often not just once but regularly, for varying periods of time. Separation can also occur because the child is removed from a parent because of concern for the child's welfare or safety. The impact of the separation is likely to depend upon a range of factors, for example, the age of the child, the length of the separation, the nature of the existing attachment between the parent and child and the availability of other attachment figures (including siblings). Parents with schizophrenia are particularly likely to be separated from children on admission to hospital (Hipwell and Kumar, 1996).

A third area for consideration is the risk to the child's development. There is considerable evidence to suggest that children's cognitive, social and emotional adjustment and later psychological functioning are impaired by having a parent with a mental illness (Cantwell and Baker, 1984; Feldman *et al.*, 1987; Shih, 1996; Zima *et al.*, 1996; Palmer, 1998). Consider the following:

> A growing body of evidence reveals that children of mentally ill parents are at increased risk for the development of psychopathology and for a full range of adjustment problems. Nevertheless some children of mentally ill parents still function well. (Shih, 1996, p. 5424)

The longer-term risk to children's development can be seen in studies of adults who grew up with a parent with a mental illness, which found significant effects later in life (Thompson, 1998) and even into the third generation (Williams, 1998). Evidence suggests this impact may be mediated by children's perception and understanding of the mental illness of the parent (Scherer *et al.*, 1996). Locus of control, that is the extent to which a family member is seen as being responsible for the symptoms or not, may be related to the impact of the illness on the functioning of the family (Robinson, 1996).

Feldman *et al.* (1987) suggest:

> Childhood behavior disorders are associated with a complex array of interrelated factors. Among the foremost are the at-risk child's relationships with his or her mother, the concentration of mentally ill persons in the child's current family, and the child's ability to participate in outside activities. (book jacket)

But since researchers tend to ignore sibling relationships, we may well speculate whether it was not found as a significant factor, because it was not looked for. Feldman *et al.* (1987) highlight the resilience of some children to the impact of parental mental illness.

There is a possibility that children who have parents with a mental illness may be more likely to form insecure attachments (Palmer,

1998). Specifically, depression is the form of mental illness particularly associated with differences in children's attachment classifications (Seifer *et al.*, 1996). Depressed parents may be unable to provide a stimulating environment for their children. Depression has also been found to be associated with vulnerability on measures of children's intellectual functioning and attention by Grunebaum and Cohler (1982). They also point to the significance of resilience, in part because their findings were quite surprising:

> Ironically, the most competent children have recurrently schizophrenic mothers; these children appear to have been able to selectively ignore maternal psychopathology and to take advantage of other adults as caretakers and teachers during periods of increased maternal psychopathology. (abstract)

One of the gravest concerns that professionals have with mentally ill parents is the risk of the parent killing the child. This fear is well founded. Parents who are extremely ill (for example psychotic) may involve children in their delusional thinking. This may be a very significant risk factor. A parent may be suicidal and believe that the child(ren) are better joining them in death than continuing to live. Falkov (1996) in his study of 100 cases of child abuse fatality found that 32 contained clear indication of parental psychiatric difficulty. Sanders *et al.* (1999) encountered two cases (from fourteen cases of fatal abuse or neglect by parent) in which parents committed suicide taking children with them (in one case one child, in the other two children). Such dire consequences highlight the need for very careful assessments when a parent has a mental disorder (Cassell and Coleman, 1995; Jacobsen *et al.*, 1997; Louis *et al.*, 1997; Ramsay *et al.*, 1998).

It is concerning that frequently parents are not aware of the impact of their mental illness on their children even when requiring hospitalisation (Stormont *et al.*, 1997). But, where it is accepted, working with mentally ill parents on parenting skills can be helpful and enable them to provide better care for their children (Soda, 1998). However, to be effective, such interventions must take into consideration the effects of the mother's environment and the mother's strengths, and consider what may be the obstacles to participation in the programme and to achieving personal parenting goals (Oyserman *et al.*, 1994).

The fourth theme concerns the interaction of parental mental illness with other forms of disadvantage, which themselves might influence the children's development. Parents with a mental illness are frequently unable to hold positions of employment, or develop a career in accord with their capabilities because of breaks in employment due to hospitalisations. For that reason and others, their standard of living may be below that of other families; they may be poorer families. Socioeconomic status has been found to be a significant mediating variable between the impact of parental mental illness and children's cognitive development (Sameroff *et al.*, 1983). Housing may also be related to mental illness. For example, connections have been found between 'symptoms of a probable lifetime major mental illness' and being a homeless mother (Zima *et al.*, 1996).

The fifth and final theme is the question of children taking on a caring role in relation to parents. Children may be put in the position of caring for their parent if their mental disorder renders them less capable. In such situations children are occasionally described as 'parentified', that is, although the term is variously defined, they have come to take on the role of the parent in relation to their parent. Consider the two following definitions:

> Parentification was defined as an on-going family interactional pattern in which a child had been excessively and inappropriately assigned roles and responsibilities normally reserved for adults. (Marx, 1999, p. 3753)

and

> children who are compelled to perform the role of parent at the expense of their own developmentally appropriate needs and pursuits. (Chase, 1999, abstract)

Depending upon the level of need and upon the support available from within the family, from the extended family and from a social support network, the amount of care provided by the young carer could vary from 'helping out' to providing 'extensive and basic care' for the parent. In its working definition of 'young carer', government guidance noted the following:

> Nor does the term refer to those children who accept an age appropriate role in taking responsibility for household tasks in homes with a disabled, sick or mentally ill parent. (Social Services Inspectorate, 1996)

The concept of 'young carer' can be variously construed as noted by Blyth and Waddell (1999):

> the language used to describe 'young carers' in families conflicts with the language used in the field of child protection. Depending on professional

or agency orientation a young person in a given situation may be perceived as either a 'young carer' (implying role and responsibility) or 'at risk' (implying dependency, lack of responsibility and vulnerability). (p. 30)

The impact of parental mental illness on sibling relationships

To begin with, severe mental illness may influence parents in terms of whether or not they have further children. For example, it was found that following severe puerperal mental illness, 80 per cent of mothers avoided further pregnancies during the following six years (compared with 56 per cent of the control group) (Bagedahl-Strindlund, 1997); a family with this particular type of problem may be less likely to have siblings at all and, consequently, fewer sibling relationships.

Generally, those studies that tell us most about the influence of parental mental illness on sibling relationships, in view of the lack of literature on the topic, are those that look at the impact on relationships within the family broadly – a factor found to be related to the quality of the sibling relationships. Dickstein *et al.* (1998), for example, instead of restricting the focus of their exploration to marital and parent-child impacts of maternal mental illness also looked at whole family functioning. They found that:

In general, families with maternal mental illness were characterized by unhealthy family-unit functioning, decreased marital satisfaction, and poor interaction quality. (p. 34)

However, they also contend that in a family with a mentally ill parent, other aspects of family functioning may promote resilience (see below). Barnes (1996) also locates parental mental illness in the context of a family systems approach in terms of both the intimate relationships within the family and the relations that the family has with the wider social context.

Two further themes worth developing here are resilience and being in the role of a young carer (a theme which also relates to the next section on siblings of children with a disability). Resilience is an important theme to emerge in terms of the impact of the parent's mental illness on the child's development. Resilience can be defined as 'Normal development under difficult circumstances' (Fonagy *et al.*, 1994). Werner (1990) has identified a range of factors that promote resilience in children, categorised in terms of factors to do with the child (according to age) and factors to do with the family. Many of these are relevant to the situation where there are siblings in the family. For our purposes, it may be useful to divide the child factors into those that produce resilience for younger siblings and those for older siblings. Gender is also a significant influence in resilience.

For younger siblings, the experience of a secure attachment is resilience promoting. Attachment to an older sibling can supplement, or perhaps even compensate for, attachment to the primary carer. Indeed, it is conceivable that in some situations where the parental capacity is extremely diminished by the severity of the mental illness, the older sibling may be the *de facto* primary carer. Having a supportive family member is resilience promoting (Werner, 1990). Therefore, even if the relationship with the older sibling is not so strong as to compensate fully for the attachment to the primary care, the support of the older sibling can diminish the adverse impacts of parental mental illness upon the younger sibling. Another resilience promoting factor for young children is social play; infants who are more advanced in social play are also more resilient. We have found in looking at the recent psychological study of sibling relationships (particularly the observational work of Judy Dunn) that older siblings can be an influence promoting social play. We can speculate therefore that for a younger child, positive sibling relationships with an older sibling, where joint play is a feature, is likely to have a beneficial effect; negative sibling relationships (or less positive ones), where there is less joint sibling play, can be expected to have a less beneficial effect for younger siblings. The situation, however, is less straightforward when we look at the older sibling.

Looking at resilience promoting factors for older siblings leads us again therefore into a consideration of the impact of parental unavailability, parentification, sibling caretaking and the role of being a young carer (all of which have been previously considered). If the situation with the younger sibling was relatively straightforward, the situation regarding the older sibling entails a balancing of risks of harm associated with being a carer against protective factors. At its most obvious, the risks that people have identified with sibling caretaking may be compounded by the risks associated with being a young carer for the adult; in effect the older sibling is looking after everyone in the family. We can consider whether an older sibling might be doubly disadvantaged by being in the role of carer not only for the parent (the 'parentified child') but also involved in sibling caretaking. This could perhaps be a prescription for a very poor outcome for the older sibling.

However, for the older children in families, resilience has been found to be associated with being characterised by pronounced social maturity and a sense of responsibility (Werner, 1990), aspects that may well go along with being a young carer.

There are three factors that are likely to be very significant here. The first is the availability of support to the parent from agencies such as health and social services in the form of adequate and well-coordinated services. The second is the provision of support to the young carer in his or her own right. If we consider recent work which explored young carers' own views of their situations (Thomas *et al.*, 2001), 'Most young people were not seeking to be 'rescued' from their role and what they saw as their responsibilities toward their family' (p. 6), but they were looking for good support in that role and information. As noted by Aldridge and Becker (1993):

> young carers' needs in terms of services were modest. All of them said that what they needed most was 'someone to talk to', someone who would befriend them, understand their circumstances, empathise and represent them without further threat of a 'cascade of intervention' or separation from their families. (p. 385)

Young carer support groups have been found to be particularly useful. In the year 2000 there were approximately 100 young carers groups throughout the UK, serving 5,000 of an estimated 51,000 young carers in the UK (Bibby and Becker, 2000). Meeting the information needs of young carers is also found to be particularly useful. Both of these factors will ensure that the personal needs of the young carer are met and are not sacrificed to the role they are undertaking.

The third significant factor is recognition of the value of the role they are undertaking. Consider, for example, the following:

> there are many situations in which children must perform parental functions and will continue to perform them until they are adults. These children fare better when their parental roles are acknowledged and honored; when, in other words, the adults can consistently and congruently name, respect, and honor the adult functions that the children perform for the family. It is the author's contention that children get into difficulty not because they perform parentified functions in families, but rather because (1) their parentified functions either go unrecognized, and/or (2) they are incongruent with other expectations for their behavior, and/or (3) they are impossible to perform. (Coale, 1999, abstract)

Where siblings are closer in age, unequal distribution of the young caring role within the home can make the burden of caring that much more difficult. In their discussion of how young carers are effectively punished by family and friends, punished by the caring profession, and effectively punished by society through poverty, isolation and exclusion, Aldridge and Becker (1993) provide this very brief consideration of sibling relationships in the context of being a young carer:

> Sisters and brothers can also perpetuate this experience of punishment by avoiding caring duties or by being persistently unavailable for caring tasks. (p. 380)

Within the family the opportunity to have affectionate ties with alternative caregivers is resilience promoting for both younger and older siblings (Werner, 1990). For the younger child this might be an older sibling; for the older sibling this might be someone outside the immediate family. It is specifically noted that sibling caretaking can be a major protective factor for vulnerable children, but the availability of supplementary support of an older adult is a mediating variable determining whether the influence of the older sibling on the younger will be for good or not.

Practice Note 5.2   Children of parents with a mental illness

Jenny (38) is the mother of two girls, Clara (13) and Margaret (12). She returned to Britain about five years ago from Canada, where she had lived since she was twenty-two. She met the children's father in Canada shortly after she arrived there, and a year later they were married. Jenny separated from the father and then returned to Britain with her two girls. Their father remained in Canada.

Clara has been referred to the local child and adolescent mental health services by the family general practitioner, who in her letter of referral suggested that the problems for which the daughter is being referred probably originate in the mother, who she described as a very 'singular' individual. Clara is described as being very anxious and withdrawn, almost to the point of agoraphobia, and this has resulted in her adamantly refusing to go to school. She has not been attending for about one year at the point of referral. For Clara, attending school has always been a source of anxiety, going back as far as her early years in primary school, but cajoling, bribery, inducements, all seemed to be effective getting her to attend, even if not reducing her anxiety about attending.

Margaret, however, appears to have no difficulty with getting herself off to school every morning. She has a few friends at school and apparently appears to enjoy her time there. She does not, however, bring her friends home after school, nor invite them around at other times. She will on occasion go to their homes, but rarely. She seems happy to keep her contact with them limited to school. She performs well in school, a little above average.

The social worker interviewing Jenny was completely unprepared for what came out and was rather taken aback. She began by asking Jenny to describe Clara's problem as she sees it, and Jenny began to talk about it all being down to the unhappy experiences that Clara had because of being the focus of an international conspiracy. She stated that Clara has information about military secrets that she had learnt when they lived in Canada, and that there were people who were trying to find out from her what those secrets were. She informed the social worker that her ex-husband, Clara's father, was a spy, and that she herself was distantly related to the Lord Chief Justice, which kept herself and her children safe from being harmed, but not from being the object of investigation and probing. She told the social worker that Margaret had no such information, and therefore she was not in any danger. Her concern was exclusively for Clara.

Upon checking, the social worker was surprised to find that there was no psychiatric history, although, from Jenny's descriptions, it would appear that these beliefs had been around for a very long period of time. She wondered how Jenny had managed to 'slip through the net' of psychiatric services. In part, this was possibly because she had never acted dangerously as a result of her beliefs, and apparently did not communicate this to many people. She was relatively isolated in her day-to-day contact.

Consider

1. How might the involvement of one child and not the other in Jenny's psychiatric difficulties influence the nature of the relationship between Clara and Margaret?

2. Now that mother's condition is known, how might the nature of the sibling relationship between the two sisters be developed as a foundation to help them cope with Jenny's difficulties?

3. Is there a role for an emphasis on the sibling relationship in addressing Clara's school difficulties? If so, what is it?

Children with disabilities

Disability amongst children has long been a focus in the literature on sibling relationships. As a theme, it also reverberates with the previous theme of differential treatment, because disability can be a factor leading to differential treatment of siblings within families. Therefore, this sub-theme (disability and parental differential treatment) will be considered, but only after we have explored some of the issues around siblings and disability more generally.

The weight of the literature on disabled siblings is focused on the question: what is the impact of having a sibling with a disability on the non-disabled child in the family? There is a substantial body of literature on this subject, mostly beginning from the mid-1980s, and much of it is contradictory. However, it is possible to challenge this emphasis in research as perhaps being in itself disablist in its orientation.

First, it marginalises the disabled child – the orientation of the question is to find out how this particular aspect of the disabled child, the disability, affects the non-disabled child as an individual. There seems to be an importance attached to the non-disabled sibling that is lacking in relation to the disabled sibling. The reciprocal questions which might put the child with the disability at the centre do not seem to have nearly as much focus, for example questions such as:

- How does having a non-disabled sibling affect a child with a disability?
- What characteristics of the non-disabled sibling affect the disabled sibling and in what ways?

Presumably, to address this, one would have to compare disabled children who have a disabled sibling with disabled children who have a sibling that is not. No such research has been undertaken.

Secondly, this orientation presumes that the disability is the over-riding factor in determining the child's impact on his or her sibling. Ideologically, we have come a long way in defining best practice in working with children with disabilities as seeing them as children first and as people with disabilities second. This principle of best practice means seeing a disabled child as having not only special needs that may need to be addressed, but also, very importantly, having the same needs as all children which also must be addressed, and which certainly must not be marginalised in the process of attempting to address special needs. The child's personality, character, likes and dislikes, etc., behind the disability, must not be overlooked, but given the same consideration as these aspects would be given for any child where an assessment of need is undertaken. The research focus, however, on the impact of a child's disability on his or her sibling's growth and development ignores the child behind the disability, and gives little consideration to variations in character, behaviour, temperament, etc. of the disabled child that might contribute to the impact he or she has on his non-disabled brother or sister. The focus is exclusively on his or her disability. This may well be colluding with a perception of disabled siblings as more broadly 'less able' by virtue of their disability, a disempowering view. The disability may be a powerful influence, but the child behind the disability is marginalised.

And, further, as has been pointed out, the focus of research in this area is on the siblings as individuals and not on the relationship between them. Shifting the focus of research to the contribution of the *child* with the disability (and *not* just the contribution of his or her disability) to the quality of the sibling relationship may be a useful avenue to explore.

In practice, it is as important to take into consideration the sibling relationships of a child with a disability as it is, or should be, for children in any other situation where assessment and intervention with a view to service delivery are being considered. If there were two points of good practice in relation to sibling relationships where one child is disabled that should arise from this discussion they would be that (a) the contribution that the disabled child makes to the sibling relationship on the basis of him- or herself as an individual should be considered (apart from his or her disability), and (b) the contribution of *both* children to the quality of the sibling relationship should be considered.

Most, but not all, studies looking at the impact of disability on siblings of the disabled child have found negative and significant findings, and it is those that we shall first consider. It is common for non-disabled siblings to feel anger and guilt, caused by a feeling of being ignored and unappreciated, an awareness of the psychological and financial demands placed on the family by the disabled child, and reactions on the part of acquaintances to the disabled sibling (Seligman, 1983). Children may be thrust into parenting roles before they are ready and may carry excessive responsibility for the disabled sibling, which may lead to resentment, guilt and subsequent psychological disturbance. Greater effects were found for lower socioeconomic families (fewer financial resources), smaller families (well siblings have to assume a greater share of the caretaking), and for sisters (who also often have greater caretaking responsibilities). Parental expectations for the non-disabled sibling may be excessive to compensate for the inability of the disabled sibling to fulfil parental expectations. Seligman (1983) suggests three factors contribute to the maladjustment of siblings of a disabled child: anxiety over 'catching' the disability, a lack of communication within the family about the condition of the disabled child, and negative parental responses and attitudes towards the disabled child.

Siblings of disabled children may experience feelings of shame (Bloch *et al.*, 1994). Sibling rivalry and hostility may be exacerbated, and these feelings may lead to fear and guilt in the non-disabled child (McKeever, 1983). Such siblings are likely to experience considerable ongoing stress. Ordinal position, sex and age of the healthy child, family socioeconomic status and characteristics of the specific condition are all factors influencing the impact on the non-disabled sibling. Risk of problems for the non-disabled sibling is greater when (a) the family is small, (b) the non-disabled sibling is younger than the disabled child, (c) the disability is severe, and (d) the sibling's disability is not easily understood by the normal sibling (Clausen, 1984). Another literature review, which found siblings of disabled children to be at risk of developing psychological difficulties, noted 'At particular risk are older females in small, low-socioeconomic-status families who assume excessive caretaking responsibilities for their impaired sibling' (Hannah and Midlarsky, 1985). Their subsequent work focused on the deterioration in social and academic performance of a sibling of a disabled child, which they considered might be related to the family's means of coping with the prolonged stressor. Birth order and gender were found to be *interactively* related in terms of psychological impairment. This means that for brothers, non-disabled siblings who were younger than the disabled sibling (especially when close in age) were more psychologically impaired than brothers who were older, but for sisters it was the other way round. For them, non-disabled sisters who were older than the disabled sibling were more psychologically impaired (Breslau, 1982). It is tempting to speculate that for the boys this may be because their needs are not being met, at the expense of family effort to meet the needs of the disabled sibling, whereas for sisters it may be because of the extra responsibility they carry for the disabled sibling, but this may be oversimplistic in view of our previous consideration of risk and protective factors in sibling caretakers and young carers. Dyson (1989) didn't find differences in self-concept, behaviour problems or social competence, but differences did emerge in relation to aggression and hyperactivity.

Other factors that contribute to variations in the non-disabled siblings' adjustment are family size, socioeconomic status (SES), and characteristics of the disabled child (Gallagher and Powell, 1989). Atkins (1989) found similar variables affect the degree of risk to the non-disabled sibling: (a) parental anxieties, attitudes, and expectations; (b) family resources; (c) sex, age and ordinal position of the non-disabled child; and (d) severity of the disability.

Most of the above factors are attributes or status indicators, what Bronfenbrenner and Crouter (1983) describe as 'social address' variables. The impact on the non-disabled sibling may also be related to process variables. For example, the way in which the parents break the news of a sibling's disability, the parents' expectations of the non-disabled siblings in relation to the disabled sibling, and, in particular, the parental expectation that non-disabled siblings will never separate from the family (to provide continued support to the parents in their raising of the disabled child) which itself creates a 'handicap' for the non-disabled sibling, are all related to non-disabled siblings' adjustment (Lapalus-Netter, 1989). Children may be concerned about the future of their disabled sibling, feel lonely, encounter difficulties with their peers and often do not know why their disabled sibling is different from other children (Bagenholm and Gillberg, 1991). This suggests perhaps a need for open and honest communication about the special needs of the sibling with the disability (Frank, 1996). Support for the non-disabled sibling's self-esteem and self-confidence is suggested as a way to avoid the possible negative impact of having a disabled sibling. The need for open and honest communication about the disability of a sibling is noted as well by Slade (1988), who describes four areas as being significant in predicting the adjustment of children with a disabled sibling: (1) parental attention to the disabled child; (2) sex and position in the family of the non-disabled sibling; (3) types of problems experienced by the disabled sibling; and (4) child-rearing practices used by the parents with the non-disabled sibling.

An interesting finding by McHale et al. (1986) was that children with a disabled brother or sister rated their family relationships as less cohesive than children with a non-disabled sibling, but their mothers rated their sibling relationships more positively. Significantly, they found that age, gender and family size did not appear to make as much difference to the quality of the relationship between siblings as perceptions of parental favouritism, coping ability or concerns about the disabled child's future. McHale and Gamble (1987, 1989) found, however, that, contrary to the contention about sibling care-giving in relation to a disabled child's being the cause of adjustment problems in the non-disabled sibling, other factors were as significant, if not more so: the behaviour of the disabled child (especially aggressive behaviour); the behaviour of the mother; and especially the child's dissatisfaction with differential treatment. Also, the non-disabled sibling's level of understanding of the cause of the problems of the disabled sibling was linked to adjustment difficulties. However, McHale and Harris (1992) did find a 'slight' association between sibling care-taking activity and adjustment, particularly for girls.

Not all the impacts are negative. Indeed, it is perhaps a shortcoming of research in this area that the negative outcomes for siblings of a disabled child have been overemphasised. McHale and Harris (1992) looked very closely at the nature of sibling associations with disabled and non-disabled siblings (through daily telephone calls), and found that although the overall amount of interaction was the same, there were qualitative differences in the way siblings interacted with disabled siblings compared with how they interacted with non-disabled siblings. Interaction with disabled siblings they described as being more *instrumental* (helping, teaching, caregiving), whereas interaction with non-disabled siblings tended to be more *expressive*. They noted that a feature of this distinction was the level of egalitarianism in the interaction. Dunn and McGuire (1992) note significantly in their consideration of the negative impacts:

> siblings of children with disabilities do often fall within the normal range of scores for psychological and behavioral problems: they may be at the high end of the range, but are usually below clinical cut-off points. (Dunn and McGuire, 1992, referring to the work of McHale and Gamble, 1989, p. 92)

They suggest researchers should:

> move away from an orientation that emphasizes negative outcomes and their correlates, and should employ the same models which guide research on other relationships, and integrate the findings with the sibling research literature. (p. 92)

In other words, the relationship between a child and a disabled sibling should be explored in the same way as other sibling relationships, by focusing on those factors that are associated with, and influence, the quality of the sibling relationship.

Stainton and Besser (1998) looked at the positive impacts of a child with an intellectual disability. Among the seven areas of positive impact identified by parents was a source of family unity and closeness and a source of increased tolerance and understanding. Adults recall the experience of growing up with a sibling with a disability as a source of psychological strength (Burton and Parks, 1994). If the contention were being put that because of the extra burden of care undertaken by the siblings for their disabled brother or sister, the quality of the sibling relationship is likely to be adversely affected, then the work of Pruchno *et al.* (1996) would suggest otherwise on both counts. They found that mothers of disabled children (a) did not feel that the non-disabled siblings provided much practical help, and (b) considered there to be strong, close ties between the children. Dunn (1988a) notes the significance of McHale and Gamble's (1987) study because of its methodology (daily telephone calls), which allowed the researchers to assess the sibling relationship more fully than had been able to be achieved through interviews or retrospective data. She notes that it is:

> established . . . that children with disabled siblings are more considerate and kind to their siblings, suggesting a connection with the reported high incidence of altruism, tolerance and humanistic concerns in adults who had grown up with a handicapped sibling. (Dunn, 1988a, pp. 123–4)

So far, we have considered studies finding differences. Some studies, however, have found either no difference, or indeed have been critical of studies finding differences. For example, Bischoff and Tingstrom (1991) looked at behavioural and psychological characteristics of siblings of children with disabilities and found no significant differences on measures of behaviour problems, social competence or self-esteem. However, the siblings did perceive their mothers to be more partial to their disabled sibling. Parents in their study indicated a greater difference in status/power between the child and his or her younger sibling. Damiani (1999), who reviewed the research on the caring responsibilities of non-disabled siblings for disabled siblings, concluded that there was no evidence for the existence of higher levels of responsibility for siblings of children with disabilities. Neither was there any evidence that such responsibility was a psychological risk factor for the non-disabled sibling. This seems, however, to go against the bulk of research in this area.

It is rather difficult to get an overview of the impact that having a sibling with a disability produces because of the apparently conflicting findings. Summers *et al.* (1994) attempted to draw together some of the themes from the research. They note that much of the literature that finds harmful consequences for non-disabled siblings lacked a control group. Their results produced both negative and positive findings. They report that 77 per cent of the highest-quality findings suggested no behavioural differences. However, they also reported that siblings of children with a disability did show greater anxiety, withdrawal, aggression, agonism and dominance, but with an equally strong tendency to higher levels of prosocial behaviour.

A final issue to consider in this subsection on disability is the connection with parental differential treatment, an issue previously considered in Chapter 3. A number of studies have considered the issue of differential treatment in relation to a disabled sibling. McHale and Pawletko (1992) and Wolf *et al.* (1998) also looked at this issue. McHale and Pawletko explored the connections between differential treatment and (a) the adjustment of both children and (b) the sibling relationship. The results indicated higher levels of differential treatment in the families with a disabled child. Features of differential treatment were found to be related both to children's adjustment and to the sibling relationships. However, as previously noted, it is the child's experience of the treatment being different (and unfairly so) which is the significant factor, more than the actual difference in the way the children are treated. Children can see justifications for differential treatment, and in such cases there may not be the adverse sequelae that arise when children perceive the differential treatment as being unfair. For example, McHale and Gamble (1989) found that children with a mentally disabled sibling reported more caregiving, more maternal negativity and poorer adjustment but they also found that the child's satisfaction of differential treatment of self, compared with the disabled sibling, was associated with the child's level of adjustment. McHale and Harris (1992) describe three aspects of differential treatment, two of which there was no evidence to support. They did not find that children with a disabled sibling were neglected relative to their age. Neither were they subjected to different forms of discipline. However, they were involved in higher levels of household tasks. McHale and Harris (1992) place a considerable emphasis on the subjective experience for the non-disabled sibling, 'the meanings children attribute to different forms of differential treatment' (p. 95). Referring to the work of McHale and Pawletko (above), they note that this may be mediated by children having the cognitive capacity to appreciate that fairness does not always mean being treated exactly the same. This may require a relatively sophisticated understanding.

Helping non-disabled siblings

Pearson and Sternberg (1986) describe sibling support groups as part of a programme developed for families of disabled children. Drawing on clinical experience and addressing the issue of how to help siblings of a child with a long-term illness or disability, McMahon (1992) observes:

> Play may also help siblings who often experience loss of attention and 'containment' because of the parents' focus on the sick child. They may pick up parents' feelings of confusion and anxiety. They may also feel guilty, believing, through 'magical thinking', that they have caused their sibling to become ill. Group work, particularly for siblings of children with long-term illnesses or disabilities, can be helpful in reducing their fantasizing and their sense of isolation. (p. 132)

Practice Note 5.3   Children with disabilities

Margaret and Jim have three children, Anne (15), Tom (14) and Paula (9). Paula has Down's Syndrome and needs a lot of medication for a Down's Syndrome-related heart condition and hypothyroidism. She is under the paediatrician and receives medication which keeps her conditions quite stable. She functions at quite a good level, and educationally she has been able to attend the local primary school. She has been statemented and has special needs support provided by the local education authority. The parents working with the agencies are beginning to focus more strongly on what type of educational provision will best suit Paula when she moves to secondary school. The school feels, because she needs constant medication and medical monitoring, that she should be in a special, residential school. The worker from the multidisciplinary children-with-a-disability team feels that Paula should continue to be maintained in mainstream education with extra support services provided. The paediatrician feels that Paula could continue quite well in mainstream education.

For the parents, the home situation is a particularly significant factor. There are tensions between the children that are making the parents lean towards thinking about residential special needs provision for Paula, something they had always been strongly opposed to.

Paula gets on quite well with Anne, her older sister, who takes a special interest in her, and has done so ever since Paula's birth. The relationship is characterised by high levels of reciprocal warmth. She
spends a lot of time in joint activity with Paula and will take her occasionally to the special appointments she requires to relieve the
burden on her parents. She clearly appears to enjoy time spent in
the company of her sister. Tom, on the other hand, has tended to avoid
Paula as much as possible. He is a rather sensitive young person, and
the parents feel that some of it may be attributable to teasing he was
subjected to by children at school when he was younger. He does not
like to be seen with Paula, and will try to avoid family outings as much
as possible, going to extreme lengths to find excuses not to come.
Further than that, however, he is rather unkind to Paula, and will, frequently, if no one is looking and he thinks he can get away with it,
pinch her, or give her a slight knock, for no apparent reason. When
confronted about this behaviour by his parents or his older sister, he
will invariably deny it. The unkind way he treats Paula is beginning to
be a concern for Anne as well as for the parents. When younger, Anne
and Tom were quite close, but that seems to be changing as Tom's
unkindness towards Paula increases.

Consider:
1. In addition to the obvious significance of Paula's relationship to
   each of her siblings, to what extent should the relationship
   between Anne and Tom be a focus as part of any assessment of
   the family?
2. In this scenario, how significant might be the influence that Paula
   might have on the relationship between Anne and Tom, and the
   influence that their relationship might have on her?
3. To what extent should there be a focus on the parental contribu-
   tion/influence in relation to the various sibling relationships?

Children living with domestic violence

Let us revisit the material in Chapter 3 (Question 4) about the interaction between family disharmony and sibling relationships (Jenkins,
1992). Families in which there is domestic violence may be considered
as families experiencing disharmony. Sibling relationships are undermined by family disharmony; siblings have relationships that are more
hostile and aggressive. But where sibling relationships are not undermined, they may be a buffer against the impact of family disharmony,
that is they may promote resilience.

Let us consider the mechanisms for these observed effects. It is logical to suggest that violence within families is reflected in family subsystems. There are likely to be correlations between spousal violence, violence towards children and violence between children. Although in the past, in cases of domestic violence, workers were comfortable making distinctions between those men who were also violent towards their children, and those who were not, this is much less likely to be the case today. Research in the UK is still in the early stages of understanding the psychological and social impact of domestic violence on children. It is only as recently as 1994 that the first British study (NCH Action for Children, 1994) exposed the devastating effects of domestic violence on children. Suh and Abel (1990) found that as many as 40 per cent of 258 women who entered a battered women's shelter between 1976 and 1986 reported that their partner had been physically abusive to the child(ren) as well. Bowker *et al.* (1988), in their study of domestic violence, found that 'wife-beaters abused children in 70 per cent of the families in which children were present' (p. 162). Farmer and Owen (1995), in their in-depth study of 44 families involved in the child protection system, found domestic violence known to social workers in 12 cases, and domestic violence in families which was not known about by the social workers in another 11 cases. Mullender (1996) explores the links between domestic abuse (both sexual and physical) and child abuse. She notes that there is more information on the overlap between physical child abuse and domestic violence than there is with child sexual abuse. This does make it difficult to extricate those influences on sibling relationships that arise from domestic violence from those arising from child abuse, which are considered in Chapter 6.

There are different theoretical perspectives accounting for the relations between the various forms of violence in families and these will have implications for how we understand the impact of domestic violence on sibling relationships. Simons and Johnson (1998), looking at patterns of intergenerational transmission of domestic violence, suggested three different models: role modelling; family relationships; and antisocial orientation. In their study of 324 Iowa families they gathered data on harsh discipline, marital strife, violence towards spouse and antisocial behaviour. They found some support for the role modelling perspective, but strongest support for the antisocial orientation model. They also found a correlation between spousal abuse and child abuse – persons who engaged in persistent marital violence tended to show aggression towards their children (and vice versa). They considered the finding of support for a general antisocial orientation within families to have specific treatment implications. This concurs with the work of Kornblit (1994) who looked at the concept of family violence, considering as syndromes of it the issues of battered women, courtship violence, child abuse, elder violence and sibling violence.

Dickstein (1988) considered the same issue, the connection between spouse abuse and other forms of domestic violence. She looked at a range of issues in connection with spouse abuse (including a multi-dimensional model of its causes). She considered the links between spouse abuse and other forms of abuse: child abuse; parental abuse; elder abuse; and, significantly for our purposes, abuse between siblings. Carter *et al.* (1988) also looked at the 'generational transfer hypothesis' in relation to male batterers, by interviewing 542 residents of battered women's shelters. They looked at whether the extent of violent socialisation of the male batterer was related directly to the extent of their violent behaviour towards their partner. They found the severity of their later battering of their partner to be directly related to their socialisation experiences, including sibling abuse in their family of origin. Stark and Flitcraft (1998) (see Chapter 6, 'Effect of being the family scapegoat') from a feminist perspective consider that the intergenerational model of the aetiology of domestic violence has the potential for victim blaming: making mothers the villains rather than the victims.

This leads one to ask how this generational transfer process might work, by considering what the impacts of domestic violence are on children and how it relates to sibling relationships in the family. Suh and Abel (1990) found that children witnessing family violence were likely to be abusive toward siblings. Also, child witnesses of spousal abuse are potential targets of physical and/or emotional abuse and may be at great risk of developing behavioural problems.

However, as is the case with many of the complex social phenomena causing concerns, there are no easy one-to-one linkages between a history of abuse in the family of origin leading to abuse in one's later family (Buchanan, 1996). Moore *et al.* (1990) highlighted this in connection with domestic violence. Whilst acknowledging that family violence may act as a predispositional factor influencing children to adopt aggressive means of problem solving, they considered that 'violence does not inevitably beget violence'. They described various factors that may ameliorate the potential harm of exposure to family violence: the child's own capacities and behaviours; the mother–child relationship; the *sibling relationships*; and the broader social context of peer interactions. McCloskey *et al.* (1995) considered whether close ties within the family buffered the children from the psychopathology found to be a possibly harmful outcome for the children of domestic violence. In their administration of specific measurement tools, they too found different forms of abuse in the home were highly inter-related; once again children of women who were victims of domestic violence were also at risk of abuse. They also found that domes-tic violence predicted psychopathology (of a general nature) in children. Significantly, they found there to be less sibling and parental warmth in families marked by aggression, although when it was present, family social support failed to buffer children.

However, given the predispositional nature of the influence of domestic violence on children, a preventive strategy may well reduce the future likelihood of such a predisposition. Frey-Angel (1989) looks at the treatment needs of children from violent families and finds using siblings a powerful tool. The approach is one that aims to change behaviours and attitudes around anger and abuse and is geared towards preventing the learning already imparted to the children from being repeated in their future adult relationships. The use of a group setting with siblings covering a wide range of ages and the rationale and methods are discussed as a way to stop the continuation of vio-lence from generation to generation. Hughes (1982), in her description of brief interventions with children in a battered women's shelter, describes the use of sibling meetings as well as individual counselling, peer group meetings and family group meetings.

McGee (2000) looks at how children experience domestic violence and has some useful observations on sibling relationships within such families. She notes, for example, that differential treatment in such families is a common pattern causing distress, abusive men tending to favour their own children over the children of other men that their partner may have, and favouring boys over girls. McGee also notes, however, that there is a need for more research into the impact of domestic violence on sibling relationships.

In considering the relevant literature on domestic violence and sibling relationships a complex pattern of counterbalancing forces emerges. Domestic violence can disturb sibling relationships; the violence between the adults is reflected in the violence between the sib-lings and produces sibling relationships characterised by less warmth. However, work with siblings has been used as a means of attempting to prevent the long-term (generational) effects of domestic violence and is used in women's refuges as part of their therapeutic programme. Nevertheless we are forced to the conclusion that in this area, as in many others, research into, and knowledge of, the impact of the adversity children within the family experience is mostly limited to the impact on them as individuals, and there is insufficient research on their relationships with each other. Even in McGee's (2000) work, where the impact of domestic violence on the children's relationships with their mother, with the abusive father (or father figure), with the extended family, and even with the peers is explored, the impact on children's sibling relationships is not. She does, however, provide some useful observations, for example in her description of how older children try to protect younger siblings in the family.

Practice Note 5.4   Children living with domestic violence

Anne (29) has just come to the Women's Refuge with her three children, Jason (9), Joanna (7) and Sophie (18 months). She has been living with Mark (24), a mechanic, for the past three years. He is the father of Sophie, but not of the two older children. Their father, Hank, an American, deserted Anne when she was pregnant with Joanna, and returned to the USA with an American woman he met in Britain. He has virtually no contact with either of his two children. He did not in fact acknowledge that Joanna was his child.

When she met Mark he was very kind and seemed to be everything she was looking for in a partner. He was very generous and kindly towards the children, although he clearly showed a preference for Joanna. He was always very attentive towards Anne. Things seemed to be going along very well until Anne became pregnant with Sophie. Mark seemed to change. He became very jealous and possessive, at times irrationally so. He would accuse Anne of seeing men when he was out at work. If she went out to do some shopping on her own, he would interrogate her upon her return, asking for details about exactly where she went, who she spoke with and the like.

It was during Anne's first trimester of the pregnancy with Sophie that Mark first struck her. At first Anne couldn't believe he had done it; in some ways, neither could Mark. But it seemed like a threshold had been crossed, and despite his protestations that it would never happen again, from that time the physical violence increased. There were several occasions when Anne feared that she would lose the baby she was carrying, following particularly severe beatings. She hoped that things would return to normal after the birth of Sophie, but instead they seemed to just get worse. Mark was very jealous of the time that Anne would devote to the baby. He insisted that there should be no changes to the previous routines. Following a particularly nasty assault, Anne took the three children with her to the refuge.

Prior to Mark's arrival, Jason and Joanna seemed to get on quite well with each other. After his arrival, however, tensions began to develop between them. There seemed to be more bickering. Anne put it down at first to Mark's overt preference for Joanna, and so tried to compensate by lavishing attention and praise on Jason. But it seemed to have no effect. In recent months, Anne noticed that the bickering and squabbling seemed to be escalating towards hitting and slapping, Jason invariably being the aggressor. Anne's concern that Jason may be modelling his aggressive behaviour on Mark was a contributing factor in her decision to leave.

She is now confronted with how to deal with her son's behaviour towards Joanna. She is worried as well that Sophie might become the target of Jason's aggressive behaviour as she gets older and begins to make her presence felt more as a demanding toddler.

Consider:

1. To what extent would you agree with Anne that Mark's differential treatment of the two children is a contributing factor to their relationship difficulties?

2. How can the workers at the Refuge assist Anne to address the sibling difficulties that appear to be the result of Mark's presence and behaviour in the family?

Summary: families requiring support and sibling relationships

This chapter has looked at four areas of practice where families may be in need of support: children of substance-abusing families; children of mentally ill parents; children with disabilities; and children living with domestic violence. In all these areas there is little direct research into the impact of these adverse circumstances on the quality of the sibling relationships, although there are relevant and interesting results from the literature.

With children of substance-abusing families, for example, we have seen that it is easy to overestimate the significance of the parents and ignore just how powerful an influence older brothers and sisters can be when looking at the likelihood of a young person becoming involved with substances – and this influence operates both ways, encouraging the young person towards substance misuse, or helping them to refrain from such use. We also found that gender was a significant factor in sibling agreement about parental alcohol abuse.

With children who have a parent with a mental illness we looked at the impact on overall family functioning and considered the relevance of resilience-thinking, and the issue of sibling caretaking (parentification) previously considered. Three issues are suggested as having an impact: agency support to parent; agency support to the young carer; and the recognition of the value of the role they are undertaking.

Research into siblings of children with a disability tends to focus on their brothers and sisters as individuals rather than on the nature of the relationship between them. It is important in research, as it is in practice, not to marginalise and disempower children with disabilities, and remember to focus on them as individuals with other character-istics besides their disabilities. Some studies have shown higher levels of maladjustment, and poorer school achievement in siblings of disabled children compared with children who have a non-disabled sibling, but the results are equivocal (as evidenced by the studies' finding no differences). Issues of sibling caretaking and differential treatment (especially as perceived by the young person) may be related to these findings. Once again, however, there were gender differences, and it is important to remember the potential positives of having a sibling with a disability (as suggested by research into the positives for parents of having a child with a disability).

Interactions between family members in violent families are com-plex and it is difficult to disaggregate the influences of domestic violence (between the adults) on children from the impact of other, more direct, forms of abuse of the children. Sibling relationships can be undermined by the violence within families although, as noted by McGee (2000), older siblings will sometimes attempt to protect younger siblings in the family. Workers have attempted to use sibling relationships, in their therapeutic in-house programmes, as a means of ensuring that the violence doesn't get carried forward into the next generation.

6 Abuse and Sibling Relationships

This chapter looks at two issues: abuse by siblings and sibling relationships where there is abuse by parents. Abuse by siblings has been more substantially addressed in the child abuse literature. This chapter will address physical and sexual abuse by siblings and, very briefly, psychological and emotional abuse. With physical abuse, the focus will be on distinguishing aggression from abuse (which can be seen as extending beyond a threshold of relative acceptability).

Sexual abuse between siblings has a myth of harmlessness associated with it. For the overwhelming majority of children, sexual relationship with an older sibling is unwanted and considered abusive. However, the more recent concerns with juvenile sexual abusers as a group reminds us that for those young individuals who become sexually predatory, the most opportunistic targets are likely to be younger children within the family. Emotional and psychological sibling abuse is a relatively neglected area.

The second focus of this chapter is abuse by parents – attempting to identify the effects of parental abuse on sibling relationships. Can sibling relationships act as a buffer against the worst consequences of parental abuse or are the relationships too damaged by the parental abuse to be effective supports? Does the type of abuse (physical, emotional, sexual or neglect) make a difference? An important issue is the extent to which children are differentially targeted in families. How do children react to parental scapegoating?

Abuse by siblings

Wiehe's work on sibling abuse (1990, 1991) deals with different forms of sibling abuse: physical, emotional and sexual. He includes narratives from victims of sibling abuse who describe the abuse, the devastation it caused in later life, and what they believe their parents could have done to prevent it. He notes excuses made by professionals have confused sibling abuse with sibling rivalry: 'Kids will be kids', 'All kids call each other names', 'Didn't you ever play doctor when you were a kid' and 'It's just normal sibling rivalry' (Wiehe, 1991, p. 2).

Sibling physical abuse

Aggression or abuse?

Sibling relationships are frequently characterised by high levels of hostility and even aggression. When does aggression become abuse? Two theoretical models provide explanations for the verbal and physical aggression between younger siblings: the 'sibling rivalry model' and the 'realistic conflict model' (Felson, 1984). In the former, the basis for the conflict is jealousy and non-realistic conflict. In the latter there are conflicts over material goods and undertaking devalued tasks because of the lack of clarity within the home about who owns what, and who has responsibilities for which tasks. Felson considers the latter model – realistic conflict – to be better supported by his evidence. Verbal aggression is more common than physical aggression, and aggression against a sibling is much more common than aggression towards children outside the home. Outside the home, males are more likely to be aggressive than females, but inside the home there is little gender difference.

Hewitt (1995) found children with siblings more likely to report being hit by them than by a non-family member, but notes this could be a reflection of the greater proportion of time spent in the company of siblings. Sibling interactions at home have a 'pivotal role' in subsequent aggressive behaviour according to the family process model of intrafamilial aggression in which the role of disruptions of parental discipline is significant (Patterson *et al.*, 1984). Rosenthal and Doherty (1984) found that child abuse, parental abuse history, unhappiness, helplessness, children's medical illness and parental condoning of the behaviour were all found to be related to higher levels of sibling aggressive behaviour. They suggest the need for external controls to prevent seriously upset children from engaging in primitive aggressive and assaultive behaviours towards their siblings.

Green (1984) describes five children ($4\frac{1}{2}$–22 years) who inflicted serious injuries on their younger siblings. The common experiences found were: perpetrators had been physically abused themselves; their families were undergoing crises which led to accentuated maternal deprivation and rejection; they were burdened with excessive care-taking for the target sibling; the target sibling was perceived as the favourite; and they had experienced the recent loss of their father or paternal caretaker. Green sees it as an intensification of normal sibling rivalry brought on by the abuser's own experience of being maltreated and deprived. The assaults were functionally adaptive for the abusers because they: (a) provided revenge against a more highly regarded sibling rival; (b) provided a venting for the rage directed towards the mother; (c) were an attention-getting device; (d) provided a sense of mastery over the trauma of their own abuse; and (e) were used to 'educate' the abusive parent.

Gender is a significant factor. Same-sex siblings appear to resemble one another in aggression (Rowe and Herstand, 1986). Male sibling pairs, however, are found to be consistently more violent than female sibling pairs (Steinmetz, 1981).

Children's perceptions of sibling aggression

How do children feel about retaliatory aggression against siblings and friends? Fifty children (ages 8–20) were asked to judge retaliation stories about characters of their own sex (Herzberger and Hall, 1993a). Aggression (both physical and verbal) was considered to be most wrong when it was directed at a younger sibling. Retaliatory aggression directed at property was considered least wrong. Retaliation against an accidental infringement was rated more wrong than where the initial action was intentional.

Gender differences were found in children's expectations of the outcomes of retaliation against siblings (Herzberger and Hall, 1993b). Boys believed that their mothers would be more disapproving of retaliation against siblings than against friends, whereas girls thought their mothers would be equally disapproving. Both groups believed retaliation would deter future aggression of friends more than siblings. They felt that younger siblings would feel worse about retaliation than older siblings. Girls expected to feel worse about retaliating against a younger sibling than boys expected to feel. The authors conclude that children's 'expectations seem to promote more aggression towards friends than siblings and to promote aggression toward siblings closer in age'.

Sibling sexual abuse

'Sibling incest may easily be taken too lightly', argues Jean Renvoize (1993, p. 58) because of myths about the mutuality of sibling sexual involvement. She provides evidence to dispel those myths. Russell

(1983) observes: 'One of the consequences of the myth of mutuality may be that when brother/sister incestuous abuse is discovered or reported, there may be even less support of the victim than in other cases of abuse.' Three-quarters (78 per cent) of women who had childhood sexual experiences with their brothers considered it to be abusive. Eighty-five per cent described the experience as totally unwanted; only 2 per cent had more or less desired it.

Sexual interaction between siblings may be the most common form of incest (Laredo, 1982). Forward and Buck (1978) consider that casual sibling sexual contact occurs in nine out of ten families having more than one child, making it the most widespread form of incest, though it tends to be unreported. The impact of sexual contact between siblings is very variable from non-traumatic (even not unpleasant) to extremely traumatic. They consider that the greater the age difference, the more likely violence is to be used, which is associated with greater traumatic impact. Laredo (1982) notes as well:

> Some investigators suggest that sibling incest does not involve the stressful ties that are apparent in parent–child incest, so that sibling incest may go unnoticed and undetected ... Sibling incest may not always be a situation involving one victim and one aggressor. Both may willingly engage in the behaviour as an attempt to cope with unmet needs. Such needs may include a desire for affiliation and affection, a combating of loneliness, depression, and a sense of isolation, and a discharging of anxiety and tension due to stress. (p. 178)

Laredo appears to be confirming the mythology surrounding sibling incest described by Renvoize (1993), but he does go on to describe more violent forms of sibling incest. It is the exploitative nature of sibling sexual abuse that does the harm (Tower, 1996). If the older sibling has more power, then the younger sibling is likely to feel victimised. She also notes that sibling incest tends to occur in large families, providing less privacy, but also less supervision. Abusers tend to be the oldest brothers in these large families – although as noted by Doyle (1996) children can be abused by younger siblings, and sisters also can be the abusers. Both Finkelhor (1980) and Russell (1986) found sibling incest victims to be from large families.

This underplaying of the significance of sibling abuse may have been contributed to by Finkelhor (1980) who found that of 796 undergraduates, 15 per cent of females and 10 per cent of males had reported some type of sexual experience involving a sibling. About one quarter of these he described as exploitative (wide age difference – more than five years – or involving the use of force), and in general females were more likely to have been exploited and to feel badly about it. Earlier exploitative experiences had greater impact, suggesting that young children may be more vulnerable to trauma from sibling sex. Nevertheless, he concludes that the 'evidence weighs against an extremely alarmist view of sibling sex'.

A difficulty in sibling incest is distinguishing between experimentation and exploitation. And frequently, what starts out as experimentation may be tolerated, and in some cases even welcomed, by the victim who only later finds that she is unable to impose limits on it (Doyle, 1996). De Jong (1989) describes four criteria to be indicative of abusive behaviour in sexual interactions between cousins and siblings. The age difference must be five years or more. It must involve the use of force, threat, or authority. There should be attempted penetration. Finally, there should be injury to the victim.

Sibling sexual abusers are a subgroup of the wider category of juvenile sexual abusers. Because of the restricted mobility of adolescents (compared to adult sexual abusers), the target population are more likely to be within a restricted range of known individuals. Siblings and children whom the abuser is babysitting are the two most likely groups (Erooga and Masson, 1999). A number of studies have found siblings to feature substantially in the victims of those abused by adolescent offenders (Araji and Bosek, 1997; Kahn and Chambers; 1991; Johnson, 1988).

Let us now consider the causes, consequences and treatment of sibling sexual abuse.

Causes of sibling sexual abuse

It is tempting to think that sibling sexual abuse is linked to the abusing child having a history of having been sexually abused. This is not always the case however; other forms of abuse or family dynamics patterns are often found instead. Physical abuse was found by Adler and Schutz (1995) to be much more common than sexual abuse in the sibling abusers' background. Steele and Ryan (1997) present three hypotheses concerning sibling incest: an empty yearning and low self-esteem; a lack of empathic modelling; and the sexualisation of attempts to overcome inner conflicts. They suggest that sexually exploitative behaviour represents a fundamental inability to be empathic, appreciative of, and caring for another human being, caused by early years of unempathetic care.

Smith and Israel (1987) suggested three aspects of family dynamics might predispose a family towards sibling incest: distant, inaccessible parents; parental stimulation of sexual climate in the home; and family secrets, especially with regard to extramarital affairs. Sibling incest was also found to be associated with marital discord, parental rejection, physical discipline, negative family atmosphere, dissatisfaction with family relationships, childhood sexual abuse and the presence of a younger child in the family (Worling, 1995). Abrahams and Hoey (1994), from their single case study, suggest three contributing factors in families: (a) the physically absent father; (b) the emotionally distant mother; and (c) the surrogate parent status of the abusing older brother. Unavailability of the parents was also found to be implicated in a single case study in Hong Kong (Tsun, 1999) and in a study of 831 sexually abused individuals (De Jong, 1989). The latter identified 'intensifying the mutual dependency and sexual curiosity of brothers and sisters' as a contributing factor.

Seventeen women sexually abused by an older brother described their families as dysfunctional with rigid rules about denying feelings (LaViola, 1991). Their relationships with parents were emotionally neglectful and their relationships with brothers (except for the incest) were non-existent or physically abusive. The families had views about men and fathers as superior, endorsing control and dominance over women and children.

Dwivedi (1993) considers that sexual abuse by siblings may be an outpouring of negative feelings (resentment, anger, aggression or hatred) towards the sibling.

Consequences of sibling incest

LaViola (1991) describes four major effects of the incest: mistrust of men and women; self-esteem problems; sexual response difficulties; and intrusive thoughts of the incest. All of the women felt they were either coerced or forced into the incest activity, although only half the sample reported that there was an age differential of less than five years (see Finkelhor, 1980). Tsun's (1999) case study described the long-term impact of the abuse on the victim. The subject presented with relationship problems with her boyfriend, poor appetite, depression, insomnia, nightmares and suicidal gestures.

Canavan *et al.* (1992) suggest that professionals may not be adequately sensitised to the female experience of sibling incest since it is considered to be less traumatic for victims than other forms of incest and there are more difficulties in allocating responsibility between minors. Consequences for victims include enforced secrecy, interpersonal power differentials, influences on sexual development, individual after-effects, disturbance in family dynamics, and gender-based differences in relationship styles.

Abrahams and Hoey's (1994) case study found consequences for the victim to include recurrent failures, both socially and in the workplace, and a general dissatisfaction with life. They describe the inappropriateness of some of the professional help. Bess and Janssen (1982) found in their sample that 70 per cent of those who had recounted an experience of childhood sibling incest reported adult sexual impairment.

Rudd and Herzberger (1999) found no evidence to suggest that brother–sister incest was less harmful or traumatic than father–daughter incest in its consequences. Factors like duration of the abuse and the association of harmful sequelae with the use of force appeared in both forms of abuse, and use of force was slightly higher in the sibling incest cases.

The consequences of discovery of sibling sexual abuse for mothers can be devastating. It can upset very important ideas about their roles as mothers, for example the notion of treating all children the same (Hooper, 1992). Sometimes these mothering agendas can interfere with effective action to protect children. Even when it is discovered, there may be effective self-deceptions operating.

Treatment of sibling incest

It is important to address the multiple needs of the members of the family when sibling sexual abuse first comes to light (Christensen, 1990). Treatment of sibling incest offenders in the context of their families highlights poor boundaries, the impact on the victim and the necessity for hierarchical reconstruction (DiGiorgio-Miller, 1998). A key process in the treatment is the development of a safety plan to prevent the occurrence of future offences. This didn't happen in a case described by Lew (1990) where the older sibling resumed the abuse some time after the initial disclosure and action taken by the mother.

Hackett *et al.* (1998) describe the therapeutic work undertaken with young men who sexually abuse their siblings. They look at myths surrounding sibling incest and the ways to challenge them. They emphasise the need to adopt a safe and appropriate approach to treatment, utilising a 'holistic' method. They also consider the need for therapeutic work with the victim and with the whole family, and with those caring for the abusers.

Hargett (1998) looked at the process of reconciling the victim and perpetrator in sibling incest. It is noted that intervention and treatment are likely to produce familial separation, which leaves less options for reunification. In order for reunification to be achieved, following appropriate therapy for all parties, the following issues are crucial to be addressed: safety, vigilance, perpetrator accountability, perpetrator pathos and victim contribution.

Many of the processes described above are similar to the issues of working with father–daughter abuse. But there are three distinctive issues. First, there are *different* myths that need to be addressed. There are myths associated with the normality of sexual interaction between brothers and sisters, and myths associated with the harmlessness of it. Secondly, there is likely to be an underestimation of the significance of the sibling relationship (when compared with the parent–child relationship). The work needs to be undertaken in the context of knowledge of some of the themes developed in this book: that sibling relationships are an important source of support in later life after parents have died; that they are a potential source of support in adversity; and that even at the best of times they are probably characterised by ambivalence, mixing elements of hostility and warmth, negativity and positivity. This is not to say that invariably efforts should be made to rehabilitate sibling relationships where sibling sexual abuse has transpired; there will be situations when this is neither feasible nor appropriate. Rather, such decisions need to be taken on the basis of knowledge about the long-term developmental course and significance of sibling relationships. As adults, victims may also have concerns about whether the abuser's orientation towards sexual interaction with children was confined to the sibling relationship, or whether, as an adult, he presents a threat to other children, for example within the family (their own children, nieces and nephews), or indeed outside the family (Doyle, 1996).

Thirdly, the period of sibling incest often lasts longer, even into adulthood (Tsun, 1999; Doyle, 1996).

Sibling psychological and emotional abuse

In comparison with sibling physical and sexual abuse, there is very little written about sibling psychological abuse. In the area of adult–child relations, consideration of emotional abuse is particularly problematic for a number of reasons. There are clearly issues about establishing links between parental behaviour and consequences. For example, because a parent speaks severely to a child does not mean that the child will be irreparably psychologically harmed; it is a question of how much, how often, how severely. Several authors have looked at the issue of parental psychological and emotional maltreatment of children (O'Hagan, 1993; Iwaniec, 1995; Garbarino *et al.*, 1997). Many of the difficult definitional issues that they identify apply in the case of siblings as well.

Whipple and Finton (1995) describe psychological sibling maltreatment as a common, but unrecognised, form of child abuse. They note its harmful effects, and suggest that such impaired intrafamilial interactions are often an indicator of larger problems within the family.

Several researchers looked at verbal as well as physical aggression seeing it as a form of psychological abuse, depending upon the extent and context. As with parental psychological and emotional abuse, it is more helpful to place the emphasis on the effects of the abusive behaviour rather than on the behaviour itself. Thus, given that siblings are frequently unkind, and hurtful, and may say unpleasant things to each other, whether it is abusive or not will depend on whether the verbal behaviour has the effect of undermining the sibling's confidence, self-esteem and value as an individual. This may depend upon a number of other factors, an important one being the extent to which parental behaviour is consistent with, or counterbalances, the sibling behaviour.

Practice Note 6.1   Sibling abuse

Jennifer recalled that her older brother, Peter, had begun to involve her in sexual activities, which escalated until, in their mid-teens, it reached the point just short of full sexual intercourse. When Jennifer was 13, and Peter 15, because of her concerns about where it would ultimately go, she disclosed what was happening in her family. In other respects, Jenny was actually quite fond of her brother; she sort of looked up to him. He seemed to be very popular at school (which she was not), and he seemed to find it easy to make friends. She wished that she could be more like him, and in part it was this that contributed to her acceding to his pressure to comply. The abuse started out as mutual exploration, and at first, she did not object. Over time, however, he expected more and more, and when she began to feel that she did not want to take it further, and even to stop altogether, he was more and more insistent that they should continue and take it further. He never forced her, but he used persuasive arguments to overcome her resistance. He would tell her it was not wrong (although in the latter stages she certainly believed it was), and if she *really* didn't want to as well, then she would not have gone along with what they had done so far.

Jennifer's father, Michael, worked on an off-shore oil rig, and was consequently away for long periods of time. Jennifer often thought that if he had had a different type of job, this would never have happened. Jennifer's mother, Sarah, was preoccupied with her own mother's health (Jennifer's maternal grandmother), as she suffered from chronic emphysema, which severely limited her ability to do things for herself. She was too proud to accept much help from the local social services, and so Sarah tried to provide as much as she could. As the grandmother lived in a village some fifty miles away, and Sarah's travelling was restricted to use of buses, it often meant that Jenny's mum was away for most of the evening, at least two or three times a week, occasionally more. Peter and Jenny spent a lot of unsupervised time together.

Although on several occasions Jenny had tried to hint to her mother about what was going on (spelling out hypothetical situations, talking about a 'friend of a friend', etc.), her mother never seemed to pick up on what was being said, and offered advice, etc. on the information received, at face value. Jenny believed, even at the time when she finally disclosed, that her mother was truly ignorant of what was going on in the home.

Consider:
1. Is it possible to separate out the abuse from the overall quality of the relationship? Jenny has talked about an otherwise positive relationship with her brother? Should this be seen as part of a 'grooming' process – an inherent part of the abuse, or as a part of the relationship apart from the abuse?
2. What would be the implications for the nature of the work done with Jenny in relation to her brother? Would the abuse be an indicator for a complete severance of the relationship between Jenny and her brother or not? What might be the factors pointing one way or the other?
3. How might the social worker's knowledge of the long-term sigificance of sibling relationships (i.e. sibling relationships in adulthood and later life) influence intervention?

Sibling relationships and abuse by parents

How does the abuse of one child in the family by a parent or parents influence other children in the family, and their relationships? Can positive sibling relationships buffer the impact of abuse? Might they promote resilience?

In our previous consideration of the complexity of sibling relationships, and with the knowledge of the complexity of the aetiology of child abuse, we should not be surprised if the connection between abuse and sibling relationships is complex, perhaps having different impacts associated with different types of abuse and perhaps being dependent upon other variables as well.

Parental physical abuse and sibling relationships

Apart from the harm of growing up in the same family environment (e.g. Oliver *et al.*, 1978; Lynch and Roberts, 1982) there has been very little written about how physical abuse of one child affects the other children in the family. If, for example, we know that it is not good for a child's mental health to see her father assaulting her mother, we might speculate about what impact it might have to witness her father (or mother) behaving violently towards her brothers and sisters.

Children who have been abused view their families more negatively than children from non-abuse families but there is little difference *within* families between how the abused children view the family and how their non-abused siblings view the family (Halperin, 1983). Also, *siblings* of abused children view their families more negatively than children in the families where no abuse has occurred. In effect, the child does not have to be the one who is abused to feel bad about the family.

Leavitt *et al.* (1998) suggest that children who have experienced severe trauma and disruptions to their attachment (as might be the case with many abused children), develop inter-sibling relationships that interfere with ordinary development, disrupt the establishment of healthy sibling relationships, undermine the opportunity to benefit from connections with adults and inhibit the working through of traumatic experiences. They describe four distinct patterns of sibling relationships: absent; adult lockout; half and half; and the trauma shield. They suggest five goals in treatment. The therapist must endeavour to suspend problematic sibling relationships to create room for bonding with caring adults. She must enable the child to transfer attachment behaviours and impulses to a receptive adult. There should be a focus on resuming healthy individual development. The child should be helped to form more adaptive sibling connections, and finally, there should be an emphasis on expressing shared traumatic content.

Child abuse fatality and sibling relationships

Sanders (1999) suggests that British child protection is understandably tuned into avoiding child abuse fatalities, although such a zero-tolerance approach has risks as well for potential over-intrusive intervention into the lives of families that might do better without it (Department of Health, 1995). A fatality through abuse is not only a tragedy for the child and the parents, and a source of tremendous anxiety for professionals; it is also a severe loss for the siblings in the family. In the context of child abuse and child protection, the work of Newlands and Emery (1991) is important because by looking at siblings they have highlighted an association between child abuse and cot death, i.e. that many cases diagnosed as sudden infant death syndrome (SIDS) may actually be missed cases of infant homicide. They found much higher rates of SIDS amongst siblings of children on child protection registers when compared to the national average (five times as high). They conclude that the possibility of child homicide should be seriously considered in such cases. Likewise, Southall (1997) found, in a covert video surveillance study of Munchausen Syndrome by Proxy, disturbingly high rates of SIDS in siblings of these children (twelve out of forty-one), and four of the parents subsequently admitted suffocating eight of those twelve children.

Reder *et al.* (1993) found, in their study of fatality inquiries, that the majority (66 per cent) of the children who died were the youngest or only child of the household (see Table 6.1).

TABLE 6.1 ORDINAL POSITION OF FATALLY ABUSED CHILDREN

Position	Number
Eldest	5
Middle	6
Youngest	10
Only child	11

Source: Reder et al., 1993.

They also considered the issue of scapegoating, general family context and siblings of these children. There were twenty-three households that contained other children at the time of the fatality, and of those, in twelve households at least one other sibling was being abused at the same time as the child who ultimately died. In several cases they consider that the abuse of the sibling was severe enough to have resulted in fatality. They suggest that the violence or neglect in the families was often a general caretaking pattern, which 'does not support a contention that one child is invariably singled out for abuse' (p. 53). The key word here is 'invariably', and they go on to attempt to understand, however, why 'there were cases in which only one child was abused; and in the households where many children were abused, why was one mistreated so badly that s/he died?' (p. 53). In some cases it is clear that *which* child died was a matter of chance. However, they continue:

> with other children we can propose certain meanings that they had for their caretakers which contributed to their deaths. Some of the meanings ... are non-specific and could arise from relationship conflicts experienced within many families. Others are specific to that particular family and reflect idiosyncrasies of their experiences. (p. 53)

Reder and Fitzpatrick (1995) looked at the siblings' needs following a child abuse fatality. They looked at the immediate aftermath, the siblings' emotional needs, their later placement, subsequent children born to the family, and issues in assessment. They note for example that:

> In the majority of cases there will be a history of maltreatment, which was not confined to the child who died with all the siblings having suffered some degree of violent or neglectful abuse. The observations ... that some children are accorded a particular psychological meaning by their parents which renders them more at risk of maltreatment should not be taken as support for the notion that one particular child is singled out and scapegoated while the siblings escape unscathed. (p. 383)

Similarly, a study of child abuse fatality by Hicks and Gaughan (1995) found that of six cases (out of fourteen) that were known to the child protection services in four it was a *sibling*, and not the fatally abused child, who was the reason for the referral. This highlights, again, the uncertainty surrounding risk to *all* children in households where a child is being abused.

However, in terms of risk to the siblings – either siblings existing before the child was killed or those subsequently born – Reder and Fitzpatrick (1995) note the lack of literature on the likelihood of parents' killing (or seriously abusing) a child a second time. They note that in three out of the thirty-five cases (nearly 10 per cent) from Reder *et al.* (1993) there was another child killed or severely injured. The Aukland Inquiry (Department of Health and Social Security, 1975) was one such case. The father, having been released from prison for the manslaughter of one of his children, was allowed to care for his other children, and was subsequently responsible for the death of another daughter.

Practice Note 6.2   Parental physical abuse and sibling relationships

One day, when Chris (aged 9½ years) was changing for P.E., his teacher, Mrs Parsons, noticed that he had bruising on both of his upper arms. When asked about it, Chris replied that his father had grabbed him and shaken him because he had been fighting again with one of his two younger brothers.

When Mrs Parsons asked if this had ever happened before, Chris admitted that it had, and reluctantly agreed to show several other bruises on his upper legs and back, which the teacher could see were at various stages of healing. She thought the bruise on the back looked like it had a straight edge. Chris then said that it wasn't likely to happen so much in the future, because he was really going to try a lot harder to get on with his brothers. He then added, however, that sometimes they deliberately set out to get him in trouble and he wasn't sure what he could do about that. Sometimes they made things up just to get him in trouble. The two brothers, Martin (8) and Michael (7), seemed to just have it in for him. He didn't know why.

Chris's family lives in a privately owned, ex-council house. His father, John, works as a builder, when he can find work; but there has not been much work in the last eighteen months. Because of the financial difficulties they are finding it very difficult to keep up the mortgage repayments and are currently facing the possibility of repossession. His mother, Sharon, has a part-time job in a local super-market, which just about brings enough in for the food. The bickering and fighting between the boys exasperates Sharon. As they do not respond to her, she tries to get her husband to sort them out, although she doesn't approve when he uses the belt on Chris.

In school, Chris is well liked by his classmates. He is quiet and shows little spontaneity, but has an engaging sense of humour. His attendance at school is good. Prior to the current incident, the school have had no particular concerns about Chris. They did notice, however, that, although Chris got on well with other children, it was somewhat surprising that he spent so little time with his brothers during free time, and when they were together, they did not seem to be very friendly.

Consider:

1. This is presented as a case in which the sibling conflict is contributing to physical abuse (a common enough scenario). Consider, however, the reverse, that the tensions within the family and the abuse may be influencing the way in which the siblings interact with each other.
2. To what extent might gendered perceptions of sibling relationships (this is the way brothers are!) be contributing to a parenting approach that quickly goes up-tariff to more extreme measures?
3. What practical advice can a professional working with the family offer to improve the relationships between the three brothers?

Parental sexual abuse and sibling relationships

Let us consider the risk of sexual abuse of siblings in a family where sexual abuse is disclosed. Haugaard and Repucci (1988) considered there to be little literature about the concerns of siblings when one child in a family has been identified as having been sexually abused. They note that there is very little interest in the literature concerning the effects of incest on the siblings of the victim. And yet, siblings may be as confused as the mother about whom to support, victim or perpetrator (James and Nasjleti, 1983).

A common pattern is for the adult male in the family to abuse one child after another as they 'come of age' within the family, and each may be unaware that other children are being abused. Ainscough and Toon (1993) describe this process in a subsection headed 'It must be my fault because he didn't abuse my sisters and brothers or anyone else':

As Elaine's story shows, sisters (and brothers) may each spend years believing they are the only one in the family who has been abused. If one person has been keeping the abuse secret other people have probably been doing the same thing ... Thirty years after her own abuse Sandra discovered that three of her brothers had also been abused ... In the Wakefield Survivors' groups at least 40 per cent of the women's abusers are known to have abused other children. (pp. 42–3)

One can speculate on how sexual abuse can influence sibling relations if the siblings are actually unaware that other siblings in the family either have been, or are being, abused. To begin with, it can create within children a sense of being different, alone, and isolated, which may influence their relationships with other children. Even after disclosure, siblings who have been abused may not wish to disclose.

Another possible, and indeed fairly common, impact of intrafamilial sexual abuse on sibling relationships is one of blame. Non-abused siblings in the family may not believe the abused sibling and may blame him or her for the aftermath of the disclosure. Glaser and Frosh (1993) describe this in relation to reconstituted families: 'In the not uncommon cases of stepfather–stepdaughter sexual abuse, the siblings may experience the loss of their biological father, and blame the abused child for this loss' (p. 136). However, this can also occur in families which are not reconstituted, but where younger children have not yet been the focus of the abuser's attention. A further impact on the sibling relationship is that siblings who have not been abused may feel rejected because they have not been selected for the abusive attention (Glaser and Frosh, 1993). They may not truly understand how terrifying the experience is and may see it in terms of preferential treatment rather than ill treatment.

Moore (1992), in her description of the work that needs to be undertaken with family members where sexual abuse has taken place, includes work with siblings. She says:

> At least one session must be given to the other children. Split loyalties have to be addressed. They may be jealous of the attention the abused child was given originally and is now getting. They may be angry with the child for breaking up the family. Perhaps they are guilty at not noticing what was going on and therefore not preventing the abuse. (p. 68)

Worse than feeling guilty about not knowing, they may feel devastated that they suspected but felt powerless to do anything about it. Several areas for consideration in respect of siblings where abuse has taken place are suggested (Moore, 1992, p. 181):

1. How have siblings been affected by abuse?
2. Significant information?
3. Is work required with siblings?

Renvoize (1993) also describes the work that needs to be done with siblings of sexually abused children. Even where siblings were ignorant of the abuse, they will be dramatically affected by the consequences of the disclosure. They may be afraid of being removed from the home, especially if one or more brothers and/or sisters have already been removed. They therefore need to be present at early meetings of the family to be reassured and to prevent them from attempting to make a scapegoat of the disclosing sibling(s). They will need to be involved in the family's attempts at healing, to minimise the impact for them of the disturbance to family life that inevitably follows disclosure. And, of course, the possibility of the siblings' having been abused must be explored as well (Green, 1988; Haugaard and Repucci, 1988; Schmitt *et al.*, 1976; Sgroi, 1982).

Non-abused siblings may collude with the abuser to protect themselves (Tower, 1996). In a fairly complex family drama, the siblings may not be aware that the victim believed her compliance to be a means to protect them from being abused. They may, however, 'set up' the victim for the continuation of the abuse. They may act out of self-preservation, and aid the abuser rather than the abused.

> The importance of their own sense of security in the collusion behaviour of siblings is undeniable. These brothers and sisters recognize that keeping the secret is necessary for the continuation of the family unit ... Some siblings attempt to intervene on behalf of the victim, but because of their powerlessness as children, they are usually thwarted. (Tower, 1996, p. 170)

Whether because of collusion or powerlessness, siblings are likely to experience guilt. They too need help (Tower, 1996):

> Whether in family therapy or through some type of individual therapy or program, the needs of the siblings should be addressed. They have experienced the same dysfunctional, abusive home setting as the victim and also have the potential to grow up to be unhappy needy adults. (p. 316)

Hooper (1992) also describes collusive elements in the relations between siblings when one is being abused. Walker *et al.* (1988) note that the reactions of siblings may include anger and blame towards the abused sibling for the disruption caused to the family. In addition, they too are likely to experience psychological distress.

Practice Note 6.3   Parental sexual abuse

Katie (12 years) is the middle of three children in the Wolfe family. The others are Mark (14) and Louise (8). Their father, Paul, is an executive in the building industry, and their mother is a supply schoolteacher. The family live in a fairly affluent part of town, and are reasonably well off.

One day Katie revealed to a friend at school what had been going on at home, and the friend strongly urged her to tell one of the teachers, which she did. This began a chain of events that Katie was very unhappy about, but it did bring to an end the escalating abuse she had been experiencing since she was 9.

It was a very traumatic time for her following the initial disclosure. There was an investigation; she was taken to a police station (that didn't look like a police station) to give an interview on videotape, in which she recounted what had been going on over the years. Her brother and sister were interviewed as well to find out if they had had similar experiences. The most disturbing aspect for Katie, however, was that her father had to move out of the family home and agree not to have contact with *any* of the children, until further notice. This was her worst fear come true, and what her father used to tell her would happen if she ever told anyone. Fortunately, Katie was able to remain at home, and so there was less disruption to daily routine. Unfortunately, however, it got out at school; everybody seemed to know about it, and again this was something that Katie was afraid would happen.

In the first week, Katie's brother and sister held back nothing in telling Katie what they thought. Neither of them believed her to begin with. They thought that she was making the whole thing up to get more attention because she was the least favoured of the three. Their dad was closer to Mark because they were both football fans, and to Louise simply because she was the baby of the family. On weekends, when Mark would have gone to the football match with his dad, he made sure that Katie knew about it. 'If dad were here . . .', he would say to her. On one occasion, when Katie had some of her schoolwork laid out on the kitchen table, Louise came up and drew all over it with a crayon. Louise could hardly bring herself to talk to her older sister, and mostly just ignored her.

It was clear to Katie that both her brother and sister blamed her for what happened. She tried to discuss this with her mother, but her mother was not as 'together' as she usually was, and was struggling to adjust to the change in the family's circumstances, and to make sense of what was happening. She wasn't sure if she believed Katie either.

After several months, however, it was clear that her mother was coming around to believing what Katie had disclosed. It was in part because of the detail of Katie's description of what her father had done and her recognition of her husband's bedroom manner in Katie's description. It was then that the confusion, despair and misery began to change to anger towards her husband.

Mark and Louise, however, were still locked in disbelief. It took several weeks for Katie's mother to be able to persuade them that Katie was telling the truth. Even then, however, there continued to be problems. Mark was insistent that Katie should still not have told anyone. He thought that she should have kept it within the family. He even suggested that she should have continued to endure it; at least that way, the family would still be together and they could work things out. When Louise was told that Katie was telling the truth, she didn't really understand what the 'truth' was. Mrs Wolfe felt it best not to share too much of the detail with her. Louise, therefore, sided with Mark and felt that Katie still should not have told. Katie didn't know how to tell her sister that one of the things she was concerned about was that she might be next in line for the abuse. Louise was now coming up to the age when the abuse first began with her. For Katie, it was not only a case of ending the abuse by her father that she was enduring, but ensuring that her younger sister, Louise, did not experience the same thing.

Consider:
1. What can be done to help Mark and Louise empathise with their sister's predicament at the point of disclosure?
2. How can the mother help to rebuild the relationships between Katie and her siblings?
3. How can the worker facilitate this?

Parental psychological/emotional abuse and sibling relationships

Doyle (2001) looked at the situation of fourteen survivors of emotional abuse and found that other family members, including siblings, provided more support even than the non-abusing parent. In looking at that support, however, she did find variations. Where there were substantial age gaps between the survivor and the sibling (e.g. five cases where the gap was 7–12 years) the support was very limited. In four cases, she noted 'the abuser pursued a policy of "divide and rule" among family members so that siblings did not support each other' (p. 393). In another four cases, the siblings were indeed able to provide support for each other.

It is possible for parents to be emotionally abusive to several or even all the children in a family (Doyle, 2001), but a very common situation is one where a particular child is selected for extreme differentially negative treatment – scapegoating. In four of the fourteen cases described by Doyle (2001), there is an element of differential treatment. There are also situations in which the children in the family may scapegoat other children without the parent's knowledge or sanction.

What do we mean by scapegoat?

The origins of the scapegoat are rooted in Yom Kippur, the Jewish Day of Atonement, and is marked by fasting, confession to God of sins committed during the last year, and prayers for forgiveness. In the Old Testament, the sins of the people are 'confessed' to a goat who is then taken from the town and released in the wilderness (Leviticus, 16, 20–2). Thus the 'scapegoat' was a vessel for all the sins/evils which are driven out.

Dare (1993) describes the scapegoating process within the family, noting, however, that whilst in the biblical scene, the goat is evicted from the community, 'Surprisingly, perhaps, eviction is unusual. Usually the scapegoated child lives miserably on the edge of the family' (p. 37).

Scapegoating is a concept arising from group dynamic and family systems theory, and has been used with families to create an awareness of a specific type of interaction pattern relevant to the presenting difficulty. Schibalski and Harlander (1982) describe the scapegoat as the family member upon whom all anxieties are vented. By turning against a scapegoat, the family members are attempting not to realise their own fears of being abandoned, of symbiotic relationships and of identity. Mook (1985) considers it a particular type of interaction which demonstrates the applicability of a general systems theory to the functioning of families and family therapy.

Thus, there can be two constructions of the scapegoat. In the more purist construction, the role of the scapegoat for the rest of the social unit – in this case the family – is an important part of understanding the mechanism underlying the selection of a member to be a scapegoat. It is to reduce anxiety, divert attention away from the true causes of difficulties, perhaps to deny responsibility for the difficulties. Like the sailors throwing Jonah off the ship to be swallowed by a great fish, the responsibility for the surrounding chaos (the great storm) is said to reside in the individual, and once Jonah is cast from the ship, the storm subsides. There is a primitive, magical thinking underlying the process. Nevertheless, there may be attributes of the individual that contribute to their being selected as the target (disability, temperament, heredity or other characteristics that mark the child as being distinctive). In the second construction there is a less functionalist approach. The evidence for the existence of the underlying processes is based on the manifestations of differential treatment which can be seen. It does not necessarily require a psychoanalytic understanding (unconscious motivation to reduce anxiety), but simply an assessment of the level of differential treatment.

How does scapegoating operate in the family?

Parents are the architects of family scapegoating but the question is how much other children in the family are involved in the process. Iwaniec (1995) has described how siblings in the family might join in with the parents in emotionally abusing a target child within a family:

> Interaction between the child and other family members (including siblings) is marked by hostility and dismissal . . . Sibling–child relationships are hostile or indifferent: siblings usually ignore the child, do not include it [sic] in their activities, and behave toward it in an aggressive and dismissive way. Because parents seldom take the side of the target child, it is smacked, pushed, and toys are frequently snatched from it. It is not unusual to see that the child is being bruised by its siblings (even the younger ones). (pp. 44–5)

Where one child is rejected by the parents, siblings may be rejecting as well, simply because they have picked up negative parental behaviour towards the rejected child, and therefore, if one is able to change parental behaviour and responses to that child, the behaviour of siblings may alter as well. Using modelling and instructions, siblings can be trained how to interact with the target child. In looking specifically at sibling interactions and scapegoating, Hendrickx (1985) found rivalrous sibling relationships with a younger sibling to be a major aspect of family scapegoating.

Crittenden (1984) found maltreatment by adults to be a significant influence on sibling interactions. Siblings interacted with the infant similarly to the way in which their mothers interacted with the infant, suggesting a style of interacting that had been learned from their mothers. Whereas adequately reared siblings increased in sensitivity towards their younger sibling with age, maltreated siblings did not. Crittenden concluded that a generational effect in the learning of parenting styles appeared as early as the third year of life.

What is the effect of being the family scapegoat on the child?

Vuchinich *et al.* (1994), in their study of families with a preadolescent referred for treatment for behaviour problems or a child at risk for conduct disorder, found a tendency to scapegoat and considered that this could undermine the ability of families to develop solutions to family problems. Stark and Flitcraft (1998) consider the scapegoat paradigm from a feminist perspective and describe an intergenerational transmission model in which a man who was abused as a child brings that violence forward into his relationship with his partner. The partner, in turn, uses the child as a scapegoat, because she is unable to cope. The authors consider the scapegoat paradigm makes mothers culpable for the violence – 'villains rather than as victims'. Using a retrospective approach, Whitmore *et al.* (1993) also challenge the scapegoat (or 'target child') hypothesis that they suggest is prevalent in the child abuse literature.

What happens when children who are scapegoated in families grow up? How are these patterns carried forward into their own families? Pillari's (1991) work on intergenerational patterns of physical and emotional abuse suggests that one person is chosen to bear the brunt of the family's anger and pain, and the threads of behaviour patterns from their original family culture are woven into the fabric of current family relationships.

Dare (1993), in his contribution to a volume on the development of hatred in children, considers that children who are given the role in the family of being irretrievably bad, and who are blamed for all the conflict within the family are likely to become full of rage and hatred. Le Gall (1998) also notes the origins of hatred between children where there is scapegoating:

> There is no point denying that, from childhood onward, siblings are capable of hating each other for reasons like parental

favouritism or because one of them always served as the scapegoat of the family. (p. 93)

Another example of the enmity that can arise between siblings in
situations of extreme differential treatment comes from Sanders
(2002):

One case highlighted differential treatment of both the favouritism and
disfavouritism variety. In this family (two older boys; two younger sisters) where mother's partner was the father of the two younger children
only, there was a clear tendency described on the part of the father to
scapegoat one of the two older boys, and to demonstrate a clear preference for one (the older) of the two younger girls: '[older sister] is always
told how wonderful she is; how she looks'. The impact of this on the
younger sister, as described by the social worker, was dramatic: 'No she
doesn't say anything, but she'll tend to go up and scram her sister'
['scram' being a local colloquialism for scratching]. (p. 262)

As the sister was only two, 'scramming' may be the only means open to
her to protest her second-class status in the family. On the other hand,
girls showing higher levels of general maturity come from families
more likely to describe themselves as flexible, trusting, cohesive,
expressive and self-sufficient, and, more significantly for our purposes,
are less likely to be caught up in the marital relationship, either as a
scapegoat or in a cross-generational coalition with either parent (Bell
and Bell, 1982).

What does one do about scapegoating?

Iwaniec (1995) describes the work that she has undertaken when
working with family patterns of rejection:

Iwaniec (1983) trained six excessively rejecting siblings in four families
by using play and modelling as a medium to teach them how to respond
to a target child in a kind way . . . The positive outcomes were attributed
to the fair and good supervision of children by parents and their positive
corrections of siblings' behaviour towards the target child. (p. 140)

Schibalski and Harlander (1982) suggest that the role of the therapist
in treating the scapegoating family is to redirect the group's aggression
away from the child and towards the therapist.

The following is an example of addressing scapegoating in a family
with twins on the child protection register (Sanders, 2002):

it was noted that [mother] treated the twins differently, appearing to reject [twin A] and favouring [twin B]; Mother admitted she did see the twins differently, that she favoured [twin B] over [twin A]. [Twin B] is like the son she lost whilst [twin A] reminds her of her ex-husband.

subsequent social work intervention with the mother noted a gradually shifting balance coming into the mother's relationship with the two girls. The issue of mother handling the two equally became a focus of intervention for both the social worker and the health visitor, and the case had an apparently positive outcome with mother coming to accept the rejected child and giving them both equal attention (p. 291)

This example highlights a successful outcome when the scapegoating is identified as a difficulty and targeted for intervention. It was less difficult here because the mother accepted the scapegoating premise, could understand why it arose and was prepared to do something about it. Usually the difficult first step is getting the family to accept the problem in terms of scapegoating.

Practice Note 6.4   Parental psychological and emotional abuse

David (8 years) and Lisa (7 years) are the children of Mary K. (age 26). Their father lived with their mother for about a year after Lisa's birth, but then left one day following a particularly bad row (one of many) with Mary. He has not been heard of since. Since then Mary has cohabited with three different partners, the last one, Richard (aged 28), being the longest standing, of eighteen months duration. She tells the children to call her partners 'Daddy', which is somewhat confusing for the children when they leave. After ex-partners have left, Mary is very belittling of them, berating them to the children.

Mary, Richard and the two children live in a council flat, on the edge of a small town. The flat is in Mary's name, a fact she continually reminds Richard of. Richard has a job in a body repair shop, which he has held for several years. He is considered to be reliable, and is well liked by his mates. He is a local lad, having been born on the same estate where he now shares a flat with Mary.

Mary and Richard's relationship is extremely turbulent. On four or five occasions, (getting more frequent recently), police have been called by neighbours, usually in the middle of the night, because of the sounds of shouting and quarrelling coming from Richard and Mary's flat. When the police have called they have found Richard and Mary in a shouting match; Mary doing most of the shouting. The children have been found huddled together in a corner of an upstairs room, too frightened to talk, but clinging to each other. The police have usually been able to separate Mary and Richard, and Richard has generally gone to stay with his parents. His parents are quite supportive of him, but they do try to persuade him to give up his relationship with Mary.

Although Mary tells Richard to go for good, and tells David and Lisa that Richard has left permanently ('good riddance to bad rubbish'), within a week or two she is asking him to come back; despite his reservations, he usually does. He has a very close relationship with David and Lisa, a significant factor influencing his return.

Mary accuses Richard of a variety of things (drug usage, physical assault against her, stealing from her and others, etc.) which appear to be unfounded. Richard, for his part, feels extremely ambivalent about the relationship, and, although he wants to leave, continues to be drawn to Mary. In addition he is afraid that he would lose contact with David and Lisa if he left for good; Mary has said as much, as a hold over him when they have been rowing.

Mary spent most of her early childhood in care, having been removed from the care of her parents at the age of 6 because of physical abuse. Mary has always maintained that what happened to her should not happen to David and Lisa, and so she has been very careful not to harm them physically. However, she appears to have no understanding of their emotional needs. In their presence, she refers to Lisa as 'that little cow', and to David as 'the sod'. She repeatedly tells Lisa that she is very plain looking, and mocks her efforts to do something about her appearance. Likewise with David, she denigrates him for his lack of 'manly' qualities, and describes him, to his face, and to others, as a 'wimp'. Mary has never physically harmed either of the children and in general provides a reasonable standard of care. They are always well turned out for school. Their clothes are clean and their personal hygiene good.

At school, neither child seems to have much confidence, either in terms of schoolwork or in making friends with the other children, although David is perhaps a bit better at this than Lisa. They spend all of their free time in each other's company. There is an obvious sense of becoming less tense when they are together that is noticeable to the teachers. Neither David nor Lisa does very well at schoolwork; both seem to have little ability to concentrate for sustained periods of time. The teacher's note that it seems like their minds are elsewhere when they should be focusing on schoolwork. The teachers describe them as 'preoccupied' or 'distrait'.

Consider:
1. To what extent might the children be being brought closer together by the emotionally hostile environment, which, were it not the case, would lead them to a less intense relationship?
2. The close relationship between David and Lisa is obviously important for them. What specific needs, not being met by their mother, are they fulfilling for each other?
3. David and Lisa are close. What factors in an emotionally abusing context might lead them to have a relationship characterised by hostility and conflict, rather than warmth?

Parental neglect and sibling relationships

Neglect is also an area where there is very little written in relation to sibling relationships. Smith and Adler (1991) found that neglected children had fewer siblings than a control group and parents of the neglected children tended to be younger.

Rosenfield-Schlichter *et al.* (1983) describe a case study which circumvented the mother of two neglected children (aged 5 and 9), to improve their poor personal cleanliness by delivering support and services to an older sibling.

Practice Note 6.5   Parental neglect and sibling relationships

In the book, *A Place Called Hope*, Tom O'Neill (1981) describes the very large family he came from, including Dennis O'Neill, a child whose death by foster carers in Wales in 1945 led to the *Curtis Report* (1946), and ultimately the Children Act 1948. He describes, in order of age, his oldest brother Cyril (fostered by the grandmother), his sister Betty, the one with the strongest, affectionate links with the parents, his older brother Charles, described as the more upright and honest member of the family, and his younger sister Rosina, described as the loyal one of the family. The three younger children, Dennis, Terrence and Frederick, he has less recall of, although he remembers Dennis as quiet, Frederick as very shy, and Terry as the 'tough guy' of the three.

O'Neill describes how, by the time of his birth, the family had already been identified as a problem family. His father – described by himself as the 'black sheep' of his own family – had already been imprisoned for a month in 1923 for child ill-treatment. O'Neill describes a situation of desperate poverty that was relatively common in the dockland area of Newport, where he was raised, and which entailed regular dealings with the local pawnbroker to make ends meet, meals made from scraps procured from the butcher and greengrocer, moving house regularly and suddenly ('moonlight flit') because of inability to pay rent, and breaking up furniture and fittings for firewood when the electricity, gas (or both) were cut off.

For 'scrumping' (taking fruit off another's fruit tree), O'Neill was sent to a remand home and then to Approved School. Three months after he was sentenced, the three youngest children in the family, Dennis (7), Terrence (5) and Frederick (2), were removed from the parents because of neglect, and both parents were imprisoned for one month (being unable to pay the £3 fine). O'Neill describes the poignancy of these events, as it was the last time the family were to be together. There were difficulties placing the three boys, and the two older ones were subsequently placed apart from Frederick. They were mistreated to such an extent that Dennis died, but Terry survived. Frederick was not seen by anyone in the family for more than thirty years until 1972, when he was visited by Tom and Terrence; upon reunion it was learned that he thought that there were only the three boys in the family. Around the same time, Tom and Terry also visited the farm in South Wales where both Terry and Dennis had been placed and where their brother Dennis had been so cruelly treated, and subsequently died.

Consider:

1. It is tempting to forget that when siblings are older they may help each other come to terms with the abusive or neglectful experiences that they may have had, either within their own family or elsewhere. How might this future healing power be promoted by actions taken today?

2. It is also useful to see this case as an illustration of how different recollections of the family may be and how these differences may need to be reconciled. For example, O'Neill describes his sister Betty's recollection of the family: 'She really believes that the authorities were to blame for everything and that there was nothing wrong with the family at all' (p. 4). Consider what evidence there may be for the statement: there is not one family, but as many 'families' within it as are seen by however many family members it contains.

Differential risk to children in families

An initial child protection conference will consider the risk of significant harm to all of the children in a family as individuals:

> When considering whether emergency action is necessary, an agency should always consider whether action is also required to safeguard other children in the same household (e.g. siblings), the household of an alleged perpetrator, or elsewhere. (National Assembly for Wales, 2000, paragraph 5.23)

The first question that needs to be considered by child protection agency is whether or not the name of a child for whom there is a clear concern about abuse or neglect should be added to the child protection register. Particularly if the answer to this question is 'Yes', a further question is 'what about other children in the family? ... what should happen to them?' This may sound simpler than it is in practice. Families that are the focus of child protection conferences are often extremely complex. Frequently, not all of the children live at home, and often children who are not the biological children of both parents (where there are two) are living in the home. Children of a younger age may be more at risk of neglect in a family than older children. Girls in a family may be considered to be at greater risk of sexual abuse than boys – particularly where one girl has already been a target. Different children in the families may have different fathers, exposing them to

TABLE 6.2 SIBLING STRUCTURE IN FAMILIES OF SEVERE ABUSE

	Number of children in the family							
	1	2	3	4	5	6	Total families	Total children
Identified children	2	8	8	13	4	3	34	38
Full siblings		5	10	20	1	5	23	41
Step- or half-siblings		1	3	19	10	4	16	37

Note: N = 116 children.
Source: From Oliver et al., 1978.

differential treatment, and sometimes to differential risk. Disability is a factor long known to make children more vulnerable to abuse (Jaudes and Diamond, 1985; Westcott, 1991).

An early study by Oliver *et al.* (1978) provides information on the sibling structure of thirty-four families in which severe abuse had taken place (see Table 6.2). Family size was large compared with the country (UK) as a whole. Families with four or more children formed 52.9 per cent of the sample compared with 8.9 per cent for the UK. Of the 78 siblings, 65 (83 per cent) were considered to be at risk of abuse (either because of their age or because the adults responsible for abuse continued to live in the family). And of these 65 children, severe or moderate physical abuse was found in 41 cases (63 per cent of the subtotal).

They noted the following clinical features in index children and siblings:

TABLE 6.3 CLINICAL FEATURES OF INDEX CHILDREN AND SIBLINGS

Clinical feature	Index children (n = 34) %	Siblings (n = 78) %
Fear of parents or other adults	42	17
Withdrawal, listlessness or drowsiness	42	20
Hyperactivity or repetitive motor activity	29	20
Persistent crying or irritability	45	34
Marked pallor	34	18

Source: Oliver et al., 1978.

Discussing physical abuse, Schmitt (1980, p.143) observes, 'There is approximately a 20% risk that a sibling of a physically abused child has also been abused at the same time.'

Creighton and Noyes (1989) looked at the percentage of siblings registered for the *same* type of abuse as the index child and found the following:

TABLE 6.4 PERCENTAGES OF SIBLINGS ADDED TO CHILD PROTECTION REGISTER UNDER THE SAME CATEGORY

Type of abuse	% siblings registered
Physical injury	11
Failure to thrive	14
Sexual abuse	23
Emotional abuse	39
Neglect	60

Browne (1995) examined risk factors to siblings:

> The dynamics of child abuse sometimes involves only one child but more often other children in the household will also be at risk. In some cases, the absence of the abused child may shift the focus of stress and frustration to another child in the family. In other families children are 'at risk' during a certain age, but if this is successfully passed the risk declines. Indeed, an older sibling of the abused child may have already been abused without detection. (pp. 118–19)

Lynch and Roberts (1982) studied siblings of 69 children from 40 abusing families and found them to be older. There were no physical injuries in the sibling group, although there had been a history of concern about their emotional care. Significantly, they found that lack of physical injury did not necessarily protect the siblings against developmental and behaviour problems and the difference between the abused and sibling groups for the occurrence of developmental delay was not statistically significant. The group with the least developmental delay were the siblings born after the abuse incident.

Stevenson and Hill (1980) discuss the particular significance of the abused child within the family, but note the danger of focusing too sharply on the risk to one child. This concern was echoed by some of the respondents in their study who felt that very often other children in a family were 'completely overlooked' (p. 68).

An early study of hospitalised abused children found evidence supporting a 'scapegoating' hypothesis, in that, in several cases, the 'sex or ordinal position of the abused child had a special significance for the abusive parent, (Elmer, 1967, p. 75). The birth of a sibling less than one year before or after the study child's admission to hospital was the factor most strongly associated with abuse. Jones *et al.* (1982) explore both the risk to siblings and the concept of scapegoating. They too emphasise the importance of not overlooking the needs of all children within an abusive family. Where children are removed because of abuse, they note that in some families the focus will simply shift to another child in the family. They also note that siblings of an abused child may themselves have been abused, but without detection.

Baher *et al.* (1976) note that:

> Although some researchers . . . have observed that often only one child in a family is singled out for abuse, the findings of [other studies] reveal a high incidence of abuse to one or more siblings of the presenting children. (p. 63)

Corby (1987) noted that procedural guidance in child protection did not cover action in respect of siblings, and consequently practice varied. Although consideration was given to safety of siblings, medical checks had not been systematically applied to ensure this. Dale *et al.* (1986) are very clear in their view that the position of siblings must be reviewed where abuse has taken place:

> initial uncertainty means assuming that the siblings are as at great a risk as the victim – not that they are at less risk because they were not harmed. (p. 50)

They highlight the importance of including siblings in the assessment, not only for the assessment of risk to them, but also because of the information they can provide. In terms of rehabilitation, they regarded sibling fighting as less serious than the means parents took to control it. O'Doherty (1982), describing hospital admissions and procedures in relation to abused children, also considers that there is significant risk to siblings when a child has been physically abused.

Regardless of whether one considers that if one child is at risk all are at risk, or one considers that risk is a differential concept applying to some children in families more than others because of idiosyncratic features (age, temperament, gender, significance of child), a thorough assessment of all children is indicated. Clearly there is no room for complacency about siblings when one child is identified by agencies as being abused. This concern needs to be on two levels. First, there is the risk that other children in the family are experiencing abuse as well – the same type or different. Secondly, in terms of developmental consequences, children who come from abusing families do poorly even if they are not abused. A child who is singled out for abuse or for neglect is very likely to come from a home where the needs of the other children, although perhaps better met than his or her own needs, are nevertheless below a level that will sustain their development.

Finally, in his autobiographical account of neglect and emotional, psychological, and physical abuse, David Pelzer (2001) highlights an example of extreme scapegoating, attributed to his being labelled as the 'bad boy' of the family by his mother. He briefly describes the impact of the abusive experience on his relationship with his two brothers (in relation to a method of abuse whereby his mother pressed his face against a mirror and compelled him to say repeatedly, 'I'm a bad boy; I'm a bad boy'):

> Whenever my brothers came into the room while I was at the mirror, they would look at me, shrug their shoulders and continue to play – as if I were not there. At first I was jealous, but soon I learned that they were only trying to save their own skins. (p. 31)

Later, he describes how they joined in the scapegoating:

> The boys who lived upstairs were no longer my brothers. Sometimes in years past, they had managed to encourage me a little. But in the summer of 1972 they took turns hitting me and appeared to enjoy throwing their weight around. It was obvious that they felt superior to the family slave. When they approached me, my heart became hard as stone, and I am sure they saw the hate etched in my face. (p. 135)

Practice Note 6.6   Differential risk

The Jenkins family has three children. Margaret (5), the oldest child, was born with a hare-lip and a cleft palate. Pauline (3) and John (21 months) were born without any congenital difficulties. They are the children of Jason and Denise Jenkins.

Approximately four months ago, the neighbours rang to refer the family because they were very concerned about the children in the family. The family had only just moved to the area (about three months before the neighbour's referral), and were living in a very run down, privately rented house in West London. The family tends to keep very much to themselves and ignores or rebuffs friendly overtures by the neighbours. The neighbours are generally concerned because, since the family moved in, they have hardly ever seen the oldest child. She goes out to school in the mornings with her mother and brother and sister, and comes back afterwards, but apart from that they never see her. Their particular concern, however, was that on two occasions they thought they could hear a child (Margaret they thought) being beaten. It sounded like it was about stealing food from the kitchen cupboard. It was much worse on the second occasion, which prompted the neighbours to alert the social services. They were particularly concerned because, being the Summer Holiday, they knew that no one would be seeing if there were any traces of visible injury on Margaret.

The family were not known to the local social services who undertook to liaise with the other local agencies. The school didn't know Margaret and her family very well, because she had only been in school for part of the last term before the Summer break. Margaret was brought and collected by her mother, who simply dropped her off and then went off without chatting to the other parents. Likewise, when she would arrive to collect her, she would not mix with the other parents, and in fact usually arrived a few minutes after the children were let out. Margaret was frequently the last child to be collected from the school play area.

The police knew Mr Jenkins because of two convictions: one for grievous bodily harm, and the other for possession of an illegal firearm. He was given probation in relation to the latter offence. The police believe that Mr Jenkins supplements his social security income with burglaries and theft, and that he takes on occasional, undeclared, casual labour. His probation officer also does not know Mr Jenkins very well but, working from previous notes, he was able to say that the previous probation officer described Mr Jenkins as an 'immature personality' who had a 'very strong anti-authority fixation'. He would continually complain to the probation officer about the way he was treated by Social Security, Housing and other official agencies.

The health visitor has seen the two younger children, and on one or two occasions has seen Margaret as well. Pauline seems to be developing normally, but there are some concerns about John, as his speech does not seem to be developing as one might expect. She indicated that weight- and height-wise he is just on the 3rd centile, and she was keeping a watching brief on him. In relation to Margaret, although her records have gone to the school nursing service, the health visitor was aware that she too was very small for her age, and that there have been a number of missed appointments in relation to Margaret's cleft palate and an assessment for speech therapy.

On the basis of further worrying information coming to light and because of the imminent danger felt to exist for Margaret, she was removed from home under an Emergency Protection Order, but the other two, not being at the same immediate risk of injury, were allowed to remain pending further assessment.

Consider:
1. How are Pauline and John likely to be affected by the physical abuse their older sister has experienced?
2. What might be the implications for the relationships between the three children of the abuse that Margaret has suffered?
3. What would one look for in the assessment to ascertain whether Pauline and John are likely to be either,
   a. at risk of physical abuse from the parents, now or in the future;
   b. at risk of some other form of abuse either because of the impact of Margaret's abuse on them, or because of being on the receiving end of the same parenting style which would promote the physical abuse of one child.

Summary: abuse and sibling relationships

When looking at the impact of abuse on the quality of the sibling relationships within a family, it becomes clear that there are very different implications depending upon the type of abuse. With physical abuse we find that abused children do not perceive their families as positively as non-abused children, and likewise that siblings of abused children perceive their families less positively than siblings from non-abuse families. However, there are no significant differences between the abused children and non-abused siblings within abusing families about how the family and its members were perceived. Abuse disrupts the establishment of healthy sibling relationships. With sexual abuse, there are very different issues in terms of the impact on sibling relationships. To begin with, siblings may not be aware of other siblings being abused. If they are aware of it, they may enter into a collusive relationship with the abuser (to protect themselves from becoming the victim). They may become locked into a victim-blaming pattern, attributing to her the causes of the disclosure consequences (removal, family break-up, imprisonment of the abuser). Work with siblings is important. With emotional abuse, we revisit the themes of scapegoating. Siblings may join the parent(s) in scapegoating the target child. With neglect, we find the issue of sibling caretaking re-emerging; one child in the family (frequently an older female) assumes a high level of responsibility for the others.

Therefore, we should be very cautious about presuming that sibling relationships can be supportive in abusive contexts. The supportive qualities of sibling relationships that one finds in other situations appear to be undermined by intrafamilial abuse although there is little empirical evidence to draw upon. There are no significant studies that specifically examine this aspect of the sibling relationship, or this aspect of abuse within families. What has been concluded here of relevance for our purposes is based upon the findings of research where the research questions were focused elsewhere, but in which there were implications for understanding sibling relationships. Why is it, we must ask, given the emphasis within government policy (e.g. the Children Act 1989) on sibling relationships, that this subject continues to be so neglected?

7 Loss and Sibling Relationships

This chapter begins with a brief consideration of the significance of sibling relationships as attachment relationships and the impact of loss on children. It will then discuss three types of loss for children and consider their impacts on sibling relationships: loss through parental divorce, loss through being looked after by the local authority and loss through death.

Sibling relationships as attachment relationships

Attachment is probably the single most important concept when working with children and families. There is insufficient space here to develop the fundamentals, but the reader is referred to a number of sources that have looked at the application of attachment concepts to working with children and families (Fahlberg, 1994; Howe, 1995; Daniel *et al.*, 1999; Colton *et al.*, 2001). Attachment as a concept and then later as a theory began with ethological studies of imprinting in ducks and geese and was then developed by Bowlby (1969) following the Second World War, when there were concerns about the possible damaging effects to young children of spending so much time in nurseries away from parental care. Bowlby warned of the dangers of 'maternal deprivation', that is the development of psychopathic and affectionless personalities. The damage of early separation was powerfully illustrated by the Robertsons (Robertson and Robertson, 1989), colleagues of Bowlby, through a series of films of young children in situations of separation. In part as a result of those films, children's wards in hospitals moved over to more liberal parental visiting (eventually to open visiting, and parents staying in with very young children), and local authorities abandoned the use of residential nurseries for very young children needing to be looked after. Rutter (1972), however, warned against alarmist views of maternal deprivation, and noted that there were a wide range of factors that influenced the outcome of maternal deprivation experiences, both in the long and short term. He accumulated evidence on the impact of separation experiences on children. In studying factors that mitigate the impact of children's separation experiences, he found it curious that studies of children's separation were considered as separations from mothers alone, when 'in fact they consist of separation from mother *and* father *and* sibs *and* the home environment' (p. 48). It is useful to note this early reference to siblings as a moderating influence on the impact of separation experiences for young children.

The homogenous and unitary quality of attachment – something one has more or less of in the relationship – was replaced in more recent years with different kinds of attachments, introducing in effect, qualitative differences in the nature of the attachment relationship. Ainsworth and colleagues (1978) developed 'The Strange Situation' as a tool to categorise attachment relationships. This is a procedure in which, under laboratory conditions, a child is put through eight 3-minute episodes involving separations from, and reunions with, the primary carer. The child's reactions to the separations and the reunions are rated, and on the basis of the ratings, the child is categorised into one of four categories: a secure attachment pattern; an insecure (anxious/avoidant) type; an insecure (anxious/ambivalent) type; and disorganised attachment. A further category has been developed for very worrying children who may be described as 'non-attached'.

Attachment is defined in terms of parental and child behaviour – in the proximity-seeking behaviour of the young child during separations. The complement of attachment is the contribution of the primary carer to the relationship, which is usually described as 'bonding'. Thus, the child attaches to the parent; the parent bonds with the child. These dual processes are mutually reinforcing in a cycle of dependency, need-arousal and need-fulfilment, described by Fahlberg (1994).

The question therefore that we wish to pose here is: are sibling relationships attachment relationships? Certainly, sibling relationships can be very close, closer indeed than the relationship between the children and their parents (Bilson and Barker, 1992). However, theoreticians tend to be somewhat reserved in describing siblings as attachment figures, preferring to retain that terminology for the primary caregiver relationships. This, however, seems unnecessarily limited both in terms of a child's psychological experience of attachment, and the restricted understanding of the needs that are met by attachment. The historical development of attachment from the field of ethology (imprinting in ducks and geese) grounds it in a relationship that is primarily biosocial, i.e. a social relationship stemming from a biological basis. However, were one to construct an understanding of attachment that was predominantly social, then the concept would be applied to relationships that had a significant history of social inter-action without necessarily involving the need to invoke a biological caregiving element. In this conception, we become attached to people because of our intimate social connections with them over time, not because of the manifestation of inbuilt biological mechanisms or because the other person feeds us and meets our other biological needs. In that sense our identity, our notion of who we are, develops in relation to the social interchanges we have with significant others in our social world, and removing them, or being removed from them, is like losing a part of one's self.

Despite being reluctant to label sibling relationships as 'attachment' relationships *per se*, however, writers have been quick to recognise how important they are in terms of social relationships *beyond attachment*, as the following suggests:

> The recognition that children have to handle social relationships beyond attachment takes us into the world of other people and new social rela-tionship − with brothers and sisters, grandparents and teachers, family and friends ... Dunn [1993, p. 46] describes various pieces of research, including her own, in which there is clear evidence that siblings can become attached to one another. They show all the responses towards their older brother or sister that other securely attached infants nor-mally show towards their mother. There is delight and happiness when a sister returns. An elder brother can act as a secure base from which to explore. There is sadness when the older children in the family are away. (Howe, 1995, p. 61)

Stewart (1983) conducted the Strange Situation (previously described) with siblings present instead of the young children being left on their own when mother left the room. It was found that over half of the older siblings engaged in caregiving behaviour, reassuring and hugging the distressed infant or attempting to distract the infant from the distress by diverting attention to the toys available. This is significant both ways. First, the majority of siblings engage in support and care-giving behaviour. But secondly, a substantial minority do not. In the first case we are struck by the older child's undertaking what could be clearly seen as attachment-promoting behaviour, even within a bio-social understanding of attachment. The infant has needs (indicated by distress), the older sibling moves in to attempt to meet those needs. But the other side of the question is why such a substantial minority don't engage in caregiving behaviour, and basically ignore the distress of the younger sibling. To this we might recall the relative lack of emphasis on sibling caretaking in Westernised societies (Minturn and Lambert, 1964), and suggest that where older siblings are less used to caring for younger siblings, they may lack the experience and confidence. They may also be less attuned to the distress of a younger child than a sibling who has been given more daily caregiving responsibilities. In support of this we might note that there are cross-cultural variations in parental attachment studies, and these variations seem, in part, to reflect different cultural parenting styles. As noted by Barnes (1995) looking at the results of a meta-analysis study of Van Ijzendoorn and Kroonenberg (1988), which described a low level of Avoidant (type A) attachments and a high level of Ambivalent (Type C) attachments in Japanese children:

> one explanation of the pattern of results from Japanese studies is that the infants were very distressed in the Strange Situation because, in their culture, they are never normally left alone at 12 months. (p. 17)

Siblings, loss and divorce/separation

We can view family disintegration and reintegration as consisting of a number of stages that families go through, with different successive associated development tasks, and potential traumatising influences. It is generally accepted that parental divorce is not good for children. As expressed by Reibstein and Bamber (1997, p. 72), 'The more disruption children experience in the process of divorce and its aftermath, the more trouble they seem to have.'

After the parental separation, there is a period of time, which may be very brief or very extended, during which the children are cared for by a single parent. The impact of sibling conflicts upon a parent who finds his/her stress-coping resources at a low level may be heightened. In many cases, divorced parents find another partner, and thereby create *de facto* step relations in the family. There are then issues for the siblings about fitting in with the new stepparent, and indeed with any children of the stepparent. Because families are located in the context of wider family networks, there are a variety of new relationships established. A developmental challenge for the children of such relationships is to get to know who's who in the new nexus of family relations. Where there are a succession of partners, this can be extremely confusing for a child who may come to regard other young people in the family as 'brothers' and 'sisters', but without having a clear understanding of the linkages.

There are three main effects of parental separation and divorce on sibling relationships. First, even where siblings remain together, as individuals they are affected by the loss of a significant carer (most frequently the father, as children, especially younger ones, tend to remain with the mother). The way they are affected, as individuals can then be expected to influence the nature of the relationship they have with each other. Secondly, siblings frequently lose their relationships with their sibling by being separated from each other as the parents establish two different homes. Where siblings do remain together, their relationship may be affected by the loss of relationship with a significant carer. Thirdly, in the aftermath of divorce and re-formation of families and remarriage, children are brought into new relationships with others who they are expected to relate to as siblings. We shall consider each of these in turn.

Where brothers and sisters remain together following parental divorce or separation

That divorce will influence sibling relationships might be inferred from the well-documented body of literature on the impact of divorce on children as individuals. For example, Hetherington and Clingempeel (1992) found children in non-divorced families to be more competent and exhibiting fewer behaviour problems than children of divorced or remarried (step)families. On the other hand, Trad (1990), focusing on the behaviours of preschool children, suggests that so-called 'normal' patterns of child development can be misleading, and that behaviours which come to be regarded as psychopathology in very young children may actually be very adaptive responses to traumatic events (one example given being that of divorce). There are three main areas of stress for children: (a) loss of access to parents; (b) change in physical surroundings; and (c) hostilities between parents with the possible intrusion of the legal system into the family (Arnold and Carnahan, 1990). Whilst the risk of harmful outcomes for children arising from divorce is high, recent thinking on risk for children, in a range of contexts, emphasises the complexity emerging from understanding resilience (Fraser, 1997). In the context of separation/divorce, single-parent status, and remarriage, Hetherington (1999) looks at the interactions of risk and protective factors identified within the individual, within the family and outside the family. A further complexity in looking at the impact of divorce has been disaggregating the influence of the various stages of divorce, the family situation pre-divorce, the actual separation and divorce experience, and the aftermath of divorce. Using longitudinal data from both the USA and the UK, Cherlin *et al.* (1993) conclude:

> Overall, the evidence suggests that much of the effect of divorce on children can be predicted by conditions that existed well before the separation occurred. These pre-divorce effects were stronger for boys than for girls ... those concerned with the effects of divorce on children should consider reorienting their thinking. At least as much attention needs to be paid to the processes that occur in troubled, intact families as to the trauma that children suffer after their parents separate. (p. 272)

Looking at the impact of divorce on younger children (boys, aged 2 to $6\frac{1}{2}$), Kier and Fouts (1989) found same-sex preferences in free play for boys from intact families, but not for young boys from divorced/separated families. In terms of sibling relationships, the reason for this may be that the stress of the separation of the parents has brought the children together (so that gender becomes less important) or on the contrary, that the pressures arising from the divorce have brought older sisters into more of an interactive role with younger siblings than older brothers (for example through increased caretaking as noted by MacKinnon, 1988). It is useful to compare this study with Spigelman *et al.* (1992) who looked at family drawings of children from divorced and non-divorced families. They suggest that in the divorce group, family relationship problems were expressed, amongst other means described, by leaving out family members from the drawings. They noted that boys from the divorce group omitted siblings from their drawings more often than girls (of both groups) and more often than boys from intact families. They did not comment on ordinal position, and so the differences may in part be attributable to that, and in part to the location of the study in Sweden, which presents perhaps different cultural constructions of the family and family members' roles within it.

There is some literature that focuses specifically on the impact of divorce and separation on the sibling relationships. The impact may be mediated by a number of intervening processes (Conger and Conger, 1996). The main sibling issues following the separation are the impact on the sibling relationships of the stress experienced in the family prior to the separation and the impact of the actual separation on the child's sibling relationships (as mediated by factors such as stress on the primary carer, poverty, parental contact). Sibling interactions in divorced families have been found to be both more negative and less positive than in married families (MacKinnon, 1988). Comparing children from intact and non-intact families, the sibling relationship is found to be better predicted by the quality of the spousal/ex-spousal relationship than by the marital status of the parents. It was found though that boys coming from divorced families had more problematic sibling relationships, particularly with younger sisters, than boys coming from intact families (MacKinnon, 1989). Boys from divorced homes were found to be more coercive and aggressive in their relationships with siblings than boys from intact homes (Hetherington, 1988). Looking at the work of both Hetherington (1988) and MacKinnon (1989), Jenkins (1992) concludes:

> there was little evidence that when children were exposed to the adverse circumstance of their parents' divorce, they used their siblings as sources of support and built up particularly close relationships with them. (p. 126)

Despite this, the positive significance of sibling relationships in the context of parental divorce has been described in a number of studies, and clearly this theme reverberates with the main contention of this book, i.e. that sibling relationships are a potential therapeutic agent for children in the context of adverse social circumstances. There is evidence that relationships between siblings of divorcing parents can have a strong facilitating influence on children's development, highlighting the aspects of mutual support and nurturance, role models and family structure (Waters, 1987). Sibling relationships are an important resource in helping children cope with the aftermath of divorce (Eno, 1985). The presence of a sibling can act as a potential buffer for young adolescents after divorce; when comparing adolescents from intact families with adolescents from divorced families, those from divorced families without siblings show more 'externalising behaviour' (Kempton *et al.*, 1991). Externalising behaviour, as defined by Anderson *et al.* (1999), can be understood as acting out, antisocial behaviour, non-compliance or aggression.

Whilst not neglecting the beneficial aspects for the older siblings of retaining a role and relationship with a younger children, as one might expect, much of the positive influence is in the reverse direction, i.e. the older child helping the younger child through the ordeal. In part this is likely to be because younger siblings, developmentally, may be more deeply affected. It is also because older children, especially those approaching adolescence, are beginning to distance themselves from the family and starting to derive more support outside the family. Therefore, one might expect, as has been found, that older children in families are better adjusted than younger ones following divorce (Kurdek, 1988). They have fewer problematic beliefs regarding the divorce and a better understanding of conflict resolution. Similarly, MacKinnon (1988), who also looked at the role of ordinal position in mediating sibling interactions in married and divorced families, found that older siblings in divorced families engaged in more caretaking behaviour; younger siblings were more likely to be the recipient of caregiving behaviour and to be more positive in their interactions. This may be because the separated parent looks for more help from the older children – help which prior to the separation may have been provided by the other parent.

Although researchers (Hetherington, 1988; MacKinnon, 1988; MacKinnon, 1989) provide us with information about the disruptive effect of divorce on sibling relationships, there is still very little that we can say about the impact of such events on the various parameters of the sibling relationship – the levels of warmth, rivalry and hostility. It is certainly not an area that is well researched.

Loss of contact between siblings following parental divorce or separation: split residence/split custody

Parental separation and divorce often leads to children losing important relationships with siblings. The separation of siblings as part of the process of divorce settlements has become more common, partly because of the increasing readiness of courts in recent years to allow men custody of their children. As noted by Hawthorne (1998):

> As many fathers have begun to assume a more active role in raising children and now want greater involvement with their children following divorce, the need to collect solid evidence on families with split residence would seem to have become more urgent. (p. 4)

Hawthorne (1998) also describes a trend for split residence children to come from larger families and to go to same-sex parents. He also found that mixed-sex sibling groups had the highest likelihood of split-residence decisions, and female-only sibling groups the lowest.

Surprisingly, he found little correlation with age (contrary to the expectation that older children are more likely to go to fathers and younger children to mothers).

It is very important to be aware of the significance of losing contact with a sibling as one of the stressors arising for children in the context of divorce (Arnold and Carnahan, 1990). Kaplan *et al.* (1991), Kaplan *et al.* (1993) look at four issues regarding split custody decisions: the impact that siblings have on each other, reasons why a court might make such a decision, the difficulties making such decisions, and the difficulties that might arise as a result of such a decision. They highlight the responsibility of clinicians to strengthen and/or improve the siblings' relationship after they are separated by divorce. They consider a number of theoretical issues in relation to sibling relationships and split custody decisions (boundary ambiguity, the psychological and physical effects of split custody, family roles and expectations, homeostatic tendencies within families, practical consequences for siblings, and the development of families as a result of such arrangements). They conclude that split custody is a threat to the sibling subsystem and should only be entered into very cautiously.

Monahan *et al.* (1993) looked at the differences between siblings in divorced families. They found that siblings who lived apart after the divorce were more different from each other than siblings who lived together following the divorce. They considered the possibility that differences between the siblings *before* the divorce might have led them to be in the group of siblings living apart, but concluded that the evidence did not support this. The differences appear to have arisen as a result of the separation following the divorce.

It is perhaps too easy to suggest that decisions to split siblings are taken too lightly, for example, where there is enmity between the children, where there is a wide age gap, or where neither parent has the means individually to care for all the children. It has also been suggested that parental motivations to split custody of children have been to avoid child support payments and to punish ex-partners (Kaplan *et al.*, 1991). However, a major factor identified by Hawthorne (1998) was the preference of the children regarding with which parent they would like to live. In 70 per cent of the cases he looked at, this was the key factor. Nevertheless, children were not altogether happy with living apart from their sibling, even though their wishes had been a key component of the decision. In a number of cases, even the parents were unhappy with the split-residence arrangements, but felt it important to accommodate the views of the children. In this age of greater emphasis on children's rights, and much more weight being given to the views of children and young people in the important decisions concerning their lives, this creates a considerable difficulty. Clearly, in some cases, children are being put in the untenable situation of expressing a preference for being with their sibling or being with a preferred parent.

Where siblings *do* separate as a result of parental divorce, it is important to ensure contact between them (Nichols, 1986). However, there may be difficulties, for example parental hostility, different family timetables, geographical distance, lack of awareness of the importance of sibling contact by parents, the artificiality of contact arrangements (often a problem for parents having contact with children), a tendency to presume that sibling contact is not important because of normal sibling antagonism and hostility, and increased hostility and aggression (especially in boys) following the divorce. Hawthorne's (1998) study found considerable emphasis put on maintaining contact between siblings separated by split-residence arrangements, as judged by the high level of contact found. He also suggests therefore a positive outcome of split residence as:

> it is conducive to both parents remaining in the lives of all the children. This is in contrast to research evidence that in sole-residence families a considerable proportion of non-residential fathers lose contact with children over the years. (p. 9)

Significantly, however, and perhaps surprisingly he found that neither children nor parents considered there to be any change in the strength of the sibling relationship before and after the divorce when split-residence arrangements were made.

New sibling relationships for children following remarriage or re-formation of family

Not all families that are broken apart by separation and divorce re-form into other families, but most do, and this process can create even more factors that complicate the picture of looking at how children adjust to the process of divorce. Approximately half of those who divorce (both men and women) are likely to remarry within five years.

Rosenberg and Hajal (1985) consider some of the characteristics of stepsibling relationships in remarried families. They note that such relationships are instantaneous, have fluid boundaries, lack a shared family history, bring a common experience of loss of original families, face sets of conflicting loyalties, experience shifts in sibling position roles and functions, experience abrupt change in family size, deal with complicated sexual boundary issues, and confront an incongruence between the individual life cycle and the family cycle. (p. 287)

They discuss these factors in comparison with the developmental tasks of divorce, and note that remarried families operate without well-developed social norms. Pasley and Ihinger-Tallman (1987) for example, noted that:

the texture of modern society has been changed dramatically by the increasing presence of the stepfamily. No longer considered the exception to the norm, the stepfamily has been thrust into the mainstream by a 50% divorce rate combined with a high incidence of remarriage. According to some estimates, 35% of children born in the 1980's will experience stepfamily living by the time they reach the age of 18. (cover)

In fact, however, the divorce 'rate' in the USA never reached 50 per cent, a statistic that, whilst oft quoted, is rather controversial.

Sanders (2002) comments on the increasing complexity of families being worked with by social workers, and notes differences in the family structures (in terms of types of sibling connections) between social workers, families receiving support services, and families with children on the child protection register. These are set out in Table 7.1.

Whereas, nearly nine out of ten social worker's brothers and sisters have two parents in common, in the families receiving family support service this proportion is less than two-thirds and in child protection families it is considerably less than half. This raises the question of the extent to which these social workers and the families they work with are likely to have the same image of 'family' as a basis for family work.

TABLE 7.1 SOCIAL WORKERS, FAMILY SUPPORT FAMILIES AND CHILD PROTECTION FAMILIES

Sibling type	Social workers	Family support families	Child protection families
Half siblings	11.8	39.3	48.8
Full siblings	88.2	60.7	39.2

Hetherington (1991) described the effects of divorce and remarriage on children's adjustment in two longitudinal studies. She found that the effects of both divorce and growing up in a single-parent (divorced) household were harder on boys than on girls. However, boys and girls were equally resistant and disrupted by the arrival of a stepfather (although boys eventually adapted to and benefited from the presence of a stepfather). Anderson *et al.* (1999), using the data from Hetherington and Clingempeel (1992), note the high risk of externalising behaviour in adolescents from remarried families.

Hetherington and Jodl (1994) describe the task of maintaining or building supportive, or at least non-destructive, sibling relationships as one of five challenges facing stepfamilies. Mekos *et al.* (1996) looked specifically at sibling issues in remarried and non-divorced families. They asked whether sibling differences are magnified and whether the links between differential treatment and sibling adjustment are stronger in remarried families. They found that there were greater intrafamilial differences and problem behaviour in remarried families where siblings did not share the same biological parent. They also found that differential treatment was more strongly related to problem behaviour in such families. Most at risk of differential treatment in such families were mother's biological child and father's stepchild. Ihinger-Tallman and Pasley (1987) described differential treatment within families as a concern of stepsiblings:

> if there were feelings of hostility or dislike between children, they generally did not extend across the entire sibling group. Rather, negative feelings were directed toward only one stepsib. When poor relations between children were mentioned, they generally stemmed from differential treatment by a parent and stepparent – a common complaint expressed by these young people. (p. 106)

It should be noted, however, that this concern was within the general context of stepsiblings being predisposed to like each other, other things being equal, and generally reporting positive feelings towards stepsiblings, a finding they attribute in part to the fact that, without separate norms for stepfamilies, the general societal expectation of affection between family members continues to predominate. Ihinger-Tallman (1987) attempts to begin the development of a theoretical model that explains the processes through which sibling bonding is affected by the divorce and remarriage of children's parents, and how sibling bonding develops or fails to develop between children in a stepfamily who previously would have had no relation to each other.

Within stepfamilies sibling relationships are generally reported to be positive, even though there may have been a considerable amount of psychological trauma to overcome on the part of the children. Sibling bonds do develop, even in stepfamilies. Of course one reason for this may be that parents forming a stepfamily are aware of the challenges facing them, and are perhaps more proactive in addressing sibling issues than parents in intact families. Parents in intact families may be more inclined to regard sibling relationships as following their natural course.

Practice Note 7.1 Siblings, loss and divorce/separation

Jane was only 17 when she met Paul, and 18 when they married. She and Paul had two children very close together, Carol and Tim. When the children were very young (2 and 3 respectively), Jane learned that Tim was having an affair with his secretary at work. The couple had counselling and tried to make a go of it, but three years later, when it was learned that Paul had been continuing his affair – but denying it – Jane had had enough, and the marriage came to an end. She insisted that her husband leave, which he did, and he moved in with his new partner. To begin with he maintained contact with the children, but when the company moved him to a new location, about fifty miles away, his contact with the children became less and less, despite Jane wishing him to keep in contact. In spite of her efforts he stopped coming to see the children, stopped sending birthday and Christmas cards and more or less just dropped out of their lives.

Jane lived on her own with the two children for several years before she met Dave, a senior accountant for a steel company, who struck Jane as being extremely trustworthy and reliable, and above all, honest. He was very fond of Carol and Tim, and they of him. He was very generous with them as well, and would buy them lavish presents for their birthdays and at Christmas. After about a year of seeing each other, Dave moved in with Jane and the children. Her divorce from Paul had not yet been finalised, but she and Dave were planning to marry once that was completed. She became pregnant with Kevin, and although they had planned to wait a little longer, both she and Dave were delighted. However, after Kevin was born, Jane began to realise that things were not right. Whilst Dave was very generous, she also noted that there were times when he seemed to be very short of money. She wondered about this, and then learned that Paul had a significant flaw in his character, he was an obsessive gambler. He was regularly at the bookmaker's placing bets on the horses. Unfortunately, he was neither a lucky gambler, nor a judicious one, and he bet more than he could afford and lost most of the time. But he was addicted. Jane had tried to persuade him to get professional help but he refused. He tried to deny that he was gambling as much as previously, but in fact, he was trying to gamble to make up his heavy losses. Soon after, Jane noticed that valuables started going missing from the home. She confronted Dave, but he denied taking them. He continued to refuse to get help. Jane was exasperated, but worse was to come, when the police knocked on their door one evening. There was evidence that Dave had embezzled large amounts of money from the steel company. Whilst waiting for the trial, he continued to deny the charges to Jane. She said if he was found guilty then the relationship was over. She had already had a relationship with someone she could not trust. Dave was tried and found guilty and sentenced to a term in prison. During that time, Jane did not visit, and made it clear that upon his release he should look for somewhere else to live. She said he could see Kevin, but that was all. They would discuss the arrangements for contact upon his release. Upon his release, he found his own place to live and arranged to see Kevin once a week on weekends. Jane agreed to this arrangement, but within herself she harboured misgivings because of her concern about the lack of contact that Carol and Tim's dad had with them. She wondered what they would make of it, especially if it were to continue.

Jane met Mark at her ceramics evening class. Mark was a single father, with a 7-year-old daughter, Mary. Both being single parents, they both felt that they had a lot in common. He had custody of his daughter because the reason for the marriage breakdown was his wife's (Sue) descent into ever more serious and dangerous drug usage. He had done everything he could to get help for her, but despite saying that she would get treatment, she continued to escalate her drug dependency, both in terms of the types of drugs she was using and the amount. At the point when he moved out, Sue was regularly injecting heroin. A serious concern for Mark was that needles and drugs would be left lying around the home whilst he was out at work, and he was very anxious about the risk to Mary. He went to live with his mother, taking Mary with him, an arrangement that worked out well, as his mother was happy to look after Mary during the day whilst he was at work. Sue would try to come round when he was at work to take Mary home with her, and so Mark applied for a residence order, which was made in his favour, thus securing Mary with him. A year later, Sue died of an accidental overdose.

Jane and Mark continued seeing each other, and their respective children appeared to get on well with each other. There were times when there appeared to be jealousy between Mary and Carol, but these were usually easy to straighten out. Mary was very fond of Kevin.

Mark was a traditionalist when it came to marriage, and did not feel that they should live together until they were married. Shortly after they were married, Liam was born. All of the older children doted on him. Kevin was perhaps a little less enthusiastic, but nevertheless proud to have a little person that he could be a big brother to.

Consider:
This case raises many issues in relation to the complexity of modern-day families:

1. There are five children in this 'reconstituted' family. How can the children be helped to understand how they are related to the other children in the family? In what ways would a genogram help?
2. In terms of full sibling relationships (two parents in common), half-sibling relationships (one parent in common) and step-sibling relationships (no parents in common), how many of each type of sibling relationship are there in this complex family (see Appendix A)?
3. Jane was worried about Kevin getting attention from his absent father, whilst Carol and Tim had no contact with their father. What advice might be given to Jane about her concerns about the differential treatment experienced by the children's different fathers?

Siblings, loss and being looked after and adopted

Generally, it is estimated that only between 10 and 20 per cent of the children entering the care system have no siblings. Millham *et al.* (1986) found that only 11 per cent of 450 children in care had no siblings of any type (full, half-, or step). Rowe *et al.* (1984) found that 84 per cent of 145 foster children they studied had full- or half-siblings. Wedge and Phelan (1986), in their four-year study of children in local authority care, found that less than one in five was an only child. Bilson and Barker (1992), in a study of 1,070 children, found that just 144 (13.5 per cent) were only children.

Ordinarily, the experience of care for the child involves not only separation from the primary caregiver, but also separation from some or all of his or her siblings; children are usually placed in separate homes (Hegar, 1988). Bilson and Barker (1992) found that where children were placed at the same time as siblings, only a quarter of all these children were placed together. Girls were more likely to be placed with all of their siblings than boys.

Kosonen (1996a) collected data on 337 adoptive and foster placements, and she too found that for the majority of children entering the care system, placement entailed separation from siblings. The most likely times for the disintegration of sibling connections was upon entering and leaving care, and she found that few children had plans which involved sibling reunification. A picture emerged of professionals lacking information about the family where they had lost contact with parents or siblings had moved away. She described the picture of siblings' lives as 'fragmented' and noted the lifelong implications for children of being separated from their brothers and sisters. She noted the tendency for children when being placed together with siblings to be in temporary placements with family relations.

Following placement of 115 children by the Children's Aid Society, a majority (53 per cent) were eventually separated from their siblings (Thorpe and Swart, 1992). Mullender (1999) notes the continuing trend for siblings to be separated as a result of being looked after or adopted:

> It is the norm in the wider community to have siblings . . . it is equally, and tragically, the norm in the care system and in adoption to be separated from some or all of them. (p. 14)

Why place siblings together?

Placement of siblings has probably received the lion's share of thinking about siblings in work with families. The main emphasis within that is on whether siblings should be placed together or separately. The Children Act 1989 (section 27(3)(b)) requires that when a local authority accommodates siblings, they should be accommodated together. Given this presumption in the Act, this has become the default position for planning, and one needs to give consideration as to whether there are legitimate reasons why children should not be placed together.

'To split or not to split', was a question posed by Jones and Niblett (1985), to which they concluded, 'To continue to make decisions about separating or maintaining sibling groups with the poverty of our current knowledge and assessment skills may pose unacceptable risks. It may be the unacceptable face of family placement in the late 1980s.' But unfortunately, sibling relationships have been, and continue to be, a neglected area of placement practice despite their vital significance (Timberlake and Hamlin; 1982; Jones and Niblett, 1985; Kosonen, 1996a).

There are good reasons why siblings should be placed together. First, siblings usually prefer to be placed together. Secondly, it preserves family links for the child – not only in terms of links with the sibling, but with the rest of the family through the sibling. Thirdly, sibling placements are associated with successful outcomes. Let us consider each of these in turn.

Siblings prefer to be placed together

Even with bickering, taunting and hostility between siblings, the relationship can provide a considerable degree of comfort when facing the anxiety of entering completely alone a new situation and encountering new people:

> Siblings typically value being placed together . . . and look to one another for support and protection . . . and for the opportunity to talk about their birth family. (Mullender, 1999, p. 9)

The fact that children ordinarily value being placed together with siblings has been found in a number of studies, but, as indicated by Kosonen (1999), children's views can be very variable, depending upon the quality of their sibling relationships. They may have views about *which* siblings they would like to be placed with (and *not* be placed with). They may have simultaneous strong views about wanting, and not wanting, to be placed with a sibling; in other words they may experience ambivalence. If not actually wanting to be placed with the sibling, they may want to live very near to the sibling so that there can be regular contact.

Placement together preserves a component of family networks

Timberlake and Hamlin (1982) emphasise the importance of sibling relationships, noting that siblings are emotionally involved with each other and co-facilitate social developmental tasks – cooperation, coping skills, individuality. The process of placement in which siblings are separated deprives children of this 'natural support network'. Separation from siblings can lead to frustration, anger and depression, and they may experience loss, worthlessness and helplessness. The authors note that this may then lead them to behave in ways that will lead to rejection.

Begun (1995), in her consideration of a range of sibling issues in placements, emphasises that a placement goal should be to preserve sibling connections, preferably through placement together rather than through separate placements with contact. Where separate placements are necessary then contact arrangements should be frequent, occur from the beginning and be very flexible. Coordination may be necessary if there are different workers responsible for different siblings.

Placement together is associated with better outcomes

There are various outcomes one could consider here – settling into the placement, psychological and emotional adjustment, the success, or otherwise, of the placement. As early as 1965, it was realised that siblings have an effect on how children settle when placed away from home. Heinicke and Westheimer (1965) observed that children admitted to a residential nursery were less distressed when admitted with a sibling. This was true even if the sibling was too young to act in a caretaking role.

There are differences in social competence, and emotional and behavioural problems between siblings who are placed together and those who are placed apart. M. Smith (1998) undertook a study of 38 very young (preschool) children, 25 of whom were placed together with their older sibling and 13 of whom were placed apart. Children who were placed with their siblings tended to have a higher level of prior psychological problems, but were also described as having fewer emotional and behavioural problems. It is difficult, however, in this study, to disaggregate those factors that emerge as a result of separation or placement with siblings, from those factors which perhaps lead to children being placed separately from, or together with, siblings, i.e. which way the cause–effect mechanism might be working.

A dissenting finding, however, of the benefits of placement together comes from Thorpe and Swart (1992) who found that separated siblings, despite having more risk factors and more placements, had fewer symptoms and better school performance during their time in foster care when compared with siblings who remained together

during placement. This suggests that placement together is not invariably an undiluted benefit for the children and that careful assessment
of the strengths and limitations of the sibling relationship is always
indicated.

Nevertheless, it does appear that the success or otherwise of a
placement depends in part on siblings. Farmer and Parker (1991)
found that children returning home from care did least well when there
were changes amongst the *children* in the household. This highlighted
for them the 'crucial importance of the child's relationships with
siblings and stepsiblings and their critical impact on the relationship
with the parents' (p. 50). Further, they found that successful home-on-
trial placements were associated with the child being placed at home at
the same time as a sibling. This finding they compare with Berridge and
Cleaver (1987) who found more success in foster placements where
children were placed with some or all of their siblings. Let us move on
now to consider situations in which children do *not* return home.

Adoption

Although the weight of the evidence does support a policy of placing
children together if possible, this does not mean that the path is
smooth when siblings are placed together. Ward (1984), writing about
adoption in Canada, stresses that sibling relationships can be more
important for children than their ties to their parents. Sibling ties
should be considered from the beginning, since early 'ad hoc separations' can be later reflected when planning for adoption. In other
words, if children get separated too early in their adoption path, they
are likely to remain separated. The needs and desires of children
regarding their sibling relationships is a crucial part of planning.
Particular consideration should be given to the strength of the sibling
ties, the influence of the 'parental child', and sibling rivalry (its sources
and uses). Where separation is necessary then contact should be
maintained and workers must ensure this. She suggests that workers
need a good level of expertise in understanding the children they are
working with, the patterns of relationships between them, and the
local resources that are available for placements.

Rushton *et al.* (1999) looked at sibling relationships of children
being placed permanently from care. This is a significant study because
it focuses on sibling interactions in long-term placements. They looked
at 72 families where 133 children had been placed, some individually

(32), the rest in 40 sibling groups. A comparison group was drawn from two local schools. Of the 32 singly placed children, 19 were placed in childfree families, and 13 were placed in families with other children already there. Most of the children in sibling groups were full siblings. In 48 of the 72 placements there were siblings who were placed elsewhere.

TABLE 7.2 SIBLINGS PLACED ELSEWHERE

Placement type	Siblings with birth family	Siblings in care elsewhere	Siblings with birth family and in care
Singly Placed	13	6	5
Sibling Group	11	9	4

Source: Rushton et al., 1999.

The siblings who remained with their birth parents were much more likely to be younger siblings and very frequently half-siblings.

Parents in the study were interviewed at three months and twelve months after placement, using a sibling relationship questionnaire. The research team found that sibling placements had better outcomes than singleton placements (in terms of not being in difficulty and not having been disrupted), but only slightly so. Parents reported high levels of conflict and rivalry among placed sibling groups, which improved somewhat over the year, and low levels of warmth between siblings. The severity of the sibling disputes was associated with high levels of strain on the parents.

For new sibling relationships (i.e. those relationships established by virtue of a child joining a family with children already in it) warmth was low, conflict was low, and rivalry was high (in comparison with the control group). Whereas warmth improved over the year, rivalry remained high. For the parents' own children, there was a picture of adjustment difficulties (64 per cent at three months; 67 per cent at twelve months). For some, the difficulties were quite significant.

Logan et al. (1998) looked at risk factors for psychological disturbance in 97 adopted children to see what features of the preplacement history might predict high problem scores after the adoption. The particular factors they explored were: racial congruence; age at placement; presence of siblings; history of abuse; number of previous placement moves; and how long the child waited for a permanent placement. Presence of siblings was associated with high problem scores. In other words, there may be good reasons for placing siblings together, but, as we have already seen, it doesn't necessarily mean that the path ahead will be smooth. There may well be challenges that may prompt carers and professionals alike to ask, 'Is it worth it?' They must be clear about the potential long-term benefits if they are to persevere when the going gets tough.

There might be a number of reasons why siblings have more problems later on in placement. First, siblings by definition will be from larger family groups, and larger groups may present more difficulties than smaller ones. To control for this, studies would have to compare sibling groups in foster/adoptive families with other foster/adoptive families with the same number of children. This type of matching is not common in studies looking at siblings in placement. A second possible reason for a higher level of difficulties is that two siblings are more likely to be affected by the problems of one of the siblings than perhaps two unrelated children in a family. In other words, whilst the problems of each of two unrelated children in placement might affect the other – because of living in the same household – it might not have the same level of impact as two siblings, who because of their closer relationship might have a closer involvement with the problems of the other.

Summarising, there is a high priority put on placing siblings together, which is not necessarily always reflected either in the placements that ultimately become available for sibling groups or in the emphasis on assessment of sibling relationships. However, where siblings can be placed together, the outcomes tend to be better, but there may be difficulties (sibling rivalry, behavioural difficulties). It can be very difficult for carers taking on a sibling group on a permanent basis. They are likely to need considerable support.

Practice Note 7.2   Siblings, loss and being looked after

There are five children in the Burton family, which has been known to the social services for many years. The children are Catherine (17), Malcolm (15), Tony (14), Doris (11) and Thomas (6). The parents are Rose and Frank Burton. They have been married for nearly twenty years. Catherine has never been in the care of the local authority, but at some point before any of the children came into care, she left to live with a paternal aunt, with the agreement of all concerned. The two older boys were made the subject of a Care Order, at different times, for offences committed both jointly and separately, before the Children Act 1989 came into effect. Malcolm was placed in a Community Home locally; Tony was placed out of the area. One factor in the decision not to place the children together was the concern that they would continue their joint offending behaviour. The pattern seemed to be one of mutual incitement to offend. Whilst Malcolm has settled reasonably well, Tony has not. He absconds regularly, and has, as a result, had to have numerous placements. He was in an assessment foster placement, but after only three days he ran away, and has not been located since; that was three weeks ago.

Shortly after Tony's Care Order was made, Mr Burton left the family home to live with another woman, who had two little children of her own, and was expecting a third that was conceived with Mr Burton. Mrs Burton, a woman of limited intellect, with very little local support, and limited resources, struggled to be able to provide a home for the children, but found that her need for stimulation and excitement meant that she would often leave the children unattended whilst she went out to meet men in the local pub. Mrs Burton was challenged about this on numerous occasions. She was reminded of the serious injuries sustained by Thomas on one such occasion when the children were left unattended, and how lucky both she and Thomas were that the injuries were not fatal. Nevertheless, she continued to leave the children unattended, and on one such occasion, they were removed and placed in care under an Emergency Protection Order. Unfortunately, because of the lack of foster homes available to take siblings, they were placed in separate foster homes, with a view towards being able to find a longer-term foster arrangement where they could be accommodated together. They seem to have settled well into their respective placements, although clearly they miss each other and often ask about their older siblings. They seem to ask about them as much as about their mother. They rarely refer to their father, although they have been to his new home, and have met the other children in his house.

Of the five children, Tony seems to be the most affected by the dissolution of the family. He is conspicuously of mixed parentage, and is clearly not the child of his father. This has caused him severe self-recrimination, and he blames himself for the fact that his father and mother split up, and that the family have all been separated. Consequently, he is unable to settle in any establishment where he has been placed.

Recently, it came out that Doris has been seeing her brother, Tony. He has been coming to the school gates when school lets out, and walking with her part of the way home, until they get near the foster home. Then he goes off. The foster carer learned this because one of the other children in the school happened to mention it to her; the child was wondering who it was that Doris often walked home with. When she described the person, the foster carer recognised the description as that of Tony.

When the other children were asked, they reluctantly admitted that Tony often came to see them as well whenever he was on the run from one or other placement. The social worker considers that Tony may feel that seeing himself as the one responsible for the break-up of the family, he has the responsibility for keeping siblings in contact with each other through himself as an intermediary.

Consider:
1. Bilson and Barker (1992) suggest that in some cases attachments to brothers and sisters can be stronger than those to parents, and describe several cases supporting this. Consider how the social worker might ensure that sufficient emphasis is given to assessing the extent to which the siblings are attached to each other in this situation.
2. Consider how the social worker might address the concerns that siblings placed together might mutually incite to deviant behaviour.
3. What practical steps might be taken to preserve and promote existing sibling relationships?

Siblings, loss and bereavement

Sulloway (1996) contends that children become closer to siblings following the loss of a parent:

> Following the loss of a parent, siblings typically become more supportive of one another as they grieve the loss. (p. 137)

Children experience bereavement differently from adults. This is true in at least three ways. First, how they respond is likely to depend upon their developmental stage. Secondly, loss is more likely to interfere with their developmental progress, which at a young age is more rapidly changing than it is for an adult. Finally, there is a greater tendency in children for stress and anxiety to be manifested somatically, through stomach-aches, headaches and other bodily disturbance. One reason for these differences is the child's developmental inability to comprehend the meaning of death. Most children of 6 years or older have some belief in the universality of death, but the understanding of personal mortality is related to both the child's cognitive development and to whether or not he or she had a death-related experience (Reilly *et al.*, 1983).

The significance of a death for the child can be related to the developmental stage of the child (S. Smith and Pennells, 1995). Children at different stages will experience and react to death differently in accordance with their stage of development. With younger children, with insufficient understanding of death, the immediate and shorter-term effects of the death of a sibling are likely to be mediated by the impact the sibling's death has on the parents and immediate caretakers, whereas the longer-term effects are likely to be progressively more influenced by the non-presence of the sibling (as well as the continuing effects of the impact of the loss on the child's parents). This is supported by findings from Leon (1986, 1990) who looked at the present and future impact of perinatal sibling death, a neglected area in the literature. Leon considers the resultant impact to be an interaction of the child's emotional and cognitive reactions with the reactions, distortions and communications of the parents. Clinical case reports suggest that an individual's disturbed responses are related to parental inability to resolve their loss, communicate accurate information about the death to the child, and assist the child in dealing with his or her feelings about death. Emphasising the family's role in mediating the child's mourning, Leon (1986, 1990) suggests that parental distortions and communications about the sibling's death can have long-range repercussions on a child's psychopathology.

McMahon (1992) links the feelings that a child may have about the death of a young sibling with the feelings he or she may have had before the baby died, and considers how this may be mediated by the child's young way of thinking:

> The death of a brother or sister often results in the surviving child feeling guilt that it [*sic*] was not the one who had died. Brothers and sisters are always in competition with one another at some level. Death gives the survivor an unfair victory and a feeling of guilty triumph, as well as of loss, sometimes so severe as to lead to emotional disturbance. (p. 138)

Krasner and Beinart (1989) describe their experiences of running a group for children who lost a sibling through a cot death. Using methods of drawings (frequently of monsters), and storytelling, the therapists helped the children to address feelings of being confused, distressed and, above all, angry. Sessions were used to help the children work through their fears and their feelings of loss.

Let us now consider the consequences of sibling loss and treatment issues.

Sibling loss: consequences

Children's reaction to loss may show itself in the form of behavioural and emotional difficulties, somatic reactions and/or school-based problems. The experience of loss requires the individual to invoke coping mechanisms and these can be divided into psychological tasks required in three different phases: early, middle and late (Baker *et al.*, 1992). Early tasks include understanding the fact that someone has died and the implications of this fact, and self-protection of themselves, their bodies and their families. Middle-phase tasks require accepting and emotionally acknowledging the reality of the loss, exploring and re-evaluating the relationship to the lost love object, and facing and bearing the psychological pain that accompanies the realisation of the loss. The late tasks require the child to evolve a new sense of personal identity that includes the experience of the loss and some identification with the deceased person, but is not limited to them. The child needs to invest in new emotional relationships without an excessive fear of loss and without a constant need to compare the new person to the dead person. The child must be able to consolidate and maintain a durable internal relationship to the lost love object that will survive over time. The child needs to be able to return to the developmental course that may have been interrupted by the experience of loss. Finally, he or she must be able to cope with the return of painful memories and feelings particularly at certain times (such as birthdays and anniversaries of the person's death).

S. Smith and Pennells (1995) draw on the work of Erikson to develop a stage model for children dealing with bereavement. They describe how children are likely to react to loss, depending upon their stage of development at the time of the loss, set out in Table 7.3. Children's reactions to loss of a sibling are complicated by a number of factors: the child's tendency to deny the reality of death; the child's feelings associated with the loss; and the manner in which the parents

TABLE 7.3 STAGES IN DEALING WITH BEREAVEMENT IN CHILDREN

Age	Behaviour
Birth to six months	Irritability, erratic eating, sleeping and crying patterns
Six months to two years	Will search for the lost object or absent caregiver showing signs of separation anxiety; may also become withdrawn, apathetic and lose interest in food, toys and outings
Two to five years	Still unable to grasp the permanence of a separation and if the caregiver is absent they will exhibit behaviours aimed at restoration. A child will cry, cling or show anger at the separation through tantrums or destructive behaviour . . . death of a significant person at this age may undermine the child's security and sense of the reliability of the world.
Five years to nine years	Age of magical thinking; children may feel they are responsible for the death because they had wished it to happen in an angry moment. The social impact of a bereavement at this stage is an additional burden; child has to cope with reactions of peers, school and the wider social environment
Pre-adolescence (9–12 years)	Awareness of the finality of death, that death is common to all living things, that it is universal and inevitable, can lead to recognising the possibility of their own death which may induce psychosomatic symptoms; at this stage children often deny their loss
Adolescence	Grief reaction begins to approximate that of adulthood. Could be increased dependence upon surviving relatives, possibly leading to confusing and conflicting emotions; some adolescents report feeling suicidal; question meaning of life; may explore issues of life after death, the occult and ritualistic behaviour.

Source: Smith and Pennells, 1995.

are able to cope with the loss (Rosen and Cohen, 1981). Loss of a sibling can occur through a number of ways: accidents, disasters and chronic illness. It is important to identify potential difficulties in surviving siblings to prevent later personality difficulties (Pollock, 1986). Consequences of sibling bereavement include somatic complaints, health fears, enuresis, sleep disturbances, jealousy, guilt, depression, antisocial behaviour, school difficulties and crying spells. The role of the funeral and contact with death in helping the subjects to grieve, understand death and restore emotional equilibrium are also related to the sibling's experience of loss (Dyregrov, 1987). The onset of difficulties following sibling bereavement are linked to the deceased child's age, place of death, family size, diagnoses, sex and funeral attendance (McCown and Pratt, 1985).

Adolescence is a particularly difficult time for sibling loss – grief, personal growth and ongoing attachment are significant issues in adolescent sibling loss (Hogan and DeSantis, 1996). The inability to mourn for their siblings and the resultant isolation from family and peers caused by their insistence on a stance of normality are issues that have been described in relation to adolescents. The death of a sibling has an impact on the issues associated with adolescence – consolidation of ego identity, emotional separation from the family, greater investment in the peer group. Loss during adolescence may lead to an emotional over-investment in the family (Mufson, 1985).

A particularly traumatic component of sibling bereavement is when the loss is through homicide, an unfortunately too frequent occurrence in many parts of the USA. Freeman *et al.* (1996) interviewed 15 children about five months after the murder of an older sibling and administered standard tests to the mother (Child Behaviour Checklist) both currently and retrospectively. The study used a control group. The children were found to report more internalising symptoms and more psychiatric disorders when compared with the controls and when compared with how they were seen to be retrospectively. Although the majority showed significant symptoms of depression, anxiety, post-traumatic stress disorder (PTSD) and psychosocial impairment, few received community or mental health services. In a subsequent work, Freeman (1998) discussed the coordination needed in human services agencies to provide a service to meet the 'profound and unmet needs of surviving siblings and family members of youth homicide crimes'. The need for an ethnically sensitive service is emphasised because homicide disproportionately affects young people from ethnic minorities. In addition to basic information about which people become murder victims, which people commit murders and where murders take place, one needs to consider the needs of sibling survivors of homicide, the obstacles to gaining access to needed care and how the needs of survivors can be better served by the mental health, criminal justice and school systems.

Sibling loss: treatment

Helping children come to terms with the loss of a sibling, and avoid the worst psychological and emotional consequences of such an experience requires both a coordinated service and the development of a range of skills. Exchanges between paediatricians and child psychiatrists have been found to be useful in cases of unexplained death of an older sibling (Lebovici, 1988). However, the scope of present professional training does not prepare clinicians to answer parental queries about what they should say to their surviving children and how they might cope with consequent difficulties. The use of mental health consultation may help to provide an effective service and develop an understanding of the bereavement process as it applies to siblings (DeMaso *et al.*, 1997).

Art therapy (Heiney, 1991), bereavement groups (Tonkins and Lambert, 1996) and school programmes (Goldberg and Leyden, 1998) have all been described as effective means of working with children in situations involving bereavement, (including loss of other significant persons as well as siblings, such as parents and grandparents). These methods help to foster the grief process, enhance family communication and support, preserve memories, combat the isolation that children may feel, break the barrier of silence around the subject of death and reduce the symptomatology associated with bereavement.

Practice Note 7.3   Siblings, loss and bereavement

Sister and brother, Samantha (12) and Anthony (10) Jones are close. They live with their parents in a small house in the country, which is fairly remote, and tend to spend a lot of time in each other's company. But it is not only for lack of an alternative; they have always been very close. If given the choice, they will usually choose to spend time together, rather than apart. Samantha was delighted when 'Antnee' (her pet name which she still uses to refer to him) was born and took great pleasure in being allowed and able to do things for him like feed him (when he was old enough), play little stimulation games with him (Peep-O), and even read to him. There have been, as might be expected, the odd disagreement here and there, but their parents have been very pleasantly surprised about how well they get along with each other, so much so that they wonder what all the fuss is about, when they hear other parents talk of sibling rivalry, and the difficulties with squabbling, bickering, and even aggression between brothers and sisters.

Mr Jones is a supervisor in the local chocolate factory, and Mrs Jones works as a school secretary at Samantha's high school. Every morning Mr Jones drives the family in to the local town, where they drop Anthony off at his school first, then mother and daughter at the high school, before carrying on to work. At the end of the day, Mrs Jones and her daughter walk over to Anthony's school and take the bus back home from there.

About eighteen months ago, Mrs Jones discovered a lump under her left breast. It was already fairly large by the time she first noticed it. She went to the GP and was referred for an early appointment with a specialist because of its advanced state. It was considered that the safest course was a mastectomy, and so Mrs Jones was duly admitted.

Ten months ago, during a routine follow-up, it was noted that the cancer had returned. Mrs Jones was treated with a regime of chemotherapy and radiotherapy, but after an initial period of apparent remission, the cancer returned as virulent as ever. Within three months, Mrs Jones succumbed to the cancer and died.

Mr Jones was grief-stricken. He found it very difficult to help the children with their grief; he was too much lost in his own. He deceived himself that they were old enough to understand and find ways to cope. He did feel, however, like a hypocrite, because right up to the end he and his wife had agreed to keep a brave face on it for the children, and although they knew different, they kept telling the children that she would be getting better and would be home soon.

Both children took it very hard, but Anthony seemed to show it more. He completely lost his ability to concentrate on his schoolwork, which suffered as a result. He became surly with the teachers (which was very uncharacteristic), and it seemed as though he had lost his ability to believe adults. He challenged them at every opportunity. Samantha, on the other hand, turned her grief inwards more. She seemed to lose interest in the things that she used to spend lots of time doing, horse-riding, ice-skating, drawing and painting. She seemed to spend a lot of time just moping; not engaged. She spent a lot less time in Anthony's company than she used to. Mr Jones appeared not to notice the changes in his children.

Consider:

1. It is clear that the children need help to come to terms with the loss of their mother. How might the strong bond that existed between Samantha and Anthony be affected by their grief?
2. How might this bond be used to help Samantha and Anthony help each other to adjust to the loss of their mother?

Sibling therapy: a means to help

Much of the preceding discussion has been about children losing siblings. However, there are times when siblings jointly survive a family adversity, often involving loss. Let us now consider how practitioners have attempted to use the sibling relationship to achieve a more positive adjustment for children. The reason for the emphasis here is to remind the reader of the strengths and potentials in the sibling relationships that, because of lack of knowledge and negative attitudes, may not be fully utilised when helping children.

We have already encountered the issue of treatment for sibling difficulties. Let us recap on those, and consider some others. Work on sibling issues has included the need for sibling work when children have been abused (Tower, 1996), treatment of siblings when adoptees are having difficulties (Hoyle, 1995), treatment being required following the birth of a sibling (Weintraub, 1990; Winnicott, 1980), treatment of aggression between siblings (Olson and Roberts, 1987; Adams and Kelly; 1992; Furman and McQuaid; 1992), reconciliation work between victim and perpetrator in sibling incest (Hargett, 1998) and conjoint play therapy work with abused children (Cattanach, 1992).

However, we have not yet looked at the extent to which the sibling can be used as a change agent in the therapeutic process, indeed as a co-therapist in some circumstances. Hamlin and Timberlake (1981) contend that the sibling group is rarely utilised as a viable treatment method and yet, as we have seen, siblings and sibling relationships exert powerful influences within the family system. Work with siblings can be used in conjunction with family therapy or adult treatment, as an adjunct to individual child therapy, or indeed on its own. They look at both limitations and benefits of sibling groupwork. They describe the use of sibling groups to help children cope with sibling separation and loss and to maintain sibling relationships. There are particular steps that the worker can take to involve siblings together when planning or reviewing moves in care. They argue that the sibling group can be mobilised to help children negotiate developmental tasks.

Cattanach (1992), in describing her play therapy work with abused children, looks at conjoint working with siblings. Similarly, Hunter (1993) describes play therapy work with siblings (in a Hawaiian homeless shelter). Several writers (e.g. Schibuk, 1989) have described their experiences of working conjointly with siblings ('sibling therapy') in the context of divorce and its aftermath. Ranieri and Pratt (1978, p. 418) define sibling therapy as 'an attempt to resolve conflicts among

LOSS 207

the children in a family by working with them as a group, apart from their parents'.

Such approaches can be applied also to children who are no longer living with their families, either in foster care or adoptive families. Lewis (1991), describing three types of work with African-American families involved with foster care, explores the meaning of fighting for siblings from chaotic homes and proceeds to explore the use of sibling therapy in work with such children. The focus of the work is on the most immediate issues that are necessary to effect a smooth transition home. She emphasises work that will improve their daily interactions and emphasise their mutuality. She describes this work as valuable even where children may not eventually return to their homes. Hoyle (1995), in considering the treatment of emotionally disturbed adoptees, advocates a long-term process with very specific therapeutic techniques, one of which is sibling therapy. The emphasis in a number of these other approaches is on attachment, and a range of methods for addressing this therapeutically is suggested as well (life books, genograms, ecomaps, life maps, family portraits, family rituals and role playing).

This quick tour of the range of settings and issues within which sibling therapy is being applied suggests two things to us. First, there is tremendous potential to harness the positive forces within sibling relationships to help children overcome the worst effects of adverse circumstances and occurrences. Secondly, it reminds us that it is probably a resource that is insufficiently utilised.

Summary: loss and sibling relationships

This chapter began with a consideration of sibling relationships as attachment relationships, and argues, perhaps against the tide of opinion, that sibling relationships *are* attachment relationships if one defines attachment in terms of social relationships rather than biological ones. The chapter then considered loss that children experience in the context of separating and/or divorcing parents, looking at three aspects: (a) the sibling relationship in the context of losing a parent through divorce; (b) the separation of siblings from each other in the increasingly likely scenario of the children going to different parents; and (c) the adjustment of children to new sibling relationships created by parents remarrying – stepsibs. But brothers and sisters may also experience loss, from parents, from each other, through the process of being looked after, or being placed for adoption. Here, the evidence in support of the presumption of children being placed together is considered, although it was noted that current evidence suggests that placement apart from siblings is still the norm rather than the exception. Further, the challenges for long-term carers of sibling groups are considered. Bereavement through loss of a sibling is then considered, focusing on the significance of the developmental stage a child is at when the loss occurs, and highlighting work that might be undertaken to help a bereaved sibling. The chapter ends with a consideration of the potential for siblings to act as a co-facilitator in achieving therapeutic objectives – sibling therapy.

8 Into Practice

The reader will see an underlying theme in the chronological way in which this book has reflected the developing complexity of understanding regarding sibling relationships. We began with an understanding of sibling relationships that was based on simplistic polarised conceptions, discourses, if you will, of good and evil. From mythology, legends, and folklore, brothers and sisters are portrayed as archetypes, frequently, but not invariably, aligning along gender lines (sister relationships are warm, nurturing, loyal, supportive; brother relations are rivalrous, competitive, hostile and aggressive). Relationships with siblings are characterised by love (being a primary support in a harsh world where cooperation promotes survival) and hate (rivalrous competition for scarce resources beginning with parental love, affection, and even birthright and later struggling to obtain the means of existence).

Levy, from a psychoanalytic perspective, explored the rivalry dimension of sibling relationships, attempting to be scientific and rigorous. It was an attempt to focus on a single characteristic of the sibling relationship (rivalry) and understand it from a scientific perspective – what are the correlates of rivalry in the way that brothers and sisters relate to each other? With the development of family therapy approaches, and systemic understanding we see the location of sibling relationships in a network of other relationships within the family, and with the work of Toman we have a taxonomy of sibling relationship types derived from the relatively restricted dimensions of birth order and gender.

Then we have the work of researchers like Brody, Dunn, McHale, Slomkowski and Stocker. The more recent approach looks in detail at the correlates of sibling relationships, asking a wide range of research questions about the influences on, and of, sibling relationships in our lives, from childhood to adult. I have considered a number of these important questions.

The underlying theme here is one of an increasing sophistication of our understanding, coinciding with a gradually arising awareness of the immense complexity of sibling relationships that we had previously tried to understand with simplistic conceptual tools. There are observations to make here. First, this is a natural process of scientific discovery – researching an issue leads to more and more sophisticated questions that need to be asked. There is no shortcoming here; it is just the way things are – how we acquire knowledge. Secondly, however, we must be aware of the influence of earlier understandings on later understandings. We must be prepared to let go of earlier simplistic concepts and integrate the newer, and more sophisticated, understandings of how siblings can influence, and are influenced by, each other and the wider social network. Failure to do this is a shortcoming and must be resisted. Failure to replace earlier global conceptions of sibling relationships with more recent, empirical- and research-based understandings is rightly subject to just criticism.

What is needed is a greater practice emphasis on sibling relationships when working to support families with children in need in the community, intervening in cases of child abuse, and arranging for children to be looked after. As has been noted, it is only in placement practice that there has been any serious focus on sibling relationships. We need to focus on how we should, and could, develop a greater emphasis on sibling relationships that will counter-balance the historical parent–child orientation to child development. We know a lot more now than previously about sibling relationships, but to date, there is little evidence that the knowledge has permeated into practice.

There are three particular areas that are relevant to the task of integrating knowledge of sibling relationships into family practice. First, where sibling relationships are strong and positive, we must begin to maximise the potential of siblings to act as therapeutic agents; to use the power of sibling relationships synergistically so that each and every sibling's potential to help other siblings overcome adversity and harm is maximised. Secondly, where sibling relationships are not strong, we must learn how to build them. I do not believe that most practitioners, if given the task to improve a sibling relationship, would know how to begin (apart from promoting and maintaining contact if the siblings are separated). They have been given no input on this. There is nothing in most professional training about sibling relationships. How can we do this? What tools do we have that will help us? Finally, where sibling relationships are, or have been, abusive, then we have to work with that in the context of a fuller knowledge of the nature and long-term significance of sibling relationships. Let us now consider these three areas.

Utilising the strengths of sibling relationships

Assessing strengths in families requiring professional help has not been a prominent feature in family practice generally. Despite it being long known that strengths are important, the problem-oriented focus of professional intervention has kept family practice firmly rooted in the negative orientation towards the problems, rather than a more positive orientation towards the strengths that families have which may provide solutions.

A strengths-based approach to child-rearing in general, and child maltreatment in particular, is linked to the emphasis in recent years on understanding the operation of resilience in children. Although sibling relationships have not featured prominently in studies looking at resilience we may find they contribute positively to children's resilience in the face of adversity.

The lack of emphasis on strengths is redressed, however, in the new guidance on assessment – the *Framework for the Assessment of Children in Need and Their Families* (Department of Health *et al.*, 2000). The *Framework* provides integrated guidelines for the assessment of both children in need (Children Act 1989, section 17) and children who are at risk of abuse (Children Act 1989, section 47), arising from policy changes derived from *Child Protection: Messages from Research* (Department of Health, 1995). It is clear from the structure of the assessment categories adopted that the material builds on the previous *Looking After Children* material (Parker *et al.*, 1991). However, the *Assessment and Action Records* themselves do not appear to place a great deal of weight on sibling relationships. The emphasis is on the extent of contact between siblings who are looked after.

The *Framework* is based upon three components of assessment: the child's developmental needs, the parents' or caregivers' capacity to respond appropriately and the wider family and environmental factors. It endorses the use of existing and yet-to-be-developed questionnaires and scales for assessing families, for example:

- Strengths and Difficulties Questionnaire
- Parenting Daily Hassles Scale
- Adult Well-Being Scale
- Home Conditions Scale
- Adolescent Well-Being Scale
- Family Activity Scales (in age bands)
- Recent Life Events Questionnaire.

These scales are intended for selective use, depending upon which are appropriate for the work being undertaken. According to the guidance, they were selected from a range of questionnaires and scales available on the basis of their appropriateness and their ease of use. They do not, for example, require any formal training. The first of these scales is clearly an attempt to enable practitioners to focus on the strengths within families needing a service.

As with any intervention process, the sequence would be assessment, planning and implementation, and review. Like any other aspect of family functioning, sibling relationships would need to be assessed, so what tools do we have to assess sibling relationships? To begin with, there is the *Sibling Relationship Checklist* (Department of Health, 1991) primarily developed as a tool for practitioners. Since its appearance there has been virtually no discussion about its strengths and weaknesses as a tool, and one is inclined to believe this is because it has not been used. This may be because it can be a very time-consuming process, especially if there is more than the average number of siblings in a family. However, the tool can be useful to engage parents in focused discussion about their children's various sibling relationships. Sanders (2002) used it in a study of social work with siblings. Whereas in some cases social workers were saying that it provided information that they were aware of, but the parents were not, in others it was the other way round. In some cases, however, the tool was not found to be useful. Certainly some of the sections were less helpful and the language was not user-friendly. Overall, however, it had considerable merit as a tool.

What other tools are available? There are a number of tools for working with young children, and these lend themselves easily to working jointly with siblings, especially where not too far apart in age. The *Framework for the Assessment of Children in Need and Their Families* (Department of Health *et al.*, 2000) disaggregates the emphasis on direct work with children into four components, seeing children, observing children, talking to children, and activities with children. It is argued here that these can be undertaken with children *conjointly*, that is with brothers and sisters together at the same time.

Genograms (family trees) are a useful tool. For many years, their use in child protection has been endorsed (Department of Health, 1988), and yet it would appear that they are still not being widely used. Research I undertook examining 29 child protection files (Sanders, 2002), and more recent experience on the Postqualifying Child Care Award Programme, have convinced me that even very experienced and senior child and family workers are rarely using them as a tool for practice. An even greater value than that which genograms have for adults (workers and parents) in being able to understand complex information about complex families is the potential value that they have for the children. Any misconceptions children have about their relations to their brothers and sisters can be clarified. Doing them jointly with siblings would create opportunities for siblings to explore their connections with each other, and perhaps contribute to understanding about how they are alike, and different in various ways from, each other.

Whilst the genogram incorporates an element of family development, there are other tools for working with children that specifically focus on the longitudinal component (the life snake, 'my history'), and they too can also be used with sibling groups. They would, however, instead of being simply a longitudinal tool for the individual child, also enable the family to be seen as a theatrical stage upon which some of the children make their entrances at different times, in different ways (sibling birth, families merging, etc.), and provide for a consideration of issues of 'upstaging', and other dynamics associated with the arrival of others. It would also provide opportunities for considering the dynamics and emotional impact of siblings leaving the stage (e.g. siblings dying, siblings being separated from each other through care or family dissolution).

Building sibling relationships

There are very few publications specifically designed to help build positive sibling relationships. The work of Faber and Mazlish (1987) is a notable exception. It was a bestseller in the USA, and although targeted at a lay audience appears to put forward advice based on findings from research into sibling relationships. The material is based on parenting workshops undertaken by the authors, and is written very accessibly. For example, they use the intriguing metaphor of getting people in the group to imagine that their spouse has brought home a new spouse and instructed them to learn to get on with the new spouse; be helpful; avoid rivalry; help the new arrival to adjust, etc. – the same things a parent might typically expect a sibling to do in the face of the arrival of a new sibling. Let us look at some of the advice offered by Faber and Mazlish (1987):

> Brothers and sisters need to have their feelings about each other acknowledged.

1. Instead of dismissing negative feelings about a sibling, acknowledge the feelings;
2. Give children in fantasy what they don't have in reality;
3. Help children channel their hostile feelings into symbolic or creative outlets;
4. Stop hurtful behaviour. Show how angry feelings can be discharged safely. Refrain from attacking the attacker;
5. Avoid unfavourable comparisons;
6. Avoid favourable comparisons;
7. Instead of worrying about giving equal amounts, focus on each child's individual needs;
8. Instead of claiming equal love, show children how they're loved uniquely;
9. Equal time can feel like less;
10. Give time in terms of need;
11. Don't give your attention to the aggressor; attend to the injured party instead;
12. No more bullies; no more victims;
13. No more problem children. Instead of focusing on children's disabilities, focus on their abilities;
14. Unhelpful responses to kids who are fighting; how to respond helpfully to kids who are fighting;
15. Kids working it out;
16. When the fighting is heading toward hurting,
    1. describe
    2. establish limits
    3. separate them.

The authors describe four levels of intervention. Normal bickering does not require any intervention. However, when the situation heats up a bit (second stage), then adult intervention might be helpful. In this case, the adult should acknowledge the child(ren)'s anger, reflect each child's point of view, make sure that the problem is described with respect, and express confidence in the children's ability to find their own solution. If the situation starts to get possibly dangerous (stage three) the parent should enquire if it is real fighting or play fighting (because play fighting is permitted, but real fighting is not). The parent might wish to remind the children that play fighting is by mutual consent only. In the final stage, should the situation become definitely dangerous, then the parent should describe what they see and separate the children.

There is a lot to be said for this type of approach. Clearly much of the material relates to issues we have already discussed. For example, we have looked at the issue of whether or not parents should intervene in sibling disputes. For Faber and Mazlish (1987) it is not an all-or-none question (which any parent probably already knows) and which we concluded from an overview of the literature. There are ways to intervene which, as they suggest, allow the children to find solutions they can live with, and can raise their esteem about solution-finding abilities and skills. However, they are also clear that a weaker child should not be sacrificed to a more powerful child in the name of positive non-interventionism.

There are also, however, potential pitfalls with this approach. To begin with, one always needs to be aware of taking material from one cultural context and attempting to apply it in another. A further shortcoming of this approach, however, is that the authors fail to appreciate that creativity in a problem-solving approach (indeed creativity in any sense) is a commodity that is unequally distributed amongst the population, and whilst some may find the methods put forward very helpful for tapping into their ability to find creative solutions, others may find that the methods call upon skills and abilities that they just do not have. One can speculate on the extent to which these types of skills are present in the kinds of families that professionals work with. Although no information is given in the book, one is inclined to suspect that the Faber and Mazlish audience were predominantly articulate middle-class families. Of course, that being said, we are ever in danger of underestimating the abilities and skills that families have, even those who are hard-pressed by social disadvantage. Learning not to underestimate the abilities of client families is one of the cornerstones of developing better practice.

Working with abusive sibling relationships

Work with abusing and abused siblings is different from the work with other types of sibling difficulties. There are also likely to be differences between work with sibling abuse and work where the abuser is in a different relationship to the victim. It therefore may be that even workers who are experienced in working with adult abusers and child victims may not have the contextual understanding of the normal patterns of sibling relationships to help them understand the implications when the abuse is between siblings. What might some of these differences be? We will look at both physical abuse and sexual abuse, separately, but first consider aspects common to both.

In both physical and sexual abuse one impact will be to impair the future sibling relationship. In view of the longevity of sibling relationships, this damage can continue for a very long time, well into old age. Whereas many siblings are coming together later in life to provide each other with support through the ageing process (even if this is not in the form of extensive contact), for siblings where abuse has taken place, this may less likely. Whilst sibling relationships in later life may be undermined by the abuse, the fact that siblings are likely to live as long as each other may also mean that the resolution, or lack of resolution of the difficulties, may extend over a longer period of time.

Sibling physically abusive relationships

Unlike relationships between parents and children, there is less of an expectation that the relationship should be a positive one. People expect siblings to be horrible to each other, or at the very least are not as surprised about it as when they learn about parents being abusive towards children. In the case of parents, the abuse violates socially accepted views about how parents should behave towards children. In the case of siblings it does not, and may even confirm stereotyped views that people have about siblings ('siblings are rivalrous, jealous and aggressive').

The task, as we have described, is for the professional to draw the line between ordinary aggressive and hostile behaviour and that which is over the line. With parents, no amount of overtly aggressive and hostile behaviour would be considered as a part of the normal parenting relationship, and would certainly not be expected or tolerated. Parents are not meant to be aggressive towards their children.

Strauss *et al.* (1980) give a useful illustration of the difference between the acceptability of sibling violence and parental abuse. They describe the fictional situation of a mother and child in a hospital emergency room. The child's face is covered with blood from a cut over his eye; his lip is swollen. They consider the amount of social disapproval if it should be the case that the others in the waiting room believe the parent to be responsible for the child's injuries. There are whispers and murmurings and 'looks of shock and revulsion' (p.76) amongst the others in the waiting room. Then, the reader is asked to imagine that the parent is not responsible for the injuries, but, as explained by the parent, they are caused by a sibling. The social disapproval transforms into sympathy for the mother. And yet, as pointed out by the authors, the injuries are the same. This example suggests to Strauss *et al.* (1980) that sibling violence is more accepted than the same violence caused by a parent. They subsequently consider the history of sibling violence and contend that violence between siblings is the most common form of violence within families.

It is to be hoped that professionals would not subscribe to the stereotypical view of sibling relationships as characterised by hostility and rivalry, but understand that sibling relationships are as multi-variate in character as individual personalities are, and therefore require an assessment as to their particular quality before making decisions.

Sibling sexually abusive relationships

With sexually abusive relationships between siblings the selection of the sibling as the target may well be opportunistic. This should not be seen as support for the denial and minimisation characteristic of abusers, but fits in with a conception of sexual abusers actively choosing targets and using grooming methods to overcome the resistance of the victim. However, as we have seen, there may be a greater tendency for force to be used in the sexual abuse carried out by siblings than by father figures. Where there are other siblings in the family, similar dynamics may operate as were found in families where the abuser was a father-figure, that is the other children may blame the victim for any consequences to the family rather than the abuser, to the point of preferring that the victim had not told in the first place, but instead continued to endure the abuse.

Laredo (1982) describes both the management of cases of sibling incest and the therapeutic considerations. For the management of cases, he focuses on the denial of the impact, a family orientation (whilst maintaining a stance of the victim's needs as being primary), the ability of the therapist to handle the disclosure, the initial contact, the need for a calm and reassuring approach, and a focus on the context of the abuse. For Laredo (1982, p. 185), 'The incest is a symptom, not the problem', thus appearing to commit himself to a family dynamic perspective on the origins of sibling incest. For the therapeutic considerations he focuses on the need for therapist determination, flexibility (in terms of being available), an ability to confront, the need for advocacy for the child victim, a willingness to address family secrets, and the wider contextual factors that may have a bearing on the sibling abuse. However, it must be noted that in many respects there are few differences between the approach that he endorses in respect of siblings, and the approach that one might adopt in working with intra-familial sexual abuse where the abuser is the father or father-figure.

Forward and Buck (1978) note the parallels between father–daughter incest and older brother–younger sister incest on the one hand, and mother–son incest and older sister–younger brother incest on the other. They, like Wiehe (1990), focus more on how to prevent sibling incest than on how to deal with it.

Summary: into practice

I have described in this chapter three important components of work with siblings: utilising the strengths, improving the relationships and working with sibling abuse. To work effectively in families where there are siblings, practitioners need to have a better understanding of sibling relationships. Family work that is based on as full an under-standing of sibling relationships as our current understanding of parenting relationships, would be much more solidly based. Whether working with families in the community to provide family support services for a child in need, working with children looked after away from home, or working in child protection situations, an under-standing of the relationships that siblings have with each other should be a significant component of both the assessment and the interven-tion. At present it is a neglected component of family work.

Appendix A

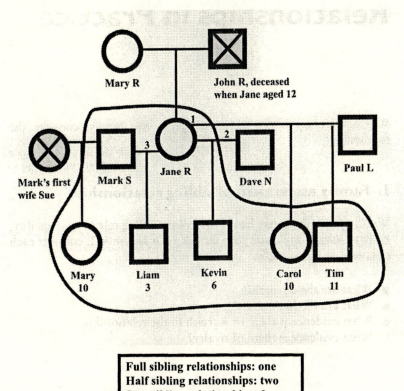

Mary R

John R, deceased when Jane aged 12

Mark's first wife Sue

Mark S

Jane R

Dave N

Paul L

Mary 10

Liam 3

Kevin 6

Carol 10

Tim 11

Full sibling relationships: one
Half sibling relationships: two
Step sibling relationships: four

FIGURE A.1 GENOGRAM IN A COMPLEX FAMILY SITUATION

Appendix B: Assessing Sibling Relationships in Practice

Where there are sibling relationships in the family, consider the following:

1. Family assessment of sibling relationships

Working with the entire family to explore sibling relationship quality, perhaps using a flip chart page set out as in Figure A.2, consider each relationship individually.

- What are the strengths?
- What are the limitations?
- What evidence is there of warmth in the relationship?
- What evidence is there of rivalry?
- What evidence is there of hostility?

2. Assessing perceived experience of differential treatment

- Are there favoured children within the families?
- Are there children in the family who are disfavoured?
- Is there agreement between family members about which children are favoured and which ones disfavoured?
- What perceptions are held by family members about how a child who is either favoured or disfavoured might influence the way the brother(s) and sister(s) get on with each other?
- If it is felt to be an issue of concern for the family, how might it be addressed?

3. Conjoint work with siblings

Undertake the following tasks with the siblings together:

■ an ecomap for each of the children (see Department of Health, 1988);
■ a family life snake (a pictorial representation of the family chronology; noting in particular the points of arrival and departures of siblings);
■ a family genogram (see Appendix A).

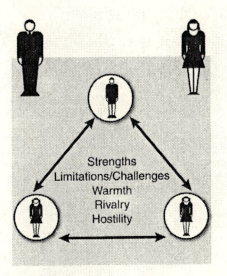

FIGURE A.2 EVALUATING SIBLING RELATIONSHIPS

References

Abarbanel, J. (1983) The revival of the sibling experience during the mother's second pregnancy, *Psychoanalytic Study of the Child*, 38: 353–79.

Abrahams, J. and Hoey, H. (1994) Sibling incest in a clergy family: a case study, *Child Abuse & Neglect*, 18(12): 1029–35.

Abramovitch, R., Corter, C., Pepler, D.J. and Stanhope, L. (1986) Sibling and peer interaction: a final follow-up and a comparison, *Child Development*, 57: 217–29.

Adams, C. and Kelly, M. (1992) Managing sibling aggression: overcorrection as an alternative to time-out, *Behavior Therapy*, 23(4): 707–17.

Adler, A. (1958) *The Individual Psychology of Alfred Adler*, New York: Basic Books.

Adler, N. and Schutz, J. (1995) Sibling incest offenders, *Child Abuse & Neglect*, 19(7): 811–19.

Ainscough, C. and Toon, K. (1993) *Breaking Free*, London: Sheldon Press.

Ainslie, R. (1999) Twinship and twinning reactions in siblings, in Akhtar, S. and Kramer, S. (eds) *Brothers and Sisters: Developmental, Dynamic, and Technical Aspects of the Sibling Relationship*, North Bergen, NJ: Jason Aronson, ch. 2, pp. 25–52.

Ainsworth, M., Blehar, M., Waters, E. and Wall, S. (1978) *Patterns of Attachment: A Psychological Study of the Strange Situation*, Hillsdale, NJ, USA: Lawrence Erlbaum.

Akhtar, S. and Kramer, S. (1999) Beyond the parental orbit: brothers, sisters, and others, in Akhtar, S. and Kramer, S. (eds) *Brothers and Sisters: Developmental, Dynamic, and Technical Aspects of the Sibling Relationship*, North Bergen, NJ: Jason Aronson, ch. 1, pp. 3–24.

Aldridge, J. and Becker, S. (1993) Punishing children for caring: the hidden cost of young carers, *Children & Society*, 7(4): 376–87.

Abramovitch, R., Corter, C. and Lando, B. (1979) Sibling interaction in the home, *Child Development*, 50: 997–1003.

Anderson, E., Greene, S., Hetherington, E. and Clingempeel, W. (1999) The dynamics of parental remarriage: adolescent, parent, and sibling influences, in Hetherington, E. (ed.) *Coping with Divorce, Single Parenting, and Remarriage: A Risk and Resiliency Perspective*, Mahwah, NJ: Lawrence Erlbaum Associates, Inc, pp. 295–319.

Angelou, M. (1969) *I Know Why the Caged Bird Sings*, New York, Random House.

Araji, S., and Bosek, R. (1997) Sexually abusive children: family, extrafamilial environments, and situational risk factors, pp. 89–118 in Araji, S. (ed.) *Sexually Aggressive Children: Coming to Understand Them*, Thousand Oaks, CA: Sage Publications, Inc., pp. 89–118.

Arnold, L. and Carnahan, J. (1990) Child divorce stress, in Arnold, L. (ed.) *Childhood Stress* (Wiley Series in Child and Adolescent Mental Health), New York, NY: John Wiley & Sons, pp. 374–403.

Atkins, S. (1989) Siblings of handicapped children, *Child and Adolescent Social Work Journal*, 6(4): 271–82.

Bagedahl-Strindlund, M. (1997) Parapartum mental illness: an interview follow-up study, *Acta Psychiatrica Scandinavica*, 95(5): 389–95.

Bagenholm, A., and Gillberg, C. (1991) Psychosocial effects on siblings of children with autism and mental retardation: a population-based study, *Journal of Mental Deficiency Research*, 35(4): 291–307.

Baher, E., Hyman, C., Jones, C., Jones, R., Kerr, A. and Mitchell, R. (1976) *At Risk: An Account of the Work of the Battered Child Research Department, NSPCC*, London: Routledge & Kegan Paul.

Baker, J., Sedney, M. and Gross, E. (1992) Psychological tasks for bereaved children, *American Journal of Orthopsychiatry*, 62(1): 105–16.

Bank, S. (1992) Remembering and reinterpreting sibling bonds, in Boer, F. and Dunn, J. (eds) *Children's Sibling Relationships: Developmental and Clinical Issues*, Hillsdale, NJ: Lawrence Erlbaum Associates, ch. 10, pp. 139–51.

Bank, S. and Kahn, M. (1997, orig. 1982) *The Sibling Bond*, New York, NY: Basic Books, Inc.

Barnes, G.G. (1996) The mentally ill parent and the family system, in Goepfert, M., Webster, J. *et al.*. (eds) *Parental Psychiatric Disorder: Distressed Parents and Their Families*, New York: Cambridge University Press, pp. 45–59.

Barnes, P. (1995) *Personal, Social and Emotional Development of Children*, Oxford/Milton Keynes: Blackwell/Open University.

Baskett, L. (1985) Understanding family interactions: most probable reactions by parents and siblings, *Child and Family Behavior Therapy*, 7(2): 41–50.

Baydar, N., Greek, A. and BrooksGunn, J. (1997) A longitudinal study of the effects of the birth of a sibling during the first 6 years of life, *Journal of Marriage and the Family*, 59(4): 939–56.

Baydar, N., Hyle, P. and BrooksGunn, J. (1997) A longitudinal study of the effects of the birth of a sibling during preschool and early grade school years, *Journal of Marriage and the Family*, 59(4): 957–65.

Beardsall, L. (1987) Sibling conflict in middle childhood, unpublished Ph.D dissertation, University of Cambridge.

Begun, A. (1995) Sibling relationships and foster care placements for young children, *Early Child Development and Care*, 106: 237–50.

Bell, J. E. (1961) *Family Group Therapy*, London: Bookstall Publications.

Bell, L. and Bell, D. (1982) Family climate and the role of the female adolescent: determinants of adolescent functioning, *Family Relations: Journal of Applied Family and Child Studies*, 31(4): 519–27.

Benko, D. (1993) Morgan le Fay and King Arthur in Malory's *Works* and Marion Zimmer Bradley's *The Mists of Avalon*: sibling discord and the fall of the round table, in Mink, J.S. and Ward, J.D. (eds) *The Significance of Sibling Relationships in Literature*, Bowling Green, OH: Bowling Green State University Popular Press.

Bennett, J. (1990) Nonintervention into siblings' fighting as a catalyst for learned helplessness, *Psychological Reports*, 66(1): 139–45.

Berndt, T. J. and Bulleit, T. N. (1985) Effects of sibling relationships on preschoolers' behaviour at home and at school, *Developmental Psychology*, 21(5): 761–7.

Berridge, D. and Cleaver, H. (1987) *Foster Home Breakdown*, Oxford: Blackwell.

Bess, B. and Janssen, Y. (1982) Incest: a pilot study, *Hillside Journal of Clinical Psychiatry*, 4(1): 39–52.

Bettelheim, B. (1976) *The Uses of Enchantment: The Meaning and Importance of Fairy Tales*, Harmondsworth: Penguin.

Bibby, A. and Becker, S. (2000) *Young Carers in Their Own Words*, London: Calouste Gulbenkian Foundation.

Bilson, A. and Barker, R. (1992) Siblings of children in care or accommodation: a neglected area of practice, *Practice*, 6(4): 307–18.

Bischoff, L. and Tingstrom, D. (1991) Siblings of children with disabilities: psychological and behavioural characteristics, *Counselling Psychology Quarterly*, 4(4): 311–21.

Blanch, A.K., Nicholson, J. and Purcell, J. (1998) Parents with severe mental illness and their children: the need for human services integration, in Levin, B.L. and Blanch, A.K. (eds) *Women's Mental Health Services: A Public Health Perspective*, Thousand Oaks, CA: Sage Publications, pp. 201–14.

Bloch, J., Margolis, J. and Seitz, M. (1994) Feelings of shame: siblings of handicapped children, in Gitterman, A. and Shulman, L. (eds) *Mutual Aid Groups, Vulnerable Populations, and the Life Cycle (2nd ed.)*, New York: Columbia University Press, pp. 97–115.

Blyth, E. and Waddell, A. (1999) Young carers – the contradictions of being a child carer, in The Violence Against Children Study Group (eds) *Children, Child Abuse and Child Protection*, Chichester: John Wiley & Sons, ch. 2, pp. 21–32.

Boer, F., Goedhart, A. and Treffers, P. (1992) Siblings and their parents, in Boer, F. and Dunn, J. (eds) *Children's Sibling Relationships: Developmental and Clinical Issues*, Hillsdale, NJ: Lawrence Erlbaum Associates, ch. 3, pp. 41–54.

Bossard, J.H.S. and Boll, E.S. (1956) *The Large Family System*, Philadelphia: University of Pennsylvania Press.

Bowen, M. (1978) *Family Therapy in Clinical Practice*, New York: Jason Aronson.

Bowker, L.H., Arbitel, M. and McFerron, J. R. (1988) On the relationship between wife beating and child abuse, in Yllö, K. and Bograd, M. (eds) *Feminist Perspectives on Wife Abuse*, Newbury Park, CA: Sage.

Bowlby, J. (1969) *Attachment and Loss*, 2 vols, London: Hogarth Press.

Breslau, N. (1982) Siblings of disabled children: birth order and age-spacing effects, *Journal of Abnormal Child Psychology*, 10(1): 85–95.

Brody, G.H. (1998) Sibling relationship quality: its causes and consequences. *Annual Review of Psychology*, 49: 1–24.

Brody, G.H. and Stoneman, Z. (1994) Sibling relationships and their association with parental differential treatment, in Hetherington, E.M., Reiss, D. and Plomin, R. (1994) *Separate Social Worlds of Siblings: The Impact of Nonshared Environment on Development*, Hillsdale, NJ: Lawrence Erlbaum Associates, Inc., ch. 5, pp. 129–42.

Brody, G.H., Stoneman, Z. and Burke, M. (1987a) Child temperaments, maternal differential behavior, and sibling relationships, *Developmental Psychology*, 23: 354–62.

Brody, G.H., Stoneman, Z. and Burke, M. (1987b) Family system and individual child correlates of sibling behavior, *American Journal of Orthopsychiatry*, 57(4): 561–9.

Brody, G.H., Stoneman, Z. and Gauger, K. (1996) Parent-child relationships, family problem-solving behavior, and sibling relationship quality: the moderating role of sibling temperament, *Child Development*, 67(3): 1289–3000.

Brody, G.H., Stoneman, Z. and McCoy, J.K. (1992a) Associations of maternal and paternal direct and differential behavior with sibling relationships: contemporaneous and longitudinal analyses, *Child Development*, 63(1): 82–92.

Brody, G.H., Stoneman, Z. and McCoy, J.K. (1992b) Parental differential treatment of siblings and sibling differences in negative emotionality, *Journal of Marriage and the Family*, 54: 643–51.

Brody, G.H., Stoneman, Z. and McCoy, J.K. (1994) Forecasting sibling relationships in early adolescence from child temperament and family processes in middle childhood, *Child Development*, 65: 771–84.

Brody, G.H., Stoneman, Z., McCoy, J.K. and Forehand, R. (1992) Contemporaneous and longitudinal associations of sibling conflict with family relationship assessments and family discussions about sibling problems, *Child Development*, 63(2): 391–400.

Brody, G.H., Stoneman, Z., Smith, T. and Gibson, N.M. (1999) Sibling relationships in rural African American families, *Journal of Marriage and the Family*, 61(4): 1046–57.

Brody, L.R., Copeland, A.P., Sutton, L.S., Richardson, D.R. and Guyer, M. (1998). Mommy and daddy like you best: perceived family favoritism in relation to affect, adjustment and family process, *Journal of Family Therapy*, 20(3): 269–91.

Bronfenbrenner, U. (1979) *The Ecology of Human Development*, Cambridge, MA, Harvard University Press.

Bronfenbrenner, U. and Crouter, A. (1983) The evolution of environmental models in developmental research, in Kessen, W. (ed.) *The Handbook of Child Psychology: Vol 1. History, Theory and Methods*, New York: John Wiley & Sons, pp. 358–414.

Brook, J., Whiteman, M., Gordon, A. and Brook, D. (1990) The role of older brothers in younger brothers' drug use viewed in the context of parent and peer influences, *Journal of Genetic Psychology*, 151(1): 59–75.

Browne, K. (1995) Predicting Maltreatment, in Reder, P. and Lucey, C. (eds) *Assessment of Parenting: Psychiatric and Psychological Contributions*, London: Routledge, ch. 8, pp. 118–35.

Bryant, B. and Crockenberg, S. (1980) Correlates and dimensions of prosocial behaviour: a study of female siblings and their mothers, *Child Development*, 51: 529–44.

Buchanan, A. (1996) *Cycles of Child Maltreatment: Facts, Fallacies and Interventions*, Chichester: John Wiley & Sons.

Buhrmester, D. (1992) The Developmental course of sibling and peer relationships, in Boer, F. and Dunn, J. (eds) *Children's Sibling Relationships: Developmental and Clinical Issues*, Hillsdale, NJ: Lawrence Erlbaum Associates, Inc., ch. 2, pp. 19–40.

Buhrmester, D. and Furman, W. (1987) The development of companionship and intimacy, *Child Development*, 58: 1101–13.

Bullock, B.M. and Dishion, T.J. (2002) Sibling collusion and problem behavior in early adolescence: toward a process model for family mutuality, *Journal Of Abnormal Child Psychology*, 30(2): 143–53.

Burton, S. and Parks, L. (1994) Self-esteem, locus of control, and career aspirations of college-age siblings of individuals with disabilities, *Social Work Research*, 18(3): 178–185.

Canavan, M., Meyer, W. and Higgs, D. (1992) The female experience of sibling incest, *Journal of Marital and Family Therapy*, 18(2): 129–42.

Cantwell, D. and Baker, L. (1984) Parental mental illness and psychiatric disorders in 'at risk' children, *Journal of Clinical Psychiatry*, 45(12): 503–7.

Carey, G. (1992) Twin imitation for antisocial behavior: implications for genetics and family research, *Journal of Abnormal Psychology*, 101: 18–25.

Carmichael, C. (1977) *Non-sexist Childraising*, Boston, MA: Beacon Press.

Carter, J., Stacey, W. and Shupe, A. (1988) Male violence against women: assessment of the generational transfer hypothesis, *Deviant Behavior*, 9(3): 259–73.

Cassell, D. and Coleman, R. (1995) Parents with psychiatric problems, in Reder, P. and Lucey, C. (eds) *Assessment of Parenting: Psychiatric and psychological contributions*, London: Routledge, ch. 11.

Cattanach, A. (1992) *Play Therapy with Abused Children*, London: Jessica Kingsley Publishers.

Chase, N.D. (1999) (ed.) *Burdened Children: Theory, Research, and Treatment of Parentification*, Thousand Oaks, CA: Sage Publications.

Cherlin, A., Furstenberg, F. Jr, Chase-Lansdale, P., Kiernan, K., Robins, P., Morrison, D. and Teitler, J. (1993) Longitudinal studies of effects of divorce on children in Great Britain and the United States, in Gauvain, M. and Cole, M. (eds) *Readings on the Development of Children*, Oxford: W.H. Freeman and Co., ch. 29, pp. 267–73.

Christensen, C. (1990) A case of sibling incest: a balancing act, *Journal of Strategic and Systemic Therapies*, 9(4): 1–5.

Cicirelli, V. (1972) The effect of sibling relationship on concept learning of young children taught by child-teachers, *Child Development*, 43: 282–7.

Cicirelli, V. (1992) *Family Caregiving: Autonomous and Paternalistic Decision Making*, London: Sage.

Cicirelli, V. (1994) Sibling Relationships in cross-cultural perspective, *Journal of Marriage and the Family*, 56: 7–20.

Cicirelli, V. (1995) *Sibling Relationships Across the Life Span*, New York: Plenum Press.

Clausen, H. (1984) Normale soskende i en familie med et handicappet barn (Normal siblings in a family with a handicapped child), *Skolepsykologi*, 21(1): 3–25.

Cleaver, H., Unell, I. and Aldgate, J. (1999) *Children's Needs – Parenting Capacity: The Impact of Parental Mental Illness, Problem Alcohol and Drug Use, and Domestic Violence on Children's Development*, London: The Stationery Office.

Coale, H. (1999) Therapeutic rituals and rites of passage: helping parentified children and their families, in Chase, N. (ed.) *Burdened Children: Theory, Research, and Treatment of Parentification*, Thousand Oaks, CA: Sage Publications, Inc., pp. 132–40.

Cohen, M. (1993) First Sisters in the English Novel: Charlotte Lennox to Susan Ferrier, in Mink, J.S. and Ward, J.D. (eds) *The Significance of Sibling Relationships in Literature*, Bowling Green, OH: Bowling Green State UP, pp. 98–109.

Colton, M., Sanders, R. and Williams, M. (2001) *An Introduction to Working with Children: A Guide for Social Workers*, London: Palgrave.

Conger, R. and Conger, K. (1996) Sibling relationships, in Simons, R. (ed.) *Understanding Differences Between Divorced and Intact Families: Stress, Interaction, and Child Outcome. Vol. 5, Understanding families*, Thousand Oaks, CA: Sage Publications, Inc., pp. 104–21.

Conger, R. and Rueter, M. (1996) Siblings, parents, and peers: a longitudinal study of social influences in adolescent risk for alcohol use and abuse, in Brody, G. (ed.) *Sibling Relationships: Their Causes and Consequences. Advances in Applied Developmental Psychology*, Norwood, NJ: Ablex Publishing Corp, pp. 1–30.

Conners, K.W. (2000) The influence of the parental relationship and parent-child relationship on sibling relationship quality, *Dissertation Abstract International: Section B – The Sciences and Engineering*, 60(11-B): 5832.

Corby, B. (1987) *Working with Child Abuse*, Milton Keynes: Open University Press.

Creighton, S. and Noyes, P. (1989) *Child Abuse Trends in England and Wales, 1983–1987*, London: NSPCC.

Crittenden, P. (1984) Sibling interaction: evidence of a generational effect in maltreating infants, *Child Abuse & Neglect*, 8(4): 433–8.

Cummings, M. (1994) Marital conflict and children's functioning, *Social Development*, 3(1): 16–36.

Curtis Report (1946) *Report of the Care of Children Committee*, London: HMSO.

Dale, N. (1989) Pretend play with mothers and siblings: relations between early performance and partners, *Journal of Child Psychology and Psychiatry*, 30(5): 751–9.

Dale, P., Murray, D., Morrison, T. and Waters, J. (1986) *Dangerous Families: Assessment and Treatment of Child Abuse*, London: Routledge.

Damiani, V. (1999) Responsibility and adjustment in siblings of children with disabilities: update and review, *Families in Society*, 80(1): 34–40.

D'Amico, E. and Fromme, K. (1997) Health risk behaviors of adolescent and young adult siblings, *Health Psychology*, 16(5): 426–32.

Daniel, B., Wassell, S. and Gilligan, R. (1999) *Child Development for Child Care and Protection Workers*, London: Jessica Kingsley Publishers.

Daniels, D., Dunn, J., Furstenberg, F. and Plomin, R. (1985) Environmental differences within the family and adjustment differences within pairs of adolescent siblings, *Child Development*, 56: 764–74.

Daniels, D. and Plomin, R. (1985) Differential experience of siblings in the same family, *Developmental Psychology*, 21: 747–60.

Dare, C. (1993) The family scapegoat: an origin for hating, in Varma, V. (ed.) *How and Why Children Hate*, London: Jessica Kingsley Publishers, ch. 3, pp. 31–45.

Deal, S.N. and MacLean, W.E. (1995) Disrupted lives: siblings of disturbed adolescents, *American Journal of Orthopsychiatry*, 65(2): 274–281.

DelGuidice, G. (1986) The relationship between sibling jealousy and presence at a sibling's birth, *Birth: Issues in Perinatal Care and Education*, 13(4): 250–4.

de Jong, A. (1989) Sexual interactions among siblings and cousins: experimentation or exploitation?, *Child Abuse & Neglect*, 13(2): 271–9.

DeMaso, D., Meyer, E. and Beasley, P. (1997) What do I say to my surviving children?, *Journal of the American Academy of Child and Adolescent Psychiatry*, 36(9): 1299–302.

den-Bak, I. and Ross, H. (1996) I'm telling! The content, context, and consequences of children's tattling on their siblings, *Social Development*, 5(3): 292–309.

Department of Health (1988) *Protecting Children: A Guide for Social Workers Undertaking a Comprehensive Assessment*, London: HMSO.

Department of Health (1991) *Patterns and Outcomes in Child Placement*, London: HMSO.

Department of Health (1995) *Child Protection: Messages from Research*, London: HMSO.

Department of Health, Department for Education and Employment, Home Office (2000) *Framework for the Assessment of Children in Need and Their Families*, London: The Stationery Office.

Department of Health and Social Security (1975) *Report of the Committee of Inquiry into the Provision and Co-ordination of Services to the Family of John George Aukland*, London: HMSO.

Dickstein, L. (1988) Spouse abuse and other domestic violence, *Psychiatric Clinics of North America*, 11(4): 611–28.

Dickstein, S., Seifer, R., Hayden, L.C., Schiller, M., Sameroff, A.J., Keitner, G., Miller, I., Rasmussen, S., Matzko, M. and Magee, K.D. (1998) Levels of family assessment: II. Impact of maternal psychopathology on family functioning, *Journal of Family Psychology*, 12(1): 23–40.

DiGiorgio-Miller, J. (1998) Sibling incest: treatment of the family and the offender, *Child Welfare*, 77(3): 335–46.

Doyle, C. (1996) Sexual abuse by siblings: the victims' perspectives, *The Journal of Sexual Aggression*, 2(1): 17–32.

Doyle, C. (2001) Surviving and coping with emotional abuse in childhood, *Clinical Child Psychology and Psychiatry*, 6(3): 387–402.

Dunbar, M. (1999) Sibling relationships and their association with parental differential treatment, paper presented at Australian Early Childhood Association Conference, *Putting Children on Top: Issues of Policy and Practice for the New Millennium*, Darwin High School, Australia, 14–17 July 1999.

Dunn, J. (1984) *Sisters and Brothers*, London: Fontana.

Dunn, J. (1988a) Annotation: sibling influences on childhood and development, *Journal of Child Psychology and Psychiatry*, 29(2): 119–27.

Dunn, J. (1988b) Connections between relationships: implications of research on mothers and siblings, in Hinde, R.A. and Stevenson-Hinde (eds) *Relationships within families*, Oxford: Oxford University Press, pp. 168–80.

Dunn, J. (1992) Sisters and brothers: current issues in developmental research, in Boer, F. and Dunn, J. (eds) *Children's Sibling Relationships: Developmental and Clinical Issues*, Hillsdale, NJ: Lawrence Erlbaum Associates, Inc., ch. 1. pp. 1–17.

Dunn, J. (1993) *Young Children's Close Relationships: Beyond Attachment*, London: Sage.

Dunn, J. (1995) *From One Child to Two: What to Expect, how to Cope and How to Enjoy Your Growing Family*, New York: Fawcett Columbine (Ballantine Books).

Dunn, J. (1996) Siblings: the first society, in Vanzetti, N., Duck, S., Hay, D., Hobfoll, S., Ickes, W. and Montgomery, B. (eds) *A Lifetime of Relationships*, Pacific Grove: Brooks/Cole Publishing Co., pp. 105–24.

Dunn, J., Brown, J. and Beardsall, L. (1991) Family talk about feeling states and children's later understanding of other's emotions, *Developmental Psychology*, 27(3): 448–55.

Dunn, J., Brown, J., Slomkowski, C., Tesla, C. and Youngblade, L. (1991) Young children's understanding of other people's feelings and beliefs: individual differences and their antecedents, *Child Development*, 62: 1352–66.

Dunn, J. and Brown, J. (1993) Early conversations about causality: content, pragmatics and developmental change, *British Journal of Developmental Psychology*, 11: 107–23.

Dunn, J. and Creps, C. (1996) Children's family relationships between two and five: developmental changes and individual differences, *Social Development*, 5(3): 230–50.

Dunn, J., Deater-Deckard, K., Pickering, K. and Golding, J. (1999) Siblings, parents, and partners: family relationships within a longitudinal community study, *Journal of Child Psychology and Psychiatry and Allied Disciplines*, 40 (7): 1025–37.

Dunn, J. and Kendrick, C. (1980) The arrival of a sibling: changes in patterns of interactions between mother and firstborn-child, *Journal of Child Psychology and Psychiatry*, 21: 119–32.

Dunn, J. and Kendrick, C. (1982) *Siblings: Love, Envy and Understanding*, Cambridge, MA: Harvard University Press.

Dunn, J. and McGuire, S. (1992) Sibling and peer relationships in childhood, *Journal of Child Psychology and Psychiatry*, 33(1): 67–105.

Dunn, J. and Munn, P. (1986) Sibling quarrels and maternal intervention: individual differences in understanding and aggression, *Journal of Child Psychology and Psychiatry and Allied Disciplines*, 27(5): 583–95.

Dunn, J. and Munn, P. (1987) Development of justification in disputes with mother and sibling, *Developmental Psychology*, 23(6): 791–8.

Dunn, J. and Plomin, R. (1990) *Separate Lives: Why Siblings are So Different*, New York: Basic Books.

Dunn, J., Plomin, R. and Nettles, M. (1985) Consistency of mothers behavior toward infant siblings, *Developmental Psychology*, 21(6): 1188–95.

Dunn, J., Slomkowski, C. and Beardsall, L. (1994) Sibling relationships from the preschool period through middle childhood and early adolescence, *Developmental Psychology*, 30(3): 315–24.

Dunn, J., Slomkowski, C. Beardsall, L. and Rende, R. (1992) Sibling relationships from the preschool period through middle childhood and early adolescence, *Developmental Psychology*, 30(3): 315–24.

Dunn, J., Slomkowski, C., Beardsall, L. and Rende, R. (1994) Adjustment in middle childhood and early adolescence: links with earlier and contemporary sibling relationships, *Journal of Child Psychology and Psychiatry*, 35(3): 491–504.

Durkin, K. (1995) *Developmental Social Psychology*, Oxford: Blackwell.

Dwivedi, K.N. (1993) Child abuse and hatred, in Varma, V. (ed.) *How and Why Children Hate: A Study of Conscious and Unconscious Sources*, London: Jessica Kingsley, ch. 4, pp. 46–71.

Dyregrov, A. (1987) Soskens reaksjoner nar et spebarn dor (Children's reactions to the death of a sibling), *Tidsskrift for Norsk Psykologforening*, 24(5): 291–8.

Dyson, L. (1989) Adjustment of siblings of handicapped children: a comparison, *Journal of Pediatric Psychology*, 14(2): 215–29.

East, P. and Rook, K. (1992) Compensatory patterns of support among children's peer relationships: a test using school friends, nonschool friends, and siblings, *Developmental Psychology*, 28(1): 163–72.

East, P.L. (1989) *Missing Provisions in Peer-Withdrawn and Aggressive Children's Friendships: Do Siblings Compensate?* Paper presented at the biennial meeting of the Society for Research in Child Development, Kansas, MO, April 1989.

Elmer, E. (1967) *Children in Jeopardy: A Study of Abused Minors and their Families*, Pittsburgh: University of Pittsburgh Press.

Eno, M. (1985) Sibling relationships in families of divorce, *Journal of Psychotherapy and the Family*, 1(3): 139–56.

Erel, O., Margolin, G. and John, R.S. (1998) Observed sibling interaction: links with the marital and the mother-child relationship, *Developmental Psychology*, 34(2): 288–98.

Erooga, M. and Masson, H. (1999) *Children and Young People Who Sexually Abuse Others: Challenges and Responses*, London: Routledge.

Faber, A. and Mazlish, E. (1987) *Siblings Without Rivalry: How to Help your Children Live Together So You Can Live Too*, New York: Avon Books.

Fahlberg, V. (1994) *A Child's Journey through Placement*, London: British Agencies for Adoption and Fostering (BAAF).

Falkov, A. (1996) *Study of Working Together 'Part 8' Reports: Fatal Child Abuse and Parental Psychiatric Disorder*, London: HMSO.

Farmer, E. and Owen, M. (1995) *Child Protection Practice: Private Risks and Public Remedies*, London: HMSO.

Farmer, E. and Parker, R. (1991) *Trials and Tribulations: Returning Children from Local Authority Care to Their Families*, London: HMSO.

Feldman, R.A., Stiffman, A.R. and Jung, K.G. (1987) *Children at Risk: In the Web of Parental Mental Illness*, New Brunswick, NJ: Rutgers University Press.

Felson, R. (1984) Aggression and violence between siblings, *Social Psychology Quarterly*, 46(4): 271–85.

Felson, R. and Russo, N. (1988) Parental punishment and sibling aggression, *Social Psychology Quarterly*, 51(1): 11–18.

Field, T. and Reite, M. (1984) Children's responses to separation from mother during the birth of another child. *Child Development*, 55(4): 1308–16.

Finkelhor, D. (1980) Sex among siblings: a survey of the prevalence, variety and effects, *Archives of Sexual Behavior*, 9(3): 171–94.

Fish, T., Dwyer McCaffrey, F., Bush, K. and Piskur, S. (1995) *Sibling Need and Involvement Profile* (SNIP), Columbus, OH: Nisonger Center.

Fonagy, P., Steele, M., Steele, H., Higgit, A. and Target, M. (1994) The theory and practice of resilience, *Journal of Child Psychology and Psychiatry*, 35(2): 231–57.

Forsythe, D. (1991) Sibling rivalry, aesthetic sensibility, and social structure in Genesis, *Ethos*, 19(4): 453–510.

Forward, S. and Buck, C. (1978) *Betrayal of Innocence: Incest and its Devastation*, Harmondsworth: Penguin.

Framo, J. (1965) Rationale and techniques of intensive family therapy in Boszormenyi-Nagy, I. and Framo, J. *Intensive Family Therapy: Theoretical and Practical Aspects*, New York: Harper and Row.

Frank, N. (1996) Helping families support siblings, in Beckman, P. (ed.) *Strategies for Working with Families of Young Children with Disabilities*, Baltimore, MD: Paul H. Brookes Publishing, pp. 169–88.

Fraser, M. (1997) *Risk and Resilience in Childhood: An Ecological Perspective*, Washington, DC: NASW Press.

Freeman, D. (1992) *Multigenerational Family Therapy*, London: Haworth.

Freeman, L. (1998) Clinical issues in assessment and intervention with children and adolescents exposed to homicide, in Hernandez, M. and Isaacs, M. (eds) *Promoting Cultural Competence in Children's Mental Health Services. Systems of Care for Children's Mental Health*, Baltimore, MD: Paul H. Brookes Publishing, pp. 185–206.

Freeman, L., Shaffer, D. and Smith, H. (1996) The neglected victims of homicide: the needs of young siblings of murder victims, *American Journal of Orthopsychiatry*, 66(3): 337–45.

Freud, S. (1917) A childhood memory from 'Dichtung and Wahrheit', *Standard Edition*, 17: 145–56.

Frey-Angel, J. (1989) Treating children of violent families: a sibling group approach, *Social Work with Groups*, 12(1): 95–107.

Fueloep, M. (1995) A versengese vonatkozo tudomanyos nezetek: II. A versenges a pszichoanalizis tuekreben (Scientific approaches to competition: II. Competition from the standpoint of psychoanalysis), *Pszichologia: Az Mta Pszichologiai Intezetenek Folyoirata*, 15(2): 157–211.

Furman, W. and Buhrmester, D. (1985) Children's perceptions of the qualities of sibling relationships, *Child Development*, 56: 448–61.

Furman, W. and Giverson, R. (1995) Identifying the links between parents and their children's sibling relationships, in Shulman, S. (ed.) *Close Relationships and*

Socioemotional Development. Vol. 7, Human Development, Norwood, NJ: Ablex Publishing, pp. 95–108.

Furman, W. and McQuaid, E. (1992) Intervention programs for the management of conflict, in Shantz, C. and Hartup, W. (eds) *Conflict in Child and Adolescent Development*, New York, NY: Cambridge University Press, pp. 402–29.

Gallagher, P. and Powell, T. (1989) Brothers and sisters: meeting special needs, *Topics in Early Childhood Special Education*, 8(4): 24–37.

Garbarino, J., Eckenrode, J. and Bolger, K. (1997) The elusive crime of psychological maltreatment, in Garbarino, J. and Eckenrode, J. (eds.) *Understanding Abusive Families: An Ecological Approach to Theory and Practice*, San Francisco: Jossey-Bass, ch. 5, pp. 101–13.

Gfroerer, J. (1987) Correlation between drug use by teenagers and drug use by older family members, *American Journal of Drug and Alcohol Abuse*, 13(1–2): 95–108.

Glaser, D. and Frosh, S. (1993) *Child Sexual Abuse* (2nd edn), London: The Macmillan Press – now Palgrave Macmillan.

Gold, D. (1989) Generational solidarity: conceptual antecedents and consequences, *American Behavioral Scientist*, 33(1): 19–32.

Goldberg, F. and Leyden, H. (1998) Left and left out: teaching children to grieve through a rehabilitation curriculum, *Professional School Counseling*, 2(2): 123–7.

Gottlieb, L. and Mendelson, M. (1990) Parental support and firstborn girls' adaptation to the birth of a sibling, *Journal of Applied Developmental Psychology*, 11(1): 29–48.

Graham, M.J. (1999) The African-centred worldview: developing a paradigm for social work, *British Journal of Social Work*, 29(2): 251–67.

Green, A.H. (1984) Child abuse by siblings, *Child Abuse & Neglect*, 8: 311–17.

Green, A.H. (1988) Special issues in child sexual abuse, in Schetky, D.H. and Green, A.H. (eds) *Child Sexual Abuse*, New York: Brunner/Mazel.

Greenbaum, M. (1965) Joint sibling interview as a diagnostic procedure, *Journal of Child Psychology and Psychiatry*, 6: 227–32.

Greenberg, J.H., Kim, H.W. and Grenley, J.R. (1997) Factors associated with subjective burden in siblings of adults with severe mental illness, *American Journal of Orthopsychiatry*, 67(2): 231–41.

Greenberg, S. (1978) *Right from the Start: A Guide to Nonsexist Child Rearing*, Boston, MA: Houghton Mifflin Co.

Griffin, E. and de la Torre, C. (1985) New baby in the house: sibling jealousy, *Medical Aspects of Human Sexuality*, 19(3): 110–16.

Grunebaum, H. and Cohler, B.J. (1982) Children of parents hospitalized for mental illness: I. Attentional and interactional studies, *Journal of Children in Contemporary Society*, 15(1): 43–55.

Hackett, S., Print, B. and Dey, C. (1998) Brother nature? Therapeutic intervention with young men who sexually abuse their siblings, in Bannister, A. (ed.) *From Hearing to Healing: Working with the Aftermath of Child Sexual Abuse* (2nd ed.), New York: John Wiley & Sons, pp. 152–79.

Halperin, S. (1983) Family perceptions of abused children and their siblings, *Child Abuse & Neglect*, 7(1): 107–15.

Hamlin, E. and Timberlake, E. (1981) Sibling group treatment, *Clinical Social Work Journal*, 9(2): 101–10.

Hannah, M. and Midlarsky, E. (1985) Siblings of the handicapped: a literature review for school psychologists, *School Psychology Review*, 14(4): 510–20.

Hannah, M. and Midlarsky, E. (1987) Siblings of the handicapped: maladjustment and its prevention, *Techniques*, 3(3): 188–95.

Hargett, H. (1998) Reconciling the victim and perpetrator in sibling incest, *Sexual Addiction and Compulsivity*, 5(2): 93–106.

Harris, J.R. (1999) *The Nurture Assumption: Why Children Turn Out the Way They Do*, New York: Touchstone Books.

Haugaard, J. and Repucci, N.D. (1988) *The Sexual Abuse of Children: A Comprehensive Guide to Current Knowledge and Intervention Strategies*, London: Jossey-Bass.

Hawthorne, B. (1998) Split-residence as a post divorce option, paper presented at Residence and Contact: Third National Conference of Family Court of Australia, Melbourne, Australia, 20–24 October 1998.

Hegar, R. (1988) Legal and social work approaches to sibling separation in foster care, *Child Welfare*, 67(2): 113–21.

Heiney, S. (1991) Sibling grief: a case report, *Archives of Psychiatric Nursing*, 5(3): 21–127.

Heinicke, C.M. and Westheimer, I.J. (1965) *Brief Separations*, Harlow, UK: Longman.

Hendrickx, J. (1985) Incompetent families and aggression, *Acta Paedopsychiatrica*, Suppl 6: 51–5.

Herzberger, S. and Hall, J. (1993a) Children's evaluations of retaliatory aggression against siblings and friends, *Journal of Interpersonal Violence*, 8(1): 77–93.

Herzberger, S. and Hall, J. (1993b) Consequences of retaliatory aggression against siblings and peers: urban minority children's expectations, *Child Development*, 64(6): 1773–85.

Hetherington, E.M. (1987) Parents, children and siblings six years after divorce, in Hinde, R.A. and Steveson-Hinde (eds) *Relations Among Relationships*, Oxford: Oxford University Press.

Hetherington, E.M. (1988) Parents, children and siblings: six years after divorce, in Hinde, R.A. and Stevenson-Hinde, J. (eds) *Relationships Wwithin Families*, Oxford: Oxford University Press, pp. 311–31.

Hetherington, E.M. (1991) Presidential address: families, lies, and videotape, *Journal of Research on Adolescence*, 1(4): 323–48.

Hetherington, E.M. (ed.) (1999) *Coping with Divorce, Single Parenting, and Remarriage: A Risk and Resiliency Perspective*, Mahwah, NJ: Lawrence Erlbaum Associates, Inc.

Hetherington, E. and Clingempeel, W. (1992) Coping with marital transitions: a family systems perspective, *Monographs of the Society for Research in Child Development*, 57(2–3) (Serial No. 227): 1–242.

Hetherington, E. and Jodl, K. (1994) Stepfamilies as settings for child development, in Booth, A. and Dunn, J. (eds) *Stepfamilies: Who benefits? Who Does Not?*, Hillsdale, NJ: Lawrence Erlbaum Associates, Inc., pp. 55–79.

Hetherington, E.M., Reiss, D. and Plomin, R. (1994) *Separate Social Worlds of Siblings: The Impact of Nonshared Environment on Development*, Hillsdale, NJ: Lawrence Erlbaum Associates, Inc.

Hewitt, J. (1995) Sources of variance affecting receipt of aggression, *Perceptual and Motor Skills*, 81(3, Pt 1): 751–4.

Hicks, R. and Gaughan, D. (1995) Understanding fatal child abuse, *Child Abuse & Neglect*, 19(7): 855–63.

Hindle, D. (1998) Growing up with a parent who has a chronic mental illness: one child's perspective, *Child and Family Social Work*, 3(4): 259–66.

Hipwell, A.E. and Kumar, R. (1996) Maternal psychopathology and prediction of outcome based on mother-infant interaction ratings (BMIS), *British Journal of Psychiatry*, 169(5): 655–61.

Hogan, N. and DeSantis, L. (1996) Adolescent sibling bereavement: toward a new theory, in Corr, C., and Balk, D. (eds) *Handbook of Adolescent Death and Bereavement*, New York: Springer Publishing Co, Inc., pp. 173–195.

Hooper, C. (1992) *Mothers Surviving Child Sexual Abuse*, London: Routledge.

Howe, D. (1995) *Attachment Theory for Social Work Practice*, London: Macmillan – now Palgrave Macmillan.

Howe, N., Aquan-Assee, J. and Bukowski, W.M. (2001) Predicting sibling relations over time: synchrony between maternal management styles and sibling relationship quality, *Merrill-Palmer Quarterly-Journal of Developmental Psychology*, 47(1): 121–41.

Hoyle, S. (1995) Long-term treatment of emotionally disturbed adoptees and their families, *Clinical Social Work Journal*, 23(4): 429–40.

Huberty, D. and Huberty, C. (1986) Sabotaging siblings: an overlooked aspect of family therapy with drug dependent adolescents, *Journal of Psychoactive Drugs*, 18(1): 31–41.

Hughes, H. (1982) Brief interventions with children in a battered women's shelter: a model preventive program, Family Relations: *Journal of Applied Family and Child Studies*, 31(4): 495–502.

Hunter, L. (1993) Sibling play therapy with homeless children: an opportunity in the crisis, *Child Welfare*, 72(1): 65–75.

Ihinger-Tallman, M. (1987) Sibling and stepsibling bonding in stepfamilies, in Pasley, K. and Ihinger-Tallman, M. (eds) *Remarriage and Stepparenting: Current Research and Theory*, New York: Guilford Press, pp. 164–82.

Ihinger-Tallman, M. and Pasley, K. (1987) *Remarriage*, London: Sage Publications.

Iwaniec, D. (1983) Social and psychological factors in the aetiology and management of children who fail-to-thrive, Unpublished PhD Thesis, University of Leicester: Department of Psychology.

Iwaniec, D. (1995) *The Emotionally Abused and Neglected Child: Identification, Assessment and Intervention*, Chichester: John Wiley & Sons.

Jacobsen, T., Miller, L.J. and Kirkwood, K.P. (1997) Assessing parenting competency in individuals with severe mental illness: a comprehensive service, *Journal of Mental Health Administration*, 24(2): 189–99.

James, B. and Nasjleti, M. (1983) *Treating Sexually Abused Children and Their Families*, Palo Alto, CA: Consulting Psychologists.

Jaudes, P. and Diamond, L. (1985) The handicapped child and child abuse, *Child Abuse & Neglect*, 9: 341–7.

Javaid, G. and Kestenberg, J. (1983) Entrancement of the mother with her young baby: implications for the older sibling, *Dynamic Psychotherapy*, 1(1): 37–51.

Jenkins, J. (1992) Sibling relationships in disharmonious homes: potential difficulties and protective effects, in Boer, F. and Dunn, J. (eds) *Children's Sibling Relationships: Developmental and Clinical Issues*, Hillsdale, NJ: Lawrence Erlbaum Associates, Inc., ch. 9, pp. 125–38.

Jeon, Y.H. and Madjar, I. (1998) Caring for a family member with chronic mental illness, *Qualitative Health Research*, 8(5): 694–706.

Johnson, T. (1988) Child perpetrators – children who molest other children: preliminary findings, *Child Abuse & Neglect*, 12(2): 219–29.

Jones, D., Pickett, J., Oates, M. and Barber P. (1982) *Understanding Child Abuse*, Sevenoaks: Hodder and Stoughton.

Jones, M. and Niblett, R. (1985) To split or not to split: the placement of siblings, *Adoption & Fostering*, 9(2): 26–32.

Jouvenot, C. (1997) Freud jaloux (A jealous Freud), *Revue Francaise de Psychanalyse*, 61(1): 11–28.

Judge, K.A. (1994) Serving children, siblings, and spouses: understanding the needs of other family members, in Lefley, H.P. and Wasow, M. (eds) *Helping Families Cope With Mental Illness. Vol. 2, Chronic Mental Illness*, Philadelphia, PA: Harwood Academic Publishers/Gordon and Breach Science Publishers, pp. 161–94.

Kahn, M.D. and Lewis, K.G. (1988) *Siblings in Therapy: Life Span and Clinical Issues*, New York: W.W. Norton and Co., Inc.

Kahn, T.J. and Chambers, H. (1991) Assessing reoffence risk with juvenile sexual offenders, *Child Welfare*, 70(3): 333–45.

Kaplan, L., Ade-Ridder, L. and Hennon, C. (1991) Issues of split custody: siblings separated by divorce, *Journal of Divorce and Remarriage*, 16(3–4): 253–74.

Kaplan, L., Hennon, C. and Ade-Ridder, L. (1993) Splitting custody of children between parents: impact on the sibling system, *Families in Society*, 74(3): 131–44.

Kelsh, N. and Quindlen, A. (1998) *Siblings*, New York: Penguin Studio.

Kempton, T., Armistead, L., Wierson, M. and Forehand, R. (1991) Presence of a sibling as a potential buffer following parental divorce: an examination of young adolescents, *Journal of Clinical Child Psychology*, 20(4): 434–8.

Kendrick, C. and Dunn, J. (1980) Caring for the second baby: effects on interaction between mother and first born, *Developmental Psychology*, 16: 303–11.

Kier, C. and Fouts, T. (1989) Sibling play in divorced and married-parent families, *Journal of Reproductive and Infant Psychology*, 7(3): 139–46.

Kingsland, L.W. (1985) *Hans Andersen's Fairy Tales*, Oxford: Oxford University Press.

Koch, H.L. (1960) The relation of certain formal attributes of siblings to attitudes held toward each other and toward their parents, *Monographs of the Society for Research in Child Development*, no. 25, no 4.

Kojima, Y (2000) Maternal regulation of sibling interactions in the preschool years: observational study in Japanese families, *Child Development*, 71(6): 1640–7.

Korbin, J. (1980) The cross-cultural context, in Kempe, C.H. and Helfer, R.E. (eds) *The Battered Child* (3rd edn), Chicago: The University of Chicago Press, ch. 2, pp. 21–35.

Kornblit, A. (1994) Domestic violence: an emerging health issue, *Social Science and Medicine*, 39(9): 1181–8.

Kosonen, M. (1996a) Maintaining sibling relationships – neglected dimension in child care practice, *British Journal of Social Work*, 26(6): 809–22.

Kosonen, M. (1996b) Siblings as providers of support and care during middle childhood: children's perceptions, *Children & Society*, 10: 267–79.

Kosonen, M. (1999) 'Core' and 'kin' siblings: foster children's changing families, in Mullender, A. (ed.) *We Are Family: Sibling Relationships in Placement and Beyond*, London: British Agencies for Adoption and Fostering (BAAF), ch. 3, pp. 28–49.

Kowal, A. and Kramer, L. (1997) Children's understanding of parental differential treatment, *Child Development*, 68(1): 113–26.

Kramer, L. and Gottman, J.M. (1992) Becoming a sibling – with a little help from my friends, *Developmental Psychology*, 28(4): 685–99.

Kramer, L. (1990) Becoming a sibling: with a little help from my friends, in Mendelson, M. (chair) Becoming a sibling: adjustment, roles and relationships, Symposium at the 7th International Conference on Infant Studies, Montreal.

Kramer, L. and Baron, L. (1995) Intergenerational linkages: how experiences with siblings relate to the parenting of siblings, *Journal of Social and Personal Relationships*, 12(1): 67–87.

Kramer, L. and Schaefer-Hernan, P. (1994) Patterns of fantasy play engagement across the transition to becoming a sibling, *Journal of Child Psychology and Psychiatry*, 35(4): 749–67.

Krasner, S. and Beinart, H. (1989) The Monday Group: a brief intervention with the siblings of infants who died from sudden infant death syndrome (SIDS), *Association of Child Psychology and Psychiatry Newsletter*, 11(4): 11–17.

Kurdek, L. (1988) Siblings' reactions to parental divorce, *Journal of Divorce*, 12(2–3): 203–19.

Lamb, M.E. (1978) The development of sibling relationships in infancy: a short-term longitudinal study, *Child Development*, 49: 1189–96.

Lamb, M.E. (1982) *Non-traditional Families: Parenting and Child Development*: Hillsdale, NJ: Lawrence Erlbaum.

Lantheir, R.P. and Stocker, C. (1992) *The Adult Sibling Relationship Questionnaire*. Denver, CO: University of Denver.

Lapalus-Netter, G. (1989) Frères et soeurs d'enfant handicapé: la souffrance inapparente (Brothers and sisters of the handicapped child: the hidden suffering), *Psychologie Medicale*, 21(2): 189–92.

Laredo, C. (1982) Sibling incest, in Sgroi, S. (ed.) *Handbook of Clinical Intervention in Child Sexual Abuse*, Lexington, MA: Lexington Books, ch. 6, pp. 177–89.

Lasky, R. (1983) Social interactions of Guatemalan infants: the importance of different caregivers, *Journal of Cross Cultural Psychology*, 14(1): 17–28.

LaViola, M. (1991) Effects of older brother – younger sister incest: a study of the dynamics of 17 cases, *Child Abuse & Neglect*, 16: 409–21.

Le Gall, D. (1998) Family conflict in France through the eyes of teenagers, in Klein, R. (ed.) *Multidisciplinary Perspectives on Family Violence*, London: Routledge, ch. 5, pp. 79–109.

Leavitt, K., Gardner, S., Gallagher, M. and Schamess, G. (1998) Severely traumatized siblings: a treatment strategy, *Clinical Social Work Journal*, 26(1): 55–71.

Lebovici, S. (1988) Rencontre des pédiatres et des psychiatres auprès de três jeunes enfants (Meeting between paediatricians and psychiatrists working with very young children), *Information Psychiatrique*, 64: 587–90.

Leder, J.M. (1991) *Brothers and Sisters: How They Shape Our Lives*. NY: Ballantine Books.

Leichtman, M. (1985) The influence of an older sibling on the separation-individuation process, *Psychoanalytic Study of the Child*, 40: 111–61.

Leon, I. (1986) Intrapsychic and family dynamics in perinatal sibling loss, *Infant Mental Health Journal*, 7(3): 200–13.

Leon, I. (1990) *When a Baby Dies: Psychotherapy for Pregnancy and Newborn Loss*, New Haven, CT: Yale University Press.

Levy, D.M. (1934) Rivalry between children of the same family, *Child Study*, vol. 11.

Levy, D.M. (1937) *Studies in Sibling Rivalry*, American Orthopsychiatry Research Monograph, no. 2.

Levy, D.M. (1941) The hostile act, *Psychological Review*, 48: 356–61.

Levy, D.M. (1943) Hostility patterns: deviations from the 'unit act' of hostility, *American Journal of Orthopsychiatry*, 13(3): 441–61.

Lew, M. (1990) *Victims No Longer: Men Recovering from Incest and Other Sexual Child Abuse*, New York: Harper & Row.

Lewin, K. (1951) *Field Theory in Social Science: Selected Theoretical Papers*, New York: Harper.

Lewis, K. (1991) A three step plan for African-American families involved with foster care: sibling therapy, mothers' group therapy, family therapy, *Journal of Independent Social Work*, 5(3–4): 135–47.

Lewis, O. (1964, orig 1961) *The Children of Sanchez*, Harmondsworth, UK: Penguin Books.

Lijembe, J. (1967) The valley between: a Muluyia's story, in Fox, L. (ed.), *East African Childhood*, Nairobi: Oxford University Press, pp. 4–7.

Logan, F., Morrall, P. and Chambers, H. (1998) Identification of risk factors for psychological disturbance in adopted children, *Child Abuse Review*, 7(3): 154–64.

Louis, A., Condon, J., Shute, R. and Elzinga, R. (1997) The development of the Louis MACRO (Mother and Child Risk Observation) forms: assessing parent-infant-child risk in the presence of maternal mental illness, *Child Abuse & Neglect*, 21(7): 589–606.

Luthar, S. and Rounsaville, B. (1993) Substance misuse and comorbid psychopathology in a high-risk group: a study of siblings of cocaine misusers, *International Journal of the Addictions*, 28(5): 415–34.

Lynch, M. and Roberts, J. (1982) *Consequences of Child Abuse*, London: Academic Press.

McCloskey, L., Figueredo, A. and Koss, M. (1995) The effects of systemic family violence on children's mental health, *Child Development*, 66(5): 1239–1261.

McCown, D. and Pratt, C. (1985) Impact of sibling death on children's behavior, *Death Studies*, 9(3–4): 323–35.

McGee, C. (2000) *Childhood Experiences of Domestic Violence*, London: Jessica Kingsley.

McGoldrick, M. and Gerson, R. (1985) *Genograms in Family Assessment*, New York: W.W. Norton & Co.

McGuire, S. and Dunn, J. (1994) Nonshared environment in middle childhood, in DeFries, J., Plomin, R. and Fulker, D. (eds) *Nature and Nurture During Middle Childhood*, Oxford: Blackwell Publishers, Inc., pp. 201–13.

McHale, S., Crouter, A., McGuire, S. and Updegraff, K. (1995) Congruence between mothers' and fathers' differential treatment of siblings: Links with family relations and children's well-being, *Child Development*, 66(1): 116–28.

McHale, S. and Gamble, W. (1987) Sibling relationship and adjustment of children with disabled brothers and sisters, *Journal of Children in Contemporary Society*, 19: 131–58.

McHale, S. and Gamble, W. (1989) Sibling relationships of children with disabled and nondisabled brothers and sisters, *Developmental Psychology*, 25(3): 421–9.

McHale, S. and Harris, V. (1992) Children's experiences with disabled and nondisabled siblings: links with personal adjustment and relationship evaluations, in Boer, F. and Dunn, J. (eds) *Children's Sibling Relationships: Developmental and Clinical Issues*, Hillsdale, NJ: Lawrence Erlbaum Associates, ch. 6, pp. 83–100.

McHale, S. and Pawletko, T. (1992) Differential treatment of siblings in two family contexts, *Child Development*, 63(1): 68–81.

McHale, S., Sloan, J. and Simeonsson, R. (1986) Sibling relationships of children with autistic, mentally retarded, and nonhandicapped brothers and sisters, *Journal of Autism and Developmental Disorders*, 16(4): 399–413.

McHale, S., Updegraff, K., Tucker, C. and Crouter, A. (2000) Step in or stay out? Parents' roles in adolescent siblings' relationships, *Journal of Marriage and the Family*, 62: 746–60.

McKeever, P. (1983) Siblings of chronically ill children: A literature review with implications for research and practice, *American Journal of Orthopsychiatry*, 53(2): 209–18.

Mackey, M. and Miller, H. (1992) Women's views of postpartum sibling visitation, *Maternal Child Nursing Journal*, 20(1): 40–9.

MacKinnon, C. (1988) Sibling interactions in married and divorced families: Influence of ordinal position, socioeconomic status, and play context, *Journal of Divorce*, 12(2–3): 221–34.

MacKinnon, C. (1989) An observational investigation of sibling interactions in married and divorced families, *Developmental Psychology*, 25(1): 36–44.

MacKinnon-Lewis, C., Starnes, R., Volling, B. and Johnson, S. (1997) Perceptions of parenting as predictors of boys' sibling and peer relations, *Developmental Psychology*, 33(6): 1024–31.

McMahon, L. (1992) *The Handbook of Play Therapy*, London: Routledge.

Maloney, M., Ballard, J., Hollister, L. and Shank, M. (1983) A prospective, controlled study of scheduled sibling visits to a newborn intensive care unit, *Journal of the American Academy of Child Psychiatry*, 22(6): 565–70.

Marsh, D.T. (1998) *Serious Mental Illness and the Family: The Practitioner's Guide*, New York: John Wiley & Sons.

Marsh, D.T. and Dickens, R.M. (1997) *Troubled Journey: Coming to Terms with the Mental Illness of a Sibling or Parent*, New York: Jeremy P. Tarcher, Inc./Penguin Putnam, Inc.

Martin, J. and Ross, H. (1995) The development of aggression within sibling conflict, *Early Education and Development*, 6(4): 335–58.

Marx, E.L. (1999) The relationship of parentification and adult adaptation in female social work graduate students, *Dissertation Abstracts International Section A – Humanities and Social Sciences*, 59(10A): 3753.

Mekos, D., Hetherington, E. and Reiss, D. (1996) Sibling differences in problem behavior and parental treatment in nondivorced and remarried families, *Child Development*, 67(5): 2148–65.

Mendelson, M. (1990) *Becoming a Brother*, Cambridge, MA: MIT Press.

Mendelson, M.J., Aboud, F.E. and Lanthier, R.P. (1994) Kindergartner relationships with siblings, peers, and friends, *Merrill-Palmer Quarterly Journal of Developmental Psychology*, 40(3): 416–35.

Merrell, S. (1995) *The Accidental Bond: How Sibling Connections Influence Adult Relationships*, New York: Fawcett Columbine.

Millham, S., Bullock, R., Hosie, K. and Haak, M. (1986) *Lost in Care*, Aldershot: Gower.

Mink, J.S. and Ward, J.D. (1993) *The Significance of Sibling Relationships in Literature*, Bowling Green, OH: Bowling Green State University Popular Press.

Minturn, L. and Lambert, W. (1964) *Mothers of Six Cultures*, New York: John Wiley & Sons.

Minuchin, S. (1974) *Families and Family Therapy*, London: Tavistock Publications.

Minuchin, S. and Fishman, C. (1981) *Family Therapy Techniques*, Cambridge, MA: Harvard University Press

Monahan, S., Buchanan, C. and Maccoby, E. (1993) Sibling differences in divorced families, *Child Development*, 64(1): 152–68.

Mook, B. (1985) Phenomenology, system theory and family therapy, *Journal of Phenomenological Psychology*, 16(1): 1–12.

Moore, J. (1992) *The ABC of Child Protection*, Aldershot: Ashgate.

Moore, T., Pepler, D., Weinberg, B. and Hammond, L. (1990) Research on children from violent families, *Canada's Mental Health*, 38(2–3): 19–23.

Mufson, T. (1985) Issues surrounding sibling death during adolescence, *Child and Adolescent Social Work Journal*, 2(4): 204–18.

Mullender, A. (1996) *Rethinking Domestic Violence*, London: Routledge.

Mullender, A. (1999) *We Are Family: Sibling Relationships in Placement and Beyond*, London: British Agencies for Adoption and Fostering.

National Assembly for Wales (2000) *Working Together to Safeguard and Promote the Welfare of Children: A Guide to Inter-Agency Worling to Safeguard and Promote the Welfare of Children*, London: The Stationery Office.

NCH Action for Children (1994) *The Hidden Victims: Children and Domestic Violence*, London: NCH.

Needle, R., McCubbin, H., Wilson, M. and Reineck, R. (1986) Interpersonal influences in adolescent drug use: the role of older siblings parents, and peers, *International Journal of the Addictions*, 21(7): 739–66.

Neubauer, P. (1982) Rivalry, envy, and jealousy, *Psychoanalytic Study of the Child*, 37: 121–42.

Neubauer, P. (1983) The importance of the sibling experience, *Psychoanalytic Study of the Child*, 38: 325–36.

Newlands, M. and Emery, J. (1991) Child abuse and cot deaths, *Child Abuse & Neglect*, 15(3): 275–8.

Newson, J. and Newson, E. (1978) *Seven Years Old in the Home Environment*, Harmondsworth: Penguin Books.

Nichols, W. (1986) Sibling subsystem therapy in family system reorganization, *Journal of Divorce*, 9(3): 13–31.

Oates, M. (1997) Patients as parents: the risk to children, *British Journal of Psychiatry*, 170 (suppl. 32): 22–7.

O'Doherty, N. (1982) *The Battered Child: Recognition in Primary Care*, London: Baillière Tindall.

O'Hagan, K. (1993) *Emotional and Psychological Abuse of Children*, Milton Keynes: Open University.

Oliver, J.E., Cox, J. and Buchanan, A. (1978) The extent of child abuse, in Smith, S. (ed.) *The Maltreatment of Children*, Lancaster, UK: MTP Press, ch. 6, pp. 121–74.

Olson, R. and Roberts, M. (1987) Alternative treatments for sibling aggression, *Behavior Therapy*, 18(3): 243–50.

O'Neill, T. (1981) *A Place Called Hope*, Oxford: Basil Blackwell.

Oyserman, D., Mowbray, C.T. and Zemencuk, J.K. (1994) Resources and supports for mothers with severe mental illness, *Health and Social Work*, 19(2): 132–42.

Palmer, S.B. (1998) The role of risk for insecure early attachment in explaining the behavioral adjustment of foster children, *Dissertation Abstracts International: Section B: The Sciences and Engineering*, 58(8B): 4493.

Parker, R., Ward, H., Jackson, S., Aldgage, J. and Wedge, P. (1991) *Assessing Outcomes in Child Care*, London: HMSO.

Pasley, K. and Ihinger-Tallman, M. (eds) (1987) *Remarriage and Stepparenting: Current Research and Theory*, New York: Guilford Press.

Patterson, G. (1984) Siblings: fellow travelers in coercive family processes, *Advances in the Study of Aggression*, 1: 173–215.

Patterson, G., Dishion, T. and Bank, L. (1984) Family interaction: a process model of deviancy training, *Aggressive Behavior*, 10(3): 253–67.

Pearson, J. and Sternberg, A. (1986) A mutual-help project for families of handicapped children, *Journal of Counseling and Development*, 65(4): 213–15.

Pelzer, D. (2001, orig. 1995) *A Child Called 'It'*, London: Orion Books.

Penning, M. and Barnes, G. (1982) Adolescent marijuana use: a review, *International Journal of the Addictions*, 17(5): 749–91.

Pepler, D., Abramovitch, R. and Corter, C. (1982) Sibling interaction in the home: a longitudinal study, *Child Development*, 52(4): 1344–7.

Perlman, H.H. (1967) A note on sibling, *American Journal of Orthopsychiatry*, 37: 148–149.

Philip, N. (1992) *The Penguin Book of English Folktales*, London: Penguin.

Pillari, V. (1991) *Scapegoating in Families: Intergenerational Patterns of Physical and Emotional Abuse*, New York: Brunner/Mazel, Inc.

Pingree, A. (1993) The Circles of Ran and Eugene MacLain: Welty's twin plots in *the Golden Apples*, in Mink, J.S. and Ward, J.D. (eds) *The Significance of Sibling Relationships in Literature*, Bowling Green, OH: Bowling Green State University Popular Press, pp. 83–97.

Plomin, R., Chipuer, H. and Neiderhiser, J. (1994), Behavioral genetic evidence for the importance of nonshared environment, in Hetherington, E.M., Reiss, D. and Plomin, R. (1994) *Separate Social Worlds of Siblings: The Impact of Nonshared Environment on Development*, Hillsdale, NJ: Lawrence Erlbaum Associates, Inc., ch. 1, pp. 1–31.

Plomin, R. and Daniels, D. (1987) Why are children within the same family so different from one another? *Behavioral and Brain Sciences*, 10: 1–16.

Pollock, G. (1986) Childhood sibling loss: a family tragedy, *Annual of Psychoanalysis*, 14: 5–34.

Prevatt-Goldstein, B. (1999) Black siblings: a relationship for life, in Mullender, A. (ed.) *We Are Family: Sibling Relationships in Placement and Beyond,* London: British Association for Adoption and Fostering (BAAF), ch. 15, pp. 194–212.

Prochaska, J. and Prochaska, J. (1985) Children's views of the causes and 'cures' of sibling rivalry, *Child Welfare*, 64(4): 427–33.

Provence, S. and Solnit, A. (1983) Development-promoting aspects of the sibling experience: Vicarious mastery, *Psychoanalytic Study of the Child*, 38: 337–51.

Pruchno, R., Patrick, J. and Burant, C. (1996) Aging women and their children with chronic disabilities: perceptions of sibling involvement and effects on well-being, *Family Relations: Journal of Applied Family and Child Studies*, 45(3): 318–26.

Rackham, A. (1973) *Grimm's Fairy Tales: Twenty Stories*, London: William Heinemann.

Raffaelli, M. (1992) Sibling conflict in early adolescence, *Journal of Marriage and the Family*, 54 (3): 652–63.

Ramsay, R., Howard, L. and Kumar, C. (1998) Schizophrenia and safety of parenting of infants: A report from a UK mother and baby service, *International Journal of Social Psychiatry*, 44(2): 127–34.

Ranieri, R. and Pratt, T. (1978) Sibling therapy, *Social Work*, 23(5): 418–19.

Reder, P., Duncan, S. and Gray, M. (1993) *Beyond Blame: Child Abuse Tragedies Revisited*, London and New York: Routledge.

Reder, P. and Fitzpatrick, G. (1995) Assessing the needs of siblings following a child abuse death, *Child Abuse Review*, 4 (Special Issue): 382–8.

Reder, P. and Lucey, C. (eds)(1995) *Assessment of Parenting: Psychiatric and Psychological Contributions*, London: Routledge.

Reese-Weber, M. (2000) Middle and late adolescents conflict resolution skills with siblings: associations with interparental and parent-adolescent conflict resolution, *Journal of Youth and Adolescence*, 29: 697–711.

Reibstein, J. and Bamber, R. (1997) *The Family Through Divorce: How You Can Limit the Damage*, London: Thorsons.

Reilly, T., Hasazi, J. and Bond, L. (1983) Children's conceptions of death and personal mortality, *Journal of Pediatric Psychology*, 8(1): 21–31.

Reiss, D., Plomin, R., Hetherington, E.M., Howe, G.W., Rovine, M., Tryon, A. and Hagan, M.S. (1994) The separate world of teenage siblings: an introduction to the study of the nonshared environment and adolescent development, in Hetherington, E.M., Reiss, D. and Plomin, R. *Separate Social Worlds of Siblings: The Impact of Nonshared Environment on Development*, Hillsdale, NJ: Lawrence Erlbaum Associates, Inc., ch. 3, pp. 63–109.

Renvoize, J. (1993) *Innocence Destroyed: A Study of Child Sexual Abuse*, London: Routledge.

Rhea, S., Nagoshi, C. and Wilson, J. (1993) Reliability of sibling reports on parental drinking behaviors, *Journal of Studies on Alcohol*, 54(1): 80–4.

Riggio, H. (2000) Measuring attitudes toward adult sibling relationships: the Lifetime Sibling Relationships Scale, *Journal of Social and Personal Relationships*, 17(6): 707–28.

Rinaldi, C. and Howe, N. (1998) Siblings' reports of conflict and the quality of their relationships, *Merrill-Palmer Quarterly-Journal Of Developmental Psychology*, 44(3): 404–22.

Robertson, J. and Robertson, J. (1989) *Separation and the Very Young*, London: Free Association Books.

Robinson, E.A.R. (1996) Causal attributions about mental illness: relationship to family functioning, *American Journal of Orthopsychiatry*, 66(2): 282–95.

Rosen, H. and Cohen, H. (1981) Children's reactions to sibling loss, *Clinical Social Work Journal*, 9(3): 211–19.

Rosenberg, E. and Hajal, F. (1985) Stepsibling relationships in remarried families, *Social Casework*, 66(5): 287–92.

Rosenfield-Schlichter, M., Sarber, R., Bueno, G. and Greene, B. (1983) Maintaining accountability for an ecobehavioral treatment of one aspect of child neglect: personal cleanliness, *Education and Treatment of Children*, 6(2): 153–64.

Rosenthal, P. and Doherty, M. (1984), Serious sibling abuse by preschool children, *Journal of the American Academy of Child Psychiatry*, 23(2): 186–90.

Ross, H., Filyer, R., Lollis, S. and Perlman, M. (1994) Administering justice in the family, *Journal of Family Psychology*, 8(3): 254–73.

Ross, H.G. and Milgram, J.I (1982) Important variables in adult sibling relationships: a qualitative study, in Lamb, M.E. and Sutton-Smith, B. (eds) *Sibling Relationships: Their Nature and Significance Across the Lifespan*, NJ: Lawrence Erlbaum.

Rowe, D. (1985) Genetic and environmental components of antisocial pairs: a study of 265 twin pairs, *Criminology*, 24: 513–32.

Rowe, D. and Gulley, G.L. (1992) Sibling effects on substance use and delinquency, *Criminology*, 30: 217–33.

Rowe, D. and Herstand, S. (1986) Familial influences on television viewing and aggression: a sibling study, *Aggressive Behavior*, 12(2): 111–20.

Rowe, D.C. and Plomin, R. (1981) The importance of nonshared (E_1) environmental influences in behavioural development, *Developmental Psychology*, 17: 517–31.

Rowe, J., Cain, H., Hundleby, M. and Keane, A. (1984) *Long Term Foster Care*, London: Batsford.

Rudd, J. and Herzberger, S. (1999) Brother-sister incest – father-daughter incest: a comparison of characteristics and consequences, *Child Abuse & Neglect*, 23(9): 915–28.

Rushton, A., Dance, C., Quinton, D. and Mayes, D. (1999) Children's relationships in late permanent placements, in Parker, R. (ed.) *Adoption Now: Messages from Research*, Chichester: John Wiley & Sons, pp. 151–5.

Russell, D. (1983) The incidence and prevalence of intrafamilial and extrafamilial sexual abuse of female children, *Child Abuse & Neglect*, 7: 133–46.

Russell, D. (1986) *Secret Trauma: Incest in the Lives of Girls and Women*, New York: Basic Books.

Rutter, M. (1972) *Maternal Deprivation Reassessed*, Harmondsworth: Penguin Books.

Rutter, M. and Quinton, D. (1987) Parental mental illness as a risk factor for psychiatric disorders in childhood, in Magnusson, D. and Oehman, A. (eds) *Psychopathology: An Interactional Perspective. Personality, Psychopathology, and Psychotherapy*, San Diego, CA: Academic Press, pp. 199–219.

Sameroff, A.J., Seifer, R. and Barocas, R. (1983) Impact of parental psychopathology: diagnosis, severity, or social status effects, *Infant Mental Health Journal*, 4(3): 236–49.

Sanders, R. (1999) *The Management of Child Protection: Context and Change*, Aldershot: Ashgate.

Sanders, R. (2002) *Siblings, Social Work and Child Abuse*, Ph.D dissertation, University of Wales Swansea.

Sanders, R., Colton, M. and Roberts, S. (1999) Child abuse fatalities and cases of extreme concern: lessons from reviews, *Child Abuse & Neglect*, 23(3): 257–68.

Sandler, I. (1980) Social support resources, stress and maladjustment of poor children, *American Journal of Community Psychology*, 8: 41–52.

Scarr, S. and Grajek, S. (1982) Similarities and differences among siblings, in Lamb, M.E. and Sutton-Smith, B. (eds) *Sibling Relationships: Their Nature and Significance Across the Lifespan*, Hillsdale, NJ: Lawrence Erlbaum Associates.

Schachter, F.F. (1982) Sibling deidentification and split-parent identification: a family tetrad, in Lamb, M.E. and Sutton-Smith, B. (eds.) *Sibling Relationships: Their Nature and Significance Across the Lifespan*, Hillsdale, NJ: Lawrence Erlbaum, pp. 123–51.

Schaefer, E. and Edgerton, M. (1981) The sibling inventory of behavior, Unpublished manuscript, Chapel Hill, NC: University of North Carolina.

Scherer, D.G., Melloh, T., Buyck, D., Anderson, C. and Foster, A. (1996) Relation between children's perceptions of maternal mental illness and children's psychological adjustment, *Journal of Clinical Child Psychology*, 25(2): 156–69.

Schibuk, M. (1989) Treating the sibling subsystem: an adjunct of divorce therapy. *American Journal of Orthopsychiatry*, 59(2): 226–37.

Schibalski, K. and Harlander, U. (1982) Beobachtungen zur Suendenbockdynamik in Psychotherapeutischen Kindergruppen (Scapegoat dynamic in group psychotherapy of children), *Dynamische Psychiatrie*, 15(5-sup-6): 251–67.

Schmitt, B. (1980) The child with nonaccidental trauma, in Kempe, C.H. and Helfer, R.E. (eds.) *The Battered Child* (3rd edn), Chicago: The University of Chicago Press, ch. 8, pp. 128–46.

Schmitt, B.D., Grosz, C.A. and Carroll, C.A. (1976) The child protection team: a problem-oriented approach, in Helfer, R.E. and Kempe, C.H. (eds) *Child Abuse and Neglect: The Family and the Community*, Cambridge, MA: Ballinger.

Seifer, R., Sameroff, A.J., Dickstein, S., Keitner, G. and Miller, I. (1996) Parental psychopathology, multiple contextual risks, and one-year outcomes in children, *Journal of Clinical Child Psychology*, 25(4): 423–35.

Seligman, M. (1983) Sources of psychological disturbance among siblings of handicapped children, *Personnel and Guidance Journal*, 61(9): 529–31.

Sgroi, S. (1982) *Handbook of Clinical Intervention in Child Sexual Abuse*, Lexington, MA: Lexington Books.

Shih, H.H. (1996) Growing up with a mentally ill parent: a phenomenological study of Chinese children in Taiwan, *Dissertation Abstracts International: Section B – The Sciences and Engineering*, 56(10B): 5424.

Shuler, S. and Reich, C.Y. (1982) Sibling visitation in pediatric hospitals: policies, opinions, and issues, *Children's Health Care*, 11(2): 54–60.

Simons, R. and Johnson, C. (1998) An examination of competing explanations for the intergenerational transmission of domestic violence, in Danieli, Y. (ed.) *International Handbook of Multigenerational Legacies of Trauma*, New York, NY: Plenum Press, pp. 553–70.

Slade, J. (1988) Why siblings of handicapped children need the attention and help of the counselor, *School Counselor*, 36(2): 107–11.

Slomkowski, C., Rende, R., Conger, K. Simons, R. and Conger, R. (2001) Sisters, brothers and delinquency: evaluating social influence during early and middle adolescence, *Child Development*, 72(1): 271–83.

Slomkowski, C., Wasserman, G., Schaffer, D., Rende, R. and Davies, M. (1997) A new instrument to assess sibling relationships in antisocial youth: the social interaction between siblings (SIBS) interview: a research note, *Journal of Child Psychology and Psychiatry*, 38(2): 253–6.

Smith, H. and Israel, E. (1987) Sibling incest: a study of the dynamics of 25 cases, *Child Abuse & Neglect*, 11(1): 101–8.

Smith, J.A.S. and Adler, R.G. (1991) Children hospitalised with child abuse and neglect: a case-control study, *Child Abuse & Neglect*, 15: 437–45.

Smith, M. (1998) Sibling placement in foster care: an exploration of associated concurrent preschool-aged child functioning, *Children and Youth Services Review*, 20(5): 389–412.

Smith, S. and Pennells, M. (1995) *Interventions with Bereaved Children*, London: Jessica Kingsley.

Social Services Inspectorate (1996) *Young Carers: Making a Start: Report of the SSI Field Work Project on Families with Disability or Illness, October 1995 – January 1996*, London: Department of Health.

Soda, M.B. (1998) Effective parenting while coping with anxiety and depression, *Dissertation Abstracts International: Section B: The Sciences and Engineering*, 59(2B): 0888.

Southall, D. (1997) Covert video recordings of life threatening child abuse: lessons for child protection, *Pediatrics*, 100(5): 735–60.

Spacks, P. M. (1986) Sisters, in Schofield, M.A. and Macheski, C. (eds) *'Sisters' Fetter'd or Free? British Women Novelists, 1670–1815*, Athens, OH: Ohio University Press, pp. 136–51.

Spigelman, G., Spigelman, A. and Englesson, I. (1992) Analysis of family drawings: a comparison between children from divorce and non-divorce families, *Journal of Divorce and Remarriage*, 18(1–2): 31–54.

Stainton, T. and Besser, H. (1998) The positive impact of children with an intellectual disability on the family, *Journal of Intellectual & Developmental Disability*, 23(1): 57–70.

Stark, E. and Flitcraft, A. (1998) Women and children at risk: a feminist perspective on child abuse, in Bergen, R. (ed.) *Issues in Intimate Violence*, Thousand Oaks, CA: Sage Publications, Inc., pp. 25–41.

Statham, J. (1986) *Daughters and Sons: Experiences of Non-sexist Childraising*, Oxford: Basil Blackwell.

Stearns, P. (1988) The rise of sibling jealousy in the twentieth century, in Stearns, C. and Stearns, P. (eds) *Emotion and Social Change: Toward a New Psychohistory*, New York: Holmes & Meier, ch. 7, pp. 193–222.

Steele, B. and Ryan, G. (1997) Deviancy: development gone wrong, in Ryan, G. D. and Lane, S. (ed.) *Juvenile Sexual Offending: Causes, Consequences, and Correction*, San Francisco, CA: Jossey-Bass Inc., Publishers, ch. 5, pp. 59–76.

Stein, N. L. and Albro, E.R. (1997) Children's and parents' understanding of conflict: evidence from past memories. Paper presented at SRCD, April, Washington, DC.

Steinmetz, S. (1981) A cross-cultural comparison of sibling violence, *International Journal of Family Psychiatry*, 2(3-sup-4): 337–51.

Steinmetz, S.K. (1977) *The Cycle of Violence: Assertive, Aggressive and Abusive Family Interaction*, New York: Praeger.

Stevenson, O. and Hill, M. (eds) (1980) *Child Abuse: Aspects of Interprofessional Cooperation*, London: George Allen & Unwin.

Stewart, R.B. (1983) Sibling attachment relationships: child-infant interactions in the strange situation, *Developmental Psychology*, 19: 192–9.

Stewart, R.B., Mobley, L.A., Van Tuyl, S.S. and Salvador, M.A. (1987) The firstborn's adjustment to the birth of a sibling: a longitudinal assessment, *Child Development*, 58: 341–55.

Stillwell, R. and Dunn, J. (1985) Continuities in sibling relationships: patterns of aggression and friendliness, *Journal of Child Psychology and Psychiatry and Allied Disciplines*, 26(4): 627–37.

Stocker, C. (1993) Siblings' adjustment in middle childhood: links with mother – child relationships, *Journal of Applied Developmental Psychology*, 14(4): 485–99.

Stocker, C. (1994) Children's perceptions of relationships with siblings, friends, and mothers: compensatory processes and links with adjustment, *Journal of Child Psychology and Psychiatry*, 35(8): 1447–59.

Stocker, C. and Dunn, J. (1990) Sibling relationships in childhood: links with friendships and peer relationships, *British Journal of Developmental Psychology*, 8(3): 227–44.

Stocker, C., Dunn, J. and Plomin, R. (1989) Sibling relationships: links with child temperament, maternal behaviour and family structure, *Child Development*, 60: 715–27.

Stocker, C., Lanthier, R.P. and Furman, W. (1997) Sibling relationships in early adulthood, *Journal of Family Psychology*, 11(2): 210–21.

Stocker, C. and McHale, S. (1992) The nature and family correlates of preadolescents' perceptions of their sibling relationships, *Journal of Social and Personal Relationships*, 9: 179–95.

Stocker, C. and Youngblade, L. (1999) Marital conflict and parental hostility: links with children's sibling and peer relationships, *Journal of Family Psychology*, 13(4): 598–609.

Stoneman, Z., Brody, G.H., Churchill, S.L. and Winn, L.L. (1999) Effects of residential instability on head start children and their relationships with older siblings: Influences of child emotionality and conflict between family caregivers, *Child Development*, 70(5): 1246–62.

Stormont, F., Crain,T., Atakan, Z., Loader, P. and Williams, C. (1997) Concerns about the children of psychiatric in-patients – what the parents say, *Psychiatric Bulletin*, 21(8): 495–97.

Strauss, M., Gelles, R. and Steinmetz, S. (1980) *Behind Closed Doors: Violence in the American Family*, New York: Anchor Press/Doubleday.

Suh, E. and Abel, E. (1990) The impact of spousal violence on the children of the abused, *Journal of Independent Social Work*, 4(4): 27–34.

Sulloway, F. (1996) *Born to Rebel: Birth Order, Family Dynamics, and Creative Lives*, London: Little, Brown and Co.

Summers, C., White, K. and Summers, M. (1994) Siblings of children with a disability: a review and analysis of the empirical literature, *Journal of Social Behavior and Personality*, 9(5): 169–84.

Taylor, M.K. and Kogan, K.L. (1973) Effects of the birth of a sibling on mother-child interactions, *Child Psychiatry and Human Development*, 4: 53–8.

Thomas, N., Stainton, T., Doubtfire, S. and Webb, A. (2001) *A Study of Young Carers in Wales: Perspectives of Children and Young People*, Report to Wales Office of Research and Development for Health and Social Care, Cardiff: The National Assembly for Wales.

Thompson, D.F. (1998) Children of parents with mental illness: the roles of temperament and family environment in adjustment, *Dissertation Abstracts International: Section B: The Sciences and Engineering*, 59(2B): 0890.

Thorpe, M. and Swart, G. (1992) Risk and protective factors affecting children in foster care: a pilot study of the role of siblings, *Canadian Journal of Psychiatry*, 37(9): 616–22.

Timberlake, E. and Hamlin, E. (1982) The sibling group: a neglected dimension of placement, *Child Welfare*, 61(8): 545–52.

Toman, W. (1994, orig. 1961) *Family Constellation: Its Effects on Personality and Social Behavior* (4th edn), London: Jason Aronson.

Tonkins, S. and Lambert, M. (1996) A treatment outcome study of bereavement groups for children, *Child and Adolescent Social Work Journal*, 13(1): 3–21.

Touris, M., Kromelow, S. and Harding, C. (1995) Mother-firstborn attachment and the birth of a sibling, *American Journal of Orthopsychiatry*, 65(2): 293–7.

Tower, C. (1996) *Child Abuse and Neglect* (3rd edn), Needham Heights, MA: Allyn and Bacon.

Trad, P. (1990) *Conversations with Preschool Children: Uncovering Developmental Patterns*, New York: W.W. Norton and Co, Inc.

Trause, M. (1981) Separation for childbirth: the effect on the sibling, *Child Psychiatry and Human Development*, 12(1): 32–9.

Treffers, P.D.A., Goedhart, A.W., Waltz, J.V. and Kouldijs, E. (1990) The systematic collection of patient data in a centre for child and adolescent psychiatry, *British Journal of Psychiatry*, 157: 744–8.

Tsun, O. (1999) Sibling incest: a Hong Kong experience, *Child Abuse & Neglect*, 23(1): 71–9.

Valsiner, J. (2000) *Culture and Human Development*, London: Sage.

Van IJzendoorn, M. and Kroonenberg, P. (1988) Cross-cultural patterns of attachment: a meta-analysis of the Strange Situation, *Child Development*, 59: 147–56.

Vandell, D.L., Minnet, A.M., Johnson, B.S. and Santrock, J.W. (1990) Siblings and friends: experiences of school-aged children, Unpublished manuscript, University of Texas.

Viorst, J. (1986) *Necessary Losses*, New York: Faxcett Columbine.

Volling, B. and Belsky, J. (1992) The contribution of mother/child and father/child relationships to the quality of sibling interaction: a longitudinal study, *Child Development*, 63(5): 1209–22.

Volling, B. and Elins, J. (1998) Family relationships and children's emotional adjustment as correlates of maternal and paternal differential treatment: a replication with toddler and preschool siblings, *Child Development*, 69(6): 1640–56.

Volling, B., Youngblade, L.M. and Belsky, J. (1997) Young children's social relationships with siblings and friends, *American Journal of Orthopsychiatry*, 67(1): 102–11.

Vuchinich, S., Wood, B. and Vuchinich, R. (1994) Coalitions and family problem solving with preadolescents in referred, at-risk, and comparison families, *Family Process*, 33(4): 409–24.

Waddell, J. (1993) Women writers as little sisters in Victorian society: *The Mill on the Floss* and the case of George Eliot, in Mink, J.S. and Ward, J.D. (eds) *The Significance of Sibling Relationships in Literature*, Bowling Green, OH: Bowling Green State University Popular Press.

Walker, A. (1983) *The Color Purple*, London: The Women's Press.

Walker, C.E., Bonner, B.L., and Kaufman, K.L. (1988) *The Physically and Sexually Abused Child: Evaluation and Treatment*, New York: Pergamon Press.

Ward, M. (1984) Sibling ties in foster care and adoption planning, *Child Welfare*, 63(4): 321–32.

Waters, B. (1987) The importance of sibling relationships in separated families, *Australian and New Zealand Journal of Family Therapy*, 8(1): 13–17.

Wedge, P. and Mantle, G. (1991) *Sibling Groups and Social Work*, Aldershot: Avebury.

Wedge, P. and Phelan, J. (1986) *Essex Child Care Survey 1981–85*, Social Work Development Unit, Norwich: University of East Anglia.

Weili, B. C. (1928) *The Behaviour of Young Children of the Same Family*, Cambridge, MA: Harvard University Press.

Weintraub, C. (1990) Telephone sessions in the treatment of a child during the therapist's absence because of threatened miscarriage, *Clinical Social Work Journal*, 18(3): 227–41.

Weisner, T. and Gallimore, R. (1977) My brother's keeper: child and sibling caretaking, *Current Anthropology*, 18(2): 169–90.

Werner, E. (1990) Protective factors and individual resilience, in Meisels, S. and Shonkoff, J. (eds) *Handbook of Early Childhood Intervention*, Cambridge: Cambridge University Press.

Westcott, H. (1991) The abuse of disabled children: a review of the literature, *Child: Care, Health and Development*, 17:243–58.

Whipple, E. and Finton, S. (1995) Psychological maltreatment by siblings: An unrecognized form of abuse, *Child and Adolescent Social Work Journal*, 12(2):135–46.

Whiting, B. and Whiting, J.W.M. (1975) *Children of Six Cultures*, Cambridge, MA: Harvard University Press.

Whitmore, E., Kramer, J. and Knutson, J. (1993) The association between punitive childhood experiences and hyperactivity, *Child Abuse & Neglect*, 17(3):357–66.

Wiehe, V. (1990) *Sibling Abuse: Hidden Physical, Emotional and Sexual Trauma*, Lexington, MA: Lexington Books/D. C. Heath and Coy.

Wiehe, V. (1991) *Perilous Rivalry: When Siblings Become Abusive*, Lexington, MA: Lexington Books.

Williams, A.S. (1998) A group for the adult daughters of mentally ill mothers: looking backwards and forwards, *British Journal of Medical Psychology*, 71(1):73–83.

Wilson, B. and Edington, G. (1982) *First Child, Second Child: What Your Birth Order Means to You*, London: Souvenir Press.

Winnicott, D.W. (1965) *The Family and Individual Development*, London: Tavistock.

Winnicott, D.W. (1980) *The Piggle: An Account of the Psychoanalytic Treatment of a Little Girl*, Harmondsworth: Penguin Books.

Wolf, L., Fisman, S., Ellison, D. and Freeman, T. (1998) Effect of sibling perception of differential parental treatment in sibling dyads with one disabled child, *Journal of the American Academy of Child and Adolescent Psychiatry*, 37(12):1317–25.

Worling, J. (1995) Adolescent sibling-incest offenders: differences in family and individual functioning when compared to adolescent nonsibling offenders, *Child Abuse & Neglect*, 19(5):633–43.

Young, M. and Willmott, P. (1957) *Family and Kinship in East London*, London: Routledge and Kegan Paul.

Zima, B.T., Wells, K.B., Benjamin, B. and Duan, N. (1996) Mental health problems among homeless mothers: relationship to service use and child mental health problems, *Archives of General Psychiatry*, 53(4):332–8.

Index

Printed in the United States
43932LVS00005B/8